RHODA BROUGHTON

To my parents,
Stanley Heller (1921–2014)
and
Anita Kempinsky Heller (1923–2021)

Rhoda Broughton

Tamar Heller

EER
Edward Everett Root, Publishers, Brighton, 2023.

EER
Edward Everett Root, Publishers, Co. Ltd.,
Atlas Chambers, 33 West Street, Brighton, Sussex, BN1 2RE, England.
Full details of our stock-holding overseas agents in America, Australia, China, Europe and Japan, and how to order our books, are given on our website.
www.eerpublishing.com

edwardeverettroot@yahoo.co.uk

We stand with Ukraine!
EER books are **NOT** available for sale in Russia or Belarus.

© Tamar Heller, *Rhoda Broughton*

ISBN: 9781915115119 Hardback
ISBN: 9781915115126 Paperback
ISBN: 9781915115133 eBook

This edition © Edward Everett Root Publishers Co. Ltd., 2023.

Key Popular Women Writers series, no.7.

Tamar Heller has asserted her right to be identified as the owner of the copyright of this Work in accordance with the copyright, Designs and Patents Act 1988 as the owner of this work.

All rights reserved. No part of this publication may be reproduced, stored in a retrieval system or transmitted in any form or by any means, electronic, mechanical, photocopying, recording or otherwise, without the prior permission of the copyright owner.

Design and production by Pageset Ltd., High Wycombe, Buckinghamshire.

KEY POPULAR WOMEN WRITERS

Series editors:
Janine Hatter and Helena Ifill.

This innovative new series delivers original and transformative, peer reviewed, feminist research into the work of leading women writers who were widely read in their time, but who have been under-represented in the canon.

The series offers critical, historical and aesthetic contributions to current literary and theoretical work. Each volume concentrates on one writer.

The first six titles are available:

- *Geraldine Jewsbury* by Abigail Burnham Bloom.
- *Florence Marryat* by Catherine Pope.
- *Margaret Oliphant* by Valerie Sanders.
- *Mrs. Henry Wood* by Mariaconcetta Costantini.
- *Frances Trollope* by Carolyn Lambert.
- *Rhoda Broughton* by Tamar Heller.

These will be followed by contracted volumes on:

- *Eliza Lynn Linton*
- *Marie Corelli*
- *Mary Elizabeth Braddon*
- *Mary Shelley*
- *Charlotte Riddell*
- *Ouida*

We are also now seeking authors for volumes on:

- *Daphne Du Maurier*
- *Edith Wharton*

The series volumes interrogate the ways in which women writers, their creative processes and published material can be considered feminist, and explore how recent developments in feminist theory can enrich our understanding of popular women's lives and literature.

The authors rethink established popular writers and their works, and rediscover and re-evaluate authors who have been largely neglected – often since their initial burst of success in their own historical period. This neglect is often due to the exclusivity and insular nature of the canon which has its roots in the Victorian critical drive to perpetuate a division between high and low culture.

In response, our definition of the "popular" is broadly interpreted to encompass women writers who were read by large sections of the public, and who wrote for the mass publishing market. The series therefore challenges this arbitrary divide, creating a new and dynamic dialogue regarding the canon's expansion by introducing readers to previously under-researched women writers who were nevertheless prolific, known and influential.

Studying the work of these authors can tell us much about women's writing, creativity and publishing practice, and about how popular fiction intervened in pressing political, social and cultural issues surrounding gender, history and women's role in society.

This is an important and timely series that is inspired by, interrogates, and speaks to a new wave of feminism, new definitions of sex and gender, and new considerations of inter-sectionality. It also reflects growing interest in popular fiction, as well as a feminist desire to broaden and diversify the literary canon.

Ultimately the series sheds light on women writers whose work deserves greater recognition, facilitates and inspires further research, and paves the way for introducing these key women writers into the canon and modern-day studies.

The series editors

DR. JANINE HATTER is an Early Career Researcher based at the University of Hull. With Nickianne Moody she has edited the volume *Fashion and Material Culture in Victorian Fiction and Periodicals,* already published by *EER.* Her research interests centre on nineteenth-century literature, art and culture, with particular emphasis on popular fiction. She has published on Mary Braddon, Bram Stoker, the theatre and identity, and Victorian women's life writing, as well as on her wider research interests of nineteenth to twenty-first century Science Fiction and the Gothic. She has edited several special journal issues: on 'Werewolves: Studies in Transformations' for Revenant, 'Gender in Victorian Popular Fiction, Art and Culture' with Nineteenth-Century Gender Studies, and 'Supernatural in the Nineteenth Century' for Supernatural Studies, as well as three special issues on 'Age and Gender in Feminist Speculative Fiction' for Femspec. Janine is conference co-organiser for the Victorian Popular Fiction Association, and co-founded the Mary Elizabeth Braddon Association.

DR. HELENA IFILL is a Senior Lecturer at the University of Aberdeen where she is Director of the Centre for the Novel. She is the Secretary of the Victorian Popular Fiction Association and editor of *Victorian Popular Fictions,* the journal of the VPFA. Her monograph, *Creating Character* was published in 2018 and she has written articles on a range of topics including sensation fiction, the Gothic, and the interactions between Victorian popular fiction and the medical sciences.

About the author

Tamar Heller, Associate Professor of English at the University of Cincinnati, is the author of *Dead Secrets: Wilkie Collins and the Female Gothic* (1992), and has co-edited *Approaches to Teaching Gothic Fiction: The British and American Traditions* (2003) and *Scenes of the Apple: Food and the Female Body in Nineteenth-and Twentieth-Century Women's Writing* (2003). She has published widely on Victorian Gothic and sensation fiction and written extensively on Rhoda Broughton, editing *Cometh Up as a Flower* for Pickering & Chatto's series *Varieties of Women's Sensation Fiction: 1855–1890* (2004), and *Not Wisely, but Too Well* for Victorian Secrets Press (2013).

Contents

Acknowledgements xi

A Note on the Text xiii

Introduction. A Plot of Her Own: Rhoda Broughton and
    Late-Victorian Women's Writing 1

Chapter 1. Passion and the Plot of a Woman's Life:
    Representing Female Desire in *Not Wisely, but Too Well* 23

Chapter 2. An Interesting Corpse: Desire, Marriage, and
    Disembodiment in *Cometh Up as a Flower* 59

Chapter 3. The Girl of the Period and Her Jealous Fiancé:
    Sexuality, Power, and the Courtship Plot in *Red as a
    Rose Is She* and *Good-bye, Sweetheart!* 85

Chapter 4. "*All* Married People Grow to Hate One
    Another": Marital Breakdown and the Adultery Plot in
    Broughton's Fiction, 1873–86 111

Chapter 5. "*A* New Woman, Not *the* New Woman!":
    Liminal Women and Ambiguous Endings in
    Broughton's Single-Volume Novels 143

Afterword. Broughton's Metafictions in the Feminist
  Classroom................................173

Notes 189

Bibliography...................................197

Index..207

Acknowledgements

I am deeply indebted to Janine Hatter and Helena Ifill for all the help they have given me on this project, and for the honour of including me in the Key Popular Women Writers Series. Thanks to John Spiers for making Edward Everett Root such a welcoming press to work with. I would also like to thank the anonymous readers who provided useful commentary on the manuscript.

Graziella Stringos is a wonderful friend and Broughton scholar. I can't thank her enough for all she has done to speed Broughton's re-evaluation, including organizing the Rhoda Broughton Centenary Conference in September, 2021, and inviting me to present the keynote on that occasion. I would also like to thank the Victorian Popular Fiction Association, both for hosting the Broughton Centenary, and for providing a fabulous community for Victorianists since being founded in 2009; several chapters of this manuscript had their start as papers delivered at annual VPFA conferences. Thanks, too, to the Taft Research Center at the University of Cincinnati for providing funding for travel to those conferences, as well as for several others at which I presented papers on Broughton. My year as a Taft Center Fellow in 2009–2010 allowed me to begin this manuscript.

I am grateful to Catherine Pope, editor of Victorian Secrets Press, which published my edition of Broughton's *Not Wisely, but Too Well*, for allowing me to use material from my introduction to that volume in chapter one.

I owe a huge debt of gratitude to Jack Mooney, who contributed a sizeable collection of materials related to Broughton—including his own painstakingly assembled notes on the reception of her work—to the University of South Carolina. Thanks again to the Taft Foundation for the grant that enabled me to spend several days in 2014 at the Jack Mooney Collection of Rhoda Broughton, and many thanks as well to the librarians who helped me with my research there.

    I would like to thank my colleague at the University of Cincinnati, Cheli Reutter, for her detailed comments on parts of this manuscript. And I am more grateful than I can say to my best friend and reader, my husband Charles Hatten, who provided expert editing and feedback on multiple versions of each chapter. Thank you to my children, Aurora and Raphael, for listening to all my conversation about "Rhoda" over the years.

A Note on the Text

As the list below details, certain sources are designated in the text by abbreviations. All correspondence between Rhoda Broughton and her publishers, Richard and George Bentley, may be found on Reel 22, Part 2, of the Bentley Archives (BA). Within my text, however, I have cited the correspondence with the Bentleys relating to Broughton's first novel, *Not Wisely, but Too Well,* as it is included in my 2013 edition of that novel. Both *Not Wisely* (*NW*) and *Cometh Up as a Flower* (*CU*), were originally serialized in *The Dublin University Magazine* (*DUM*); I cite the *DUM* versions as they appear in my editions of both novels, each of which includes a section on textual variants between the *DUM* and three-volume versions.

List of Abbreviations

BA	Bentley Archives
DUM	*Dublin University Magazine*
NW	*Not Wisely, but Too Well*
CU	*Cometh Up as a Flower*

INTRODUCTION

A Plot of Her Own: Rhoda Broughton and Late-Victorian Women's Writing

In 1929, Virginia Woolf famously declared that, in order to write fiction, "a woman must have money and a room of her own" (*A Room of One's Own*, 1929 [1957]: 4). In "Professions for Women", a speech she delivered two years later, Woolf added another, possibly even more critical, necessity for the woman writer: freedom from Victorian mores. In a memorable psychomachia, Woolf imagines a struggle between herself and the internalised embodiment of Victorian domestic ideology, the Angel in the House, a being who is "utterly unselfish" and—even more importantly— "pure" (1931 [1979]: 59). As Woolf reviews a novel by an eminent man, the Angel, warning her never to reveal her own opinion, grabs at her pen, prompting Woolf to defend herself:

> Had I not killed her she would have killed me. She would have plucked the heart out of my writing. For, as I found, directly I put pen to paper, you cannot review even a novel without having a mind of your own, without expressing what you think to be the truth about human relations, morality, sex. And all these questions, according to the Angel of the House, cannot be dealt with freely and openly ... Killing the

Angel in the House was part of the occupation of a woman writer. (1931 [1979]: 59–60)

Born in 1840—ninety-one years before Woolf dared resist the Angel in the House—the author Rhoda Broughton could attest to how hard it was for a Victorian woman to write "freely and openly" about "human relations, morality [and] sex." Like Woolf, Broughton battled the repressive influence of Victorian gender roles on female creativity. Launching her career during the heyday of domestic ideology, though, she could not defy the Angel in the House to the same extent as her modernist successor. The London publisher who initially accepted Broughton's first book, *Not Wisely, but Too Well* (1867)—a tale about a young woman's passionate love for a married man—pressured her to withdraw it after a reader for the firm declared it "the most thoroughly sensual tale I have read in English for a long time" and "as bad as any French novel" (Letters to Richard Bentley, 2 and 3 July, 1866, in *NW* 1867 [2013]: 378, 379). Broughton was only able to publish her inaugural effort after vowing to "expunge it of coarseness & slanginess, & to rewrite those passages which cannot be toned down" ([Summer of 1867], in *NW* 1867 [2013]: 381). Both the revised *Not Wisely* and *Cometh Up as a Flower* (1867), the book published in its place due to the disastrous reader's report, sold well upon their appearance in 1867, launching Broughton on a career as one of the late Victorian era's most popular writers. Yet these early works also attracted critical hostility for their portrayal of respectable young women teetering on the brink of sexual fall, with the redoubtable critic Margaret Oliphant singling out *Cometh Up as a Flower* as a prime example of the "abomination in the midst of us"—women writers who portrayed an "intense appreciation of flesh and blood" as the "natural sentiment of English girls" (1867: 268, 259). Even after Broughton moved away from the déclassé genre of sensationalism with which her first two novels were associated, critics continued to fault her stories for violating conventions designed to protect the sexual purity that Woolf identifies as the "chief beauty" of the Angel in the House (1931 [1979]: 59). Although generally impressed by her fiction, Anthony Trollope was unsettled by the unladylike extent to which Broughton's heroines make known their desires: "They throw themselves at men's heads, and when they are not accepted only think how they may throw themselves again" (cited in Wood, 1993: 42).

This book—the first full-length critical study of Broughton's work to date—participates in the ongoing re-evaluation of this long-neglected woman writer that includes (but is by no means limited to) Marilyn Wood's invaluable 1993 biography and scholarship by Helen Debenham, Pamela Gilbert, myself, and the participants in the Rhoda Broughton Centenary Conference sponsored in September 2021 by the Victorian Popular Fiction Association.[1] Broughton's lengthy career—which began in 1865 with the serialization of her first novel and ended in the year of her death, 1920—coincided with a period of seismic changes in gender roles that her fiction not only reflected but influenced. Labelled a "novelist of revolt" by one reviewer of her early work (19 October 1867, exc. In *NW,* 1867 [2013]: 436), Broughton pioneered a daring representation of female sexuality striking even in the racy context of sensation fiction, the genre in which her first two novels, *Not Wisely, but Too Well,* and *Cometh Up as a Flower,* were classified upon their publication in volume form in 1867. The term "erotic sensationalism", coined by Andrew Maunder to describe *Cometh Up as a Flower* when it was included in Pickering & Chatto's series *Varieties of Women's Sensation Fiction* (2004), captures the visceral depiction of female desire that distinguishes Broughton's contribution to sensationalism and informs her fiction even beyond that genre's heyday in the 1860s. My juxtaposition of Woolf and Broughton points to the significance of the latter as a precursor for the former: in writing fiction that insisted that women had, in Everett. F. Bleiler's words, "bodies, desires, and passions" (1981: 127), Broughton helped to create a climate in which later feminists like Woolf could more confidently defy the repressive ethos of the Victorian Angel.

Indeed, in certain ways Broughton was bolder even than Woolf in representing female sexuality. Whereas, in "Professions for Women", Woolf confesses herself unable, even after her triumph over the Angel, to write "the truth about my own experiences as a body" (1931 [1979]: 62), the serial version of Broughton's first novel, *Not Wisely, but Too Well,* includes a passage evoking the sensation of female orgasm.[2] Of course, that this passage was one of those expunged from the heavily revised triple-decker incarnation of the novel testifies to the obstacles faced by Victorian writers—especially women writers—in publishing risqué fiction. In consequence, this study will, in addition to identifying the elements that made Broughton's fiction ground-breaking in its representation of female desire, examine the complex strategies to which she was compelled to resort in order to make her work acceptable for publication.

As re-evaluative efforts have increasingly acknowledged, however, Broughton's innovative portrayal of female desire is not her sole contribution to literary history. Nor, for that matter, are her first two novels, *Not Wisely, but Too Well* and *Cometh Up as a Flower,* the only fiction she wrote, although they have, to date, been the focus of most of the renewed critical attention to her work. This attention is understandable, not only because of her daring portrayal of transgressive female sexuality in these novels, but because of their status as sensation fiction, a literary genre whose unidealised representation of women's domestic experience has largely been responsible for its scholarly re-evaluation over the past few decades. Nonetheless, the most recent Broughton scholarship reflects a broadened focus, not only in terms of examining the body of work she published after the two sensation novels of 1867—twenty-three novels and short fiction that includes distinguished supernatural tales—but in identifying such important aspects of this work as its sensitive critique of the gender inequities of Victorian and Edwardian-era marriage.

There has also been increased attention in Broughton scholarship to aesthetic concerns, including her strikingly self-conscious relation to authorship. Two of Broughton's novels—*A Beginner* (1894) and the posthumously published *A Fool in Her Folly* (1920)—are overtly metafictional in their portrayal of would-be women writers who, like Broughton herself, face hostile responses to their provocative portrayal of female sexuality but who—unlike Broughton—subsequently abandon a literary career.[3] Emphasizing the continuum between Broughton's fiction and Woolfian feminism, the heroines of both metafictions are reminiscent of Woolf's portrayal of the tragically silenced female artist, Judith Shakespeare, in *A Room of One's Own*, and their capitulation to Victorian mores contrasts with Woolf's own, modernist-era defiance of those constraints in "Professions for Women."

A Beginner and *A Fool in Her Folly* are not the only novels by Broughton with metafictional elements. For instance, Lindsey Faber and Tabitha Sparks have examined how the first-person narration of Broughton's early novel, *Cometh Up as a Flower*, self-reflexively shapes a purportedly autobiographical account into a type of fiction.[4] As this study will argue, Broughton frequently interrogates the influence of literary forms and conventions on women's lives, such as when she introduces readers to the heroine of *Not Wisely, but Too Well*, Kate Chester, as the young woman ponders the relevance of love stories to her own experience. Intertextuality, conveyed through numerous references to literary precursors in Broughton's novels, is a prominent feature of her self-conscious relation to women's authorship and reading. In her first two novels, indeed, intertextuality is well-nigh obsessive, with many pages of *Not Wisely, but Too Well* and *Cometh Up as a Flower* containing one, and often more, quotations from, or other references to, earlier literary texts. In her study of nineteenth-century women's reading practices, Kate Flint compares the first-person narrator's inclusion of poetic quotations in *Cometh Up as a Flower* to the practice among genteel young women of keeping a commonplace book, whose selection of favourite passages displayed their acquaintance with classic literature (1993: 284). Yet, if this type of allusiveness is rooted in genteel feminine experience, intertextuality also demonstrates Broughton's literary professionalism, and how seriously she defined herself as a writer in dialogue with other writers.

This dialogue with literary history is explored in an important re-evaluation of Broughton's fiction, Helen Debenham's 1996 essay on "the art of sensation" in *Not Wisely, but Too Well*. Combining Bakhtinian and feminist approaches, Debenham reads the novel's pastiche of quotations from sources in both high and low culture as a "carnivalesque heteroglossia" that is at once a "claim to ownership" of the male-dominated literary tradition and a "challenge to it" (1996: 15). According to Debenham, Broughton's allusions to classic literature and conventions bolster her tenuous authority as a young woman writer, while also enabling her to revise stereotypical depictions of women and assert her "difference from the literary establishment" that shaped them (1996: 10). As I will argue in my own reading of *Not Wisely, but Too Well* in chapter one, however, Broughton's attempts to give new meaning to what Bakhtin calls "words that are already populated with the social intentions of others" (qtd. Debenham, 1996: 11) can, particularly in regard to misogynistic representations of women, unfortunately reproduce the very ideologies they attempt to rewrite.

While many of Broughton's intertextual allusions are to male writers and male-dominated traditions, she also demonstrates an extensive knowledge of the work of women writers. An admirer of Jane Austen's novels, Broughton reproduces elements of Austenian narrative in her own fiction, and alludes as well to such notable fictional works by nineteenth-century women as Emily Brontë's *Wuthering Heights* (1847), Charlotte Brontë's *Villette* (1853), and

George Eliot's *The Mill on the Floss* (1860). Broughton's literary career was inspired by her reading a woman writer, Anne Thackeray Ritchie, whose provocatively unidealised portrayal of a young woman's experience in *The Story of Elizabeth* (1862–63) spurred her to begin *Not Wisely, but Too Well*.[5] Moreover, as I will note in subsequent chapters, several of Broughton's novels revise the plots of significant works by nineteenth-century women writers: *Not Wisely, but Too Well* reworks the tale of a would-be bigamist in *Jane Eyre* (1847); *Belinda* (1886) portrays a young woman's disastrous marriage with an elderly scholar that is clearly inspired by Dorothea's union with Casaubon in *Middlemarch* (1871); and *Good-bye, Sweetheart!* (1872) reproduces the plot trajectory of Germaine de Staël's premier novel of the female artist, *Corinne* (1807).

As is evident from this list of female precursors, Broughton was influenced by the works of women writers who not only depicted feminine experience in innovative ways, but whose work questions the disadvantaged status of women in nineteenth-century culture. As such, Broughton shares with these literary foremothers a complex, and often troubled, relation to genre. Domestic fiction, defined as either, or both, a tale of feminine experience within the home or a courtship narrative, was the predominant genre for nineteenth-century female readers and writers. Women writers with feminist leanings, however, such as Madame de Staël, the Brontës, and George Eliot, were well aware that marriage, the goal to which heroines aspire in domestic fiction, was in fact a problematic social institution that enforced the legal and economic disenfranchisement of women. Writing by feminist nineteenth-century women writers thus tends to make an uneasy truce with the marriage plot, as in *Jane Eyre*, where the overly-controlling aristocratic male must be symbolically disempowered before the heroine, who desires personal freedom, can wed him. Beginning her career as an author of sensation fiction, a genre notorious for its focus on sexual transgression, Broughton avoided traditional happy endings in her first two novels, which tragically separated the heroines from their love interests. Moving away from the controversial genre of sensationalism, though, with the publication of her third novel, *Red as a Rose Is She* (1870), Broughton found herself cast as a writer of domestic romance—Arnold Bennett called her the "typical novelist of our domesticity" (1901: 61)—even though her portrayal of marriage and heterosexual romance was resolutely unsentimental and frequently Gothic. In a chapter in her book on popular women's writing, Pamela Gilbert characterises Broughton's career in terms of generic paradox, claiming that, following the publication of her first two novels, she was "classified as a writer of love stories, long after love had ceased to be even arguably the primary theme of her novels" (1997: 113).

While Gilbert may overstate the extent to which Broughton distanced herself from romance, I agree with her thesis that love, in and of itself, is not Broughton's primary theme: at any point in her career, the topic of romance in her novels is entangled with issues of power, both in terms of women's desire for personal autonomy and the ways in which this yearning is threatened by women's disadvantaged position relative to men. In "Girls Past and Present", an essay that appeared in *Ladies Home Journal* several months after her death in June 1920, Broughton succinctly conveys her low opinion of marriage.[6] While admitting to being somewhat shocked by the emergent flapper, Broughton nonetheless applauds the modern young woman's ability to define herself outside the "nuptial yoke": "Marriage ... is to many of the girls of to-day an unessential accident, which may or may not happen to them, but which in any case cannot materially affect the serious business of their lives, their professional or political activities" (1920b: 38).

In this context, the position that Broughton filled in the literary marketplace for most of her career—purveyor of romantic fiction—is, indeed, deeply ironic. It is in this context, however, that I would like to explain the relevance to this study of the title to this introduction, "A Plot of Her Own." Obviously indebted to Virginia Woolf, to whose *A Room of One's Own* I have referred, the notion of "a plot of her own" is crucial for the woman writer who wishes to break with stereotypical, and often misogynistic, portrayals of women in traditional romantic narratives. Yet, as any creative writer can attest—and as is demonstrated by Broughton's own trail of intertextual allusion—it is impossible to define a plot that is genuinely original, and unindebted to literary forebears. As I noted in my earlier comments on Broughton's intertextuality, too, it is difficult to disentangle even an innovative portrayal of female experience from the patriarchal ideologies so frequently inherited, along with genres and conventions, from literary predecessors. Still, even if she could not define a plot entirely free from previous conventions for telling women's stories, Broughton succeeded nonetheless in creatively recasting the traditional "happily ever after" telos of domestic fiction, a creativity at its most notable in the expertly crafted, single-volume novels she produced following the demise of the triple-decker format in the 1890s. Comedies of manners which defer, ironically undercut, or even evade the traditional definition of comedy as marital closure, these late works are compelling evidence of how Broughton's representation of female experience anticipates the narrative innovations of later modernist authors, particularly of feminist modernists such as Woolf.

Spanning the Distance: A Woman Writer in Transition

Addressing the cultural impact of Broughton's fiction, Walter Sichel claimed in 1912 that it spanned "the distance between the 'Girl of the Period' and the 'New Woman'" (cited in Wood, *Rhoda Broughton*, 1993: 116)—between, in other words, Eliza Lynn Linton's figure of the rebellious young woman of the 1860s and the *fin-de-siècle* feminist. Whereas this assessment focuses on the forward-looking nature of Broughton's work—its anticipation of turn-of-the-century feminism—a later tribute, written in 1928 by Percy Lubbock, looks backward instead, portraying her as the gallant embodiment of a departed age. Saluting "our ever-memorable Rhoda", Lubbock recalls the acerbic wit that made Broughton a noted conversationalist among a wide circle of acquaintances that included such authors as Thomas Hardy, Matthew Arnold, and Henry James, the latter a dear friend despite his harsh review of her novel *Joan* (1876). For Lubbock, Broughton's "staunch" integrity and intellectual rigor were unique, yet could only have had their source in an earlier era: "we have never seen her like, nor expect in our day to see it" (1928: 34, 43).

By the end of her life, Broughton was herself aware that her once-scandalous fiction had become a relic of the past, though she depicted her association with Victorianism in less hagiographic, and wryer, terms than Lubbock. In "Girls Past and Present", she recounts with amusement that a recent visitor, "thinking to gratify me, told me that in Italy mine was the only English fiction thought innocent enough to be given as pabulum to schoolgirls" (1920b: 38). Appreciating the irony of her earlier innovations paving the way for her later obsolescence, the elderly Broughton described shifting public perceptions of her work by contrasting an iconoclastic French writer of the *fin-de-siècle* with a primly didactic mid-Victorian one: "'I began my career ... as Zola, I finish it as Miss Yonge, it's not I that have changed, it's my fellow-countrymen'" (cited in Wood, 1993: 122).

Whichever period they emphasise in Broughton's life, these descriptions—by Sichel, Lubbock, and Broughton herself—position her as a writer in, and of, transition. Whether focusing on how Broughton's fiction anticipates a nascent feminism, or looking backward to link her to a superseded age, the assessments situate her work in relation to the tumultuous social changes that occurred during her career. Yet, at the same time that Broughton's fiction defied the repressions of the Victorian era, it is also informed by the ambivalence and ideological contradictions that so often characterize literature written in periods of profound cultural transition. In the earlier part of this introduction, I stressed the most feminist aspects of Broughton's work. Yet, as this study will explore, her work has conservative elements as well.

Broughton's background made it unlikely for her to become a political radical. Hailing from an aristocratic family—the Delves Broughtons—she was, according to her friend Ethel Arnold, a "rigid Tory of the real 'old vintage' brand" (1920: 271), and her work reflects prejudices common to the elite of her day. In *Cometh Up as a Flower*, Sir Adrian Lestrange's sneering response to "'counterjumper[s]'" (1867 [2004]: 224)—working-class individuals who become wealthy through trade—captures the snobbish tone that often accompanies Broughton's representations of socially mobile characters. With its heroine's unfortunate references to Jews as "greasy" and the "offscouring of the earth" (1867 [2004]: 417), *Cometh Up* also reveals the anti-Semitism endemic among Britons of her era and class background.

In terms of gender, Broughton's fiction often contains mixed messages. Re-evaluations of *Not Wisely, but Too Well* by Pamela Gilbert, Laurence Talairach-Vielmas, and myself have traced the way that her fiction reproduces some of the same cultural anxieties about female sexuality that informed negative responses to her work,[7] and this ideological tension will be addressed in my reading of that novel here as well. Like other women writers of her generation whose work contains feminist elements, too, Broughton was ambivalent about feminism as a movement, and at times even hostile, as in *Dear Faustina* (1897), a novel which attacks the *fin-de-siècle* New Woman for which her own fiction had paved the way. Nonetheless, as the essay "Girls Past and Present" demonstrates, Broughton welcomed women's ability to privilege "professional or political activities" above marriage, and the anti-feminism of *Dear Faustina* is counteracted by an ending reminiscent of a New Woman novel, in which the heroine defers marriage to take up social work. In her personal life, too, Broughton was friends with avowed late nineteenth- and early twentieth-century feminists including Mary Cholmondeley and Marie Belloc Lowndes.[8]

Broughton's attitude toward women's newfound independence in the twentieth century was, in fact, more often wistful than hostile. In her posthumously published final novel, *A Fool in Her Folly*, the elderly narrator, Charlotte Hankey, sadly notes that the options available to young women in the post-World War I period were unknown in the mid-Victorian era in which she, like Broughton herself, came of age. In her youth, Char claims, the notion that "a couple of girls should ... betake themselves to a joint flat, to maintain which their own industries should furnish the means" would "have consigned the holder of it to Bedlam" (1920a: 9). "Girls Past and Present"—probably the last piece Broughton wrote—contains a moving passage in which she confronts her own mixed feelings about gender role change. Describing an inner conflict that recalls Woolf's struggle with the Angel in "Professions for Women", Broughton admits to being uncomfortable with the "brazen" sexuality of "the rampant virgin of to-day", but nonetheless attributes this response to her training in Victorian values:

> It is very difficult for one with that natural bias toward the past which comes with old age to judge impartially an alien world, an "alien" which to ancient eyes has a tendency to appear an "undesirable" one. It is only with an effort that one can lay prepossession and prejudice aside, can free oneself from the standards, toss away the weights and measures of one's youth; but if one can succeed in doing so, one is forced to confess that the girl of 1920 is a larger, more useful, happier being than was her grandmother[.] (1920b: 140)[9]

Broughton and the Paradoxes of Victorian Female Authorship

Before addressing, in the chapters that follow, the issues that I have raised thus far in this introduction—Broughton's complex relation both to genre and to gender role change—I would like to situate her career in an important literary and cultural context. If, by the end of her life, Broughton welcomed the new independence achieved by women, her own literary efforts to reimagine the traditional marriage plot were influenced—and constrained—by her participation in the literary marketplace, as well as by her culture's conflicting perceptions of the woman writer.

At the outset of Broughton's career, indeed, the British woman writer's situation was defined by paradox. On one hand, women writers wielded considerable cultural influence on the basis of numbers alone; in 1862, around the time that Broughton began writing her first novel, *Not Wisely, but Too Well*, the journal *Temple Bar*, which would serialise much of her work between the 1870s and 1890s, estimated that roughly two-thirds of all novels were written by women (Fryckstedt, 1986: 11). On the other hand, this cultural power was undermined by demeaning attitudes toward the female author. Since Victorian gender ideology decreed that the public, economic sphere was reserved for men, the entry of women into the literary marketplace was viewed by many with suspicion, especially given the common assumption that popular literature was not suitable for women to read, much less write, because it pandered to the unrefined tastes of the proletariat. Due to the heated controversy over sensationalism, Broughton entered the literary marketplace at a moment when anxieties about women reading and writing popular texts were at their height. Margaret Oliphant assailed Broughton's sensation novel *Cometh Up as a Flower* in a review identifying female sensation writers as those who "speak [...] the most plainly" about sexuality, and thus pose the greatest threat to the chastity that is the Victorian woman's "one duty of invaluable importance to her country and her race" (1867: 274, 275).

An anecdote that Broughton enjoyed telling in later life humorously conveys these nineteenth-century anxieties about female authorship: while browsing a train station bookstall, she discovered a packet of her novels labelled "'Rhoda Broughton, soiled but cheap'" (Wood 1993: 113). That Broughton found a bargain bundle of her novels at a railway station reflects the crucial role played by train travel in the dissemination of nineteenth-century popular fiction. Yet, while celebrating her popularity, the anecdote also associates that success with being both "cheap", or devalued, and "'soiled'"—a word redolent not only of the déclassé but of sexual fall. Linking female authorship with dirt—class degradation and even sexual contamination—the anecdote recalls Broughton's association, in the early part of her career with sensation fiction, the genre that Susan Bernstein has called "dirty reading" for women (1994: 213–30). That it is "Rhoda Broughton" who is offered for sale, rather than the individual novels, captures the overtones of prostitution that informed the nineteenth-century metaphor of "author as whore" that, as Catherine Gallagher argues, was especially problematic for the popular woman writer (1986: 39–62).

At the same time, the humour of the "'soiled but cheap'" anecdote derives in part from the discrepancy between the woman writer's symbolic commodification and her actual class position as a lady. Among her social circle, Broughton downplayed her association with the marketplace in order to stress her gentility. In her preface to Broughton's *A Fool in Her Folly,* her friend Marie Belloc Lowndes remembered her as "[c]uriously humble" about her books, and "content to regard her literary gift as a kind of elegant accomplishment", rather than as the basis for a career (Foreword, 1920: 6). Herself a feminist author of a younger generation, Lowndes attributes the plot of a failed female writer in *A Fool in Her Folly* to the "Victorian tradition" of viewing "professional authorship as not at all suitable to ladies" (1920: 6). It is reflective of negative attitudes toward female authorship that Broughton, like many other mid-Victorian women writers, chose to publish her first three novels anonymously. Even when she later published under her own name, she identified herself more as a refined gentlewoman than a successful popular writer.

Helen C. Black, who interviewed Broughton in the 1890s for the book *Notable Women Authors of the Day* (1893), found no copies of her own novels on the shelves of her tastefully decorated home: "She says that she sells them out and out at once, and then has 'done with them'" (1893: 44). Yet Broughton's diffidence about authorship was counterbalanced by an enterprising business sense. Although her decision to sell her novels "out and out"—in other words, sell their copyrights to the publisher—resulted in an unfortunate shortage of income in her old age, Broughton's extensive correspondence with Bentley's, her publishers for much of her career, reveals her efforts to obtain the best possible terms for her work, as well as her displeasure when she felt she had been denied her due.

Broughton's self-presentation as an author thus reveals a tension between her culture's contradictory images of the woman writer. Countering the perception spawned by the sensation controversy—in which the popular female author is both whore and madam, selling herself as well as corrupting female readers—Broughton adopted the persona of a genteel woman who underplayed her connection to the marketplace, even though this image conflicted in turn with the identity she assumed with her publishers, that of the literary professional who demands proper compensation for her work. An unusually sympathetic review of Broughton's sensation fiction in *The Spectator* in 1867, however, places her in a category of female authorship that, unlike those already mentioned, offered women a chance to attain genuine literary stature. Praising the "full and noble nature" of her heroines, as well as their refusal to submit to "the usual cut and dry formulas for living" (1867, in *Not Wisely* 1867 [2013]: 437), this reviewer—the one who, as I mentioned earlier, called Broughton a "novelist of revolt"—likened *Not Wisely, but Too Well* and *Cometh Up as a Flower* to "*Villette* ... the *Mill on the Floss*, [and] many another work of female genius" (1867 [2013]: 436, 438). Invoking a Romantic-era ideal of artistic inspiration, the word "genius", when applied to a woman writer, has affinities with a related nineteenth-century concept of female authorship, that of the "woman of letters", identified by Linda Peterson as an "honorific", "high-art" antithesis to the popular woman writer stereotypically associated with ephemeral, aesthetically inferior work (2009: 4,11). The two women writers to whom the *Spectator* reviewer compared Broughton, Charlotte Brontë and George Eliot, were quintessential examples of the distinguished woman writer, Eliot in being the epitome of the high-art woman of letters and Brontë in being, as Peterson says, a figure who "preserve[d] the category of artistic genius for women's authorship" (2009: 7).

The *Spectator* reviewer's inclusion of Broughton in the category of "female genius" suggests that, early in her career at least, she was seen as having the potential to be a woman of letters, rather than, as she was later classified, a popular "Queen of the Circulating Libraries." The *Spectator* reviewer's identification of Broughton as a female genius, however, comes in the context of a passage that introduces the concept only to betray ambivalence about it:

> When *Cometh Up as a Flower* first appeared, there was great dispute in quiet households as to its morality. It fluttered women as *Jane Eyre* did, and almost for the same reason, but we should no more pronounce it immoral than *Jane Eyre*. The author indulges, as we have said, in certain audacities of expression, sometimes witty to an enjoyable degree, sometimes profane, sometimes feebly flippant, and some of these audacities reveal, like some passages in *Villette*, in the *Mill on the Floss*, in many another work of female genius, a consciousness of sex which in its persistency is not either healthy or realistic. But we cannot admit that the general drift of these two books is in any degree immoral. (1867, in *Not Wisely* 1867 [2013]: 438–39)

Defending Broughton against charges of immorality, the reviewer nonetheless claims that the "consciousness of sex" in her novels "is not either healthy or realistic." In our period, the term "consciousness of sex" might be taken as a reference to sexuality, and, like Broughton's work, Eliot's and Brontë's were indeed criticised for their representation of female desire. Yet, in nineteenth-century parlance, "consciousness of sex" is more likely a description of the female genius's awareness of the power inequalities between men and women, a feminist insight that informs not only Charlotte Brontë's and Eliot's work, but may also be found in the premier nineteenth-century text both by and about the female genius, Madame de Staël's *Corinne* (1807).

Broughton's link to a genealogy of feminist literary foremothers—a topic addressed in the first section of this introduction—thus complicates her definition as an artist, associating her both with prestigious and with popular women writers, supposedly disparate groups that, in fact, were linked by similar cultural anxieties. Linda Peterson points out that the woman of letters was a figure who combined literary professionalism—and hence participation in the literary marketplace—with the type of personal life or didactic role that reassured readers as to her essential adherence to domestic feminine ideals (2009: 45–46). Yet authors such as Charlotte Brontë and George Eliot were, as previously mentioned, associated with a "consciousness of sex" which, especially in Brontë's case, attracted criticism of "coarseness" similar to that used against Broughton. And, as the *Spectator* review of Broughton's sensation fiction indicates, works by both the popular woman writer and the high-art "female genius" were criticised as much for their feminism as their depiction of female sexuality. In her 1867 *Blackwood's* diatribe, Margaret Oliphant traces the origins of sensation fiction to "the time when Jane Eyre made what advanced critics call her 'protest' against the conventionalities in which the world clothes itself" (1867: 258). In associating sensation fiction with *Jane Eyre*—the work to which the *Spectator* reviewer also compares *Cometh Up as a Flower*—Oliphant targets not Brontë's representation of female sexuality so much as her feminism, the reference to Jane Eyre's "'protest'" presumably alluding to what is probably the most explicitly feminist passage in the novel, where Jane insists that "women feel just as men feel; they need exercise for their faculties" (1847 [1996]: 116). Towards the end of her attack on sensationalism, Oliphant asserts the "vital importance" of female chastity in defiance of increasingly vocal discourses of "Women's rights" (1867: 275), an association of popular women's writing, sexual impropriety, and feminism voiced as well, in 1872, by a review in *The Athenæum* of Broughton's fourth novel, *Good-bye, Sweetheart!* Declaring that Broughton assumes the "tone and manner of a man"— a reference to her racy and informal style of writing—the reviewer accuses her of "throw[ing] down the glove as distinctly as does a female orator at a Woman's Rights convention" (1872: 585). That *Good-bye, Sweetheart!* was a revision of Madame de Staël's famous novel of female genius, *Corinne,* speaks to the overlap in the period between popular and prestigious women's writing, as well as to the association of both varieties of authorship with a feminism deemed threatening to male authority.

Like her reaction to changing gender roles, Broughton's response to the contradictory attitudes toward women's writing in her culture was ambivalent. To the extent that she, as Marie Belloc Lowndes claimed, viewed "professional authorship as not at all suitable for ladies", Broughton was reluctant to portray her literary activities as anything other than an unfortunate financial necessary. At the same time, her intertextuality, which I previously described as a dialogue with earlier writers that asserts her literary professionalism and authority, displays her affinities with nineteenth-century women of letters whose work, like hers, interrogates conventional plots about, and attitudes towards, women. Yet the role that Broughton filled in the literary marketplace, and through which she made a living—a writer of popular romance—bound her to the marriage plot despite her reservations about that institution as an option for women. In this context, Broughton's experimental revisions of the marriage plot—especially those in her late fiction—are the more impressive given marketplace pressures to produce conventional happily-ever-after endings. Ironically, however, literary modernism—a movement that championed the rewriting of Victorian conventions—delayed the recognition of Broughton's own achievements in that area by devaluing popular writers in favour of those who were not only avant-garde but self-consciously elite. Only now, after feminist scholars have questioned the exclusion of popular women writers from literary canons, can Broughton's innovations finally be acknowledged.

Summary of Chapters

Since this study examines the development of Broughton's career, its chapters are, for the most part, organised chronologically. Chapter One, "Passion and the Plot of a Woman's Life: Representing Female Desire in *Not Wisely, but Too Well*", analyses Broughton's first, and most controversial, novel, which exists in two forms—the original serialization and a heavily revised triple-decker format—because of Geraldine Jewsbury's unfavourable report objecting to its immorality. *Not Wisely* thus not only shows us Broughton's portrayal of sexuality at its most daring, but allows us to assess, by comparing the two versions, the degree to which she was compelled to censor her own work. At the same time, *Not Wisely* is a remarkably complex novel both aesthetically and ideologically. Riven by mixed messages about female desire, which it simultaneously celebrates and chastises, the text also reflects self-consciously on narrative possibilities for women's fiction and, especially in the triple-decker version of its tragic ending, questions the male narrator's definition of romance as the "main plot of a woman's life."

The second chapter, "'An Interesting Corpse': Marriage, Death, and Disembodiment in *Cometh Up as a Flower*", addresses the second novel Broughton wrote and serialised, albeit the first published in triple-decker form. Substituted by Bentley's as less offensive in its portrayal of a near-adulterous relationship than *Not Wisely*, *Cometh Up* still attracted considerable controversy, and was even, as I mentioned earlier, singled out by Margaret Oliphant as emblematic of the "abomination" of female sensationalism. Nonetheless, *Cometh Up* employs a different, and less explicitly erotic, strategy than *Not Wisely* for portraying female sexuality—a strategy I label "disembodied embodiment" because it paradoxically figures the heroine's transgressive desire through her wasting death from consumption. The novel's most visceral evocations of sexuality are reserved for the loveless marriage into which the heroine enters for economic reasons. In this sense, *Cometh Up* anticipates Broughton's critique of marriage, and its curtailment of women's sexuality and autonomy, in her subsequent novels.

Chapter Three, "The Girl of the Period and Her Jealous Fiancé: Sexuality, Power, and the Courtship Plot in *Red as a Rose Is She* and *Good-bye, Sweetheart!*", examines how Broughton's third and fourth novels, in moving away from the sensation genre to that of romance fiction, nonetheless represent heterosexual love as problematic for women. In both works, jealous and patriarchal fiancés break their engagements with the heroines after judging their behaviour transgressive of conventional femininity; in *Red as a Rose*, the lovers reconcile in Broughton's first happily-ever-after marital ending, while, in *Good-bye, Sweetheart!*, the male lead's rejection of the heroine leads to her untimely death. Engaging cultural anxieties about rebellious young women sparked by Eliza Lynn Linton's anti-feminist essay "The 'Girl of the Period'", these novels also reflect the challenges that Broughton faced at a point in her career in which she—not unlike her heroines—found herself frequently accused of being unladylike and immodest. In addition to enduring harsh reviews of her increasingly popular fiction, Broughton also struggled during this period to define her relation to the genre that was the basis for her popularity, romantic fiction. Despite its purportedly happy ending, *Red as a Rose* represents heterosexual romance in less than rosy terms, and the battle between the sexes in *Good-bye, Sweetheart!* ends in outright tragedy. In its revision of Madame de Staël's *Corinne*, too, the latter novel suggests how difficult it is for the exceptional woman—be she heroine or author—to evade the romance plot.

Chapter Four, "'*All* Married People Grow to Hate One Another': Marital Breakdown and the Adultery Plot in Fiction of the 1870s and 80s", moves from Broughton's novels about courtship to her novels about marriage—or, more accurately, marital failure—in the 1870s and 1880s, concentrating on *Nancy* (1874) and *Belinda* (1883), but also including her ghost story "The Man with the Nose" (1872), as well as *Joan* (1876) and *Doctor Cupid* (1886). The sensitive portrayal of marital incompatibility in these works expands on Broughton's earlier critique of the dangers posed by marriage to female autonomy, while her return to the adultery plot of her earlier sensation fiction responds to her readers' preference for (as she called it) "hot & strong" fare (BA, 22 June 1880, Pt. 2, Reel 2). Nonetheless, that the eponymous heroines of *Nancy*, *Belinda*, and *Joan* ultimately refuse to commit adultery speaks to the continuing taboo, even in a climate of changing sexual attitudes, against positively representing extra-marital female sexuality.

Chapter Five, "'*A* New Woman, Not *the* New Woman': Liminal Women and Ambiguous Endings in Broughton's Late Novels", explores Broughton's innovative revisions of the romance plot in the single-volume works she wrote following the demise of the triple-decker format, focusing in particular on novels that end ambiguously, suggesting, but never confirming, possible marital closure. Not only are the endings of the novels examined in this chapter ambiguous, but the heroines themselves defy easy classification. While several of the works discussed, such as *Dear Faustina* (1897) and *Concerning a Vow* (1914), are ambivalent or even hostile to the New Woman, all of these fictions sympathetically represent the plight of a figure I call the liminal woman—a female character who, like Broughton herself, is caught between Victorian and modern definitions of women's roles.

Finally, the afterward, "Broughton's Metafictions in the Feminist Classroom" addresses an important venue for re-evaluating Broughton's work: the feminist classroom. Envisioning a hypothetical course on the female *künstlerroman* from the late Victorian period through the early twentieth century, I discuss how Broughton's two metafictional novels, *A Beginner* (1894) and *A Fool in Her Folly* (1920), could be taught alongside such feminist classics as the New Woman *künstlerroman* by Broughton's friend Mary Cholmondeley, *Red Pottage,* and Virginia Woolf's "Professions for Women" and *A Room of One's Own*. Despite their apparently farcical treatment of female authorship, both *A Beginner* and *A Fool in Her Folly*—*künstlerromans* that reverse the movement toward literary success that typically defines the genre—critique the social factors silencing women's voices in ways that attest to Broughton's significance as a precursor for future women writers.

CHAPTER ONE

Passion and the Plot of a Woman's Life: Representing Female Desire in *Not Wisely, but Too Well*

> Oh! I have bought my increased refinement of a great wealth of power.
> – Rhoda Broughton to George Bentley, BA, 25 Aug. 1876, in *NW* 1867 [2013]: 384

> Since this time yesterday she had made the pleasing discovery that she was fast falling in love violently, and as it now appeared unrequitedly, with a man her superior in station, and in every respect unlikely to prove a satisfactory object for that passion which forms the main plot of a woman's life, and is only a small secondary byplay in a man's. Yes, the play of her life had begun, and whether it was to be a tragedy or a comedy who could tell?
> – *Not Wisely, but Too Well*, 1867 [2013]: 83

In 1876, Rhoda Broughton implored her publisher, George Bentley, to help her find copies of *The Dublin University*

Magazine containing the complete serialization of her novel *Not Wisely, but Too Well*, which had appeared there in 1865–66. Having just discovered an issue of the journal with the tale's final instalment—and being "struck with its much greater power than the later published version" (BA, 25 August 1876, in *NW*, 1867 [2013]: 384)—she was eager to reread the original manuscript in its entirety. The conclusions of the serial and triple-decker versions of *Not Wisely* are, indeed, markedly different. In the final scene of the serial, the male protagonist—a married man who had, on two occasions, vainly pressured the heroine to become his mistress—shoots to death first her, and then himself. In the triple-decker version, the rakish aristocrat dies in a carriage accident, and the desolate heroine becomes an Anglican nun. Broughton's removal of the serial's gory murder-suicide made good on her promise to George Bentley's father, Richard, in the wake of the derailment of *Not Wisely*'s hitherto smooth progress toward publication following Geraldine Jewsbury's disastrous reader's report of July 1866. Substituting her second novel, *Cometh Up as a Flower*, for the work that Jewsbury had assailed as "a bad style of book altogether" (BA, 2 July 1866, in 1867 [2013]: 379). Broughton approached Richard Bentley in July 1867 with the hope that he would consider a "remodelled" version of *Not Wisely* (BA, [summer of 1867], in *NW*, 1867 [2013]: 381) which, she vowed, would not only "omit all the slang and coarseness of expression", but also "soften the violence of the situations and rewrite altogether the end, which is melodramatic and savours of a Surrey theatre" (BA, Summer of 1867, in *NW*: 381).[10] By 1876, though, Broughton apparently regretted following through on this plan. Though she told Bentley that she still found the original ending "crude & coarse", she nonetheless declared "it seems to me rather fine" (BA 25 August 1876, in *NW*, 1867 [2013]: 384). Her letter to the publisher concludes with a *cri de coeur* expressing a sentiment doubtless shared by other Victorian authors forced to tame controversial work in order to bring it into print: "Oh! I have bought my increased refinement of a great wealth of power" (BA 25 August 1876, in *NW,* 1867 [2013]: 384).

Broughton's lament for her lost "power" sets the stage for the first section of this chapter, which assesses the daring of Broughton's representation of female desire by noting the extent to which she was compelled to bowdlerise it in her revisions of the serial text. These revisions tone down, not only the novel's more sexually explicit passages, but also the rebellion of the heroine, Kate Chester, against masculine authority. This latter type of bowdlerisation is culturally significant, given Kate's embodiment of a figure increasingly visible in nineteenth-century literature, most notably in women's writing: the discontented woman, or heroine who resists gender roles that inhibit her personal fulfilment. In its depiction of the discontented woman, *Not Wisely* stands at the interstices of two feminine narrative traditions, looking back to the fiction of the Brontës and the early work of Eliot on one hand while also anticipating New Woman fiction of the 1890s on the other. It was, indeed, in regard to *Not Wisely* that the *Spectator* reviewer mentioned in the introduction declared that Broughton was a "novelist of revolt" (19 October 1867, in *NW,* 1867 [2013]: 436). Citing the passage in which the lovelorn Kate cries "'Oh, why will not God let us have what we like and be happy in this world in our own way'" (1867 [2013]: 89), the *Spectator* reviewer identifies Kate's yearning for sexual fulfilment as, in fact, a longing for autonomy: "[w]hat she really loves is power" (19 October 1867, in *NW,* 1867 [2013]: 437).

It would, however, be simplistic to claim that Broughton's revisions of the serialised *Not Wisely* seriously compromise the novel's critique of Victorian women's social and sexual constraints. Not only, as I argue, did the most controversial aspects of the text resist expurgation, but in one signal instance, at least, Broughton's attempt to play down the "violence" in her novel could be said to strengthen its social criticism. As I will address toward the end of this chapter, the triple-decker ending—for all that it blunts, as

Broughton lamented, the aesthetic "power" of the serial version—arguably offers a more subversive message about marriage and sexuality than the original conclusion.

In order to do justice to the aesthetic and ideological complexity of the novel, this chapter is organised around different levels at which it can be read. Whereas the first level examines the novel's literally doubled voice—the contrast between the serial and triple-decker versions—the second level explores a type of doubleness that exists in both versions of the narrative: the tension between its sympathy with the sexually frustrated heroine on the one hand and its condemnation of her illicit desire on the other. For instance, a character in *Not Wisely* who is a clergyman warns Kate that she is the "'bait with which Satan is angling'" for the soul of her would-be seducer (1867 [2013]: 299), and the narrator berates her in similarly sententious terms for preferring "[t]hat muddy, polluted flood of earthly love" (1867 [2013]: 66) to the love of God. Predating the expurgating revisions of the serial text, such didactic interventions can partly be ascribed to Broughton's awareness, even prior to Jewsbury's report, that she could not represent a woman's adulterous passion too positively. And yet the degree to which *Not Wisely* reflects late-Victorian anxieties about female sexuality suggests that, to some extent at least, Broughton shares them. The narrator's dualistic association of "earthly love" with dirt and sin is repeated in the images of pollution and contagion that surround Kate during her stint as a district visitor in the London slums, and which, as Pamela Gilbert says, link her transgressive desire with "disease, foreign invasion, and class blending" (1997: 116).

Nonetheless, even these conservative messages are tempered by Broughton's self-conscious use of literary allusion, a practice that testifies to the role of culture in shaping attitudes toward women and ways of telling their stories. Often featuring two to three literary quotations or allusions on a single page, Broughton's first novel is a prime example of how, as Helen Debenham says,

Broughton "negotiat[es] her right of entry to and her difference from" a historically male-dominated "literary establishment" (1996:10). Demonstrating both the revisionary possibilities and the limits of using earlier, and often misogynistic, texts to represent women's experience, the intertextuality of *Not Wisely* — the third level on which I read the novel—reflects the challenges faced by a woman writer attempting to define (as I called it in the introduction) "a plot of her own."

In terms of plot, indeed, it is significant that, in a letter to George Bentley in 1871, Broughton claimed that the idea for the plot of *Not Wisely* was the "best I ever had" (BA, [late December?] 1871, in *NW* 1867 [2013]: 384). This commendation is the more striking because, in the years between the publication of the triple-decker in 1867 and her rediscovery of the "power" of the original ending in 1876, Broughton claimed to "simply <u>detest</u>" the novel, calling it "that vile 'Not Wisely'" and "a thorn in the flesh" (BA [late December? 1871] and 21 May 1871, in *NW* 1867 [2013]: 384). Repeatedly begging George Bentley—who seems simply to have ignored her—to buy back the copyright from Tinsley's, who had published it after she rejected the elder Bentley's terms, Broughton professed herself eager to "begin whitewashing Not Wisely" (BA, [February or March 1870], in *NW*, 1867 [2013]: 384), a revision of her earlier revision that would feature "different characters" and "less violence, diffuseness & vulgarity" while nonetheless preserving "the same or a nearly similar plot" (BA [late December? 1871], in *NW*, 1867 [2013]: 384). In other words, what Broughton apparently valued about her first novel— even at a time when she could find nothing else good to say about it—was a plot that depicted a woman's love for a man whom she could not marry. Such a plot, however, is at odds with the marital telos of the courtship novel, the traditional genre for representing what the narrator of *Not Wisely* calls, in the passage which serves as an epigraph to this chapter, "the passion which forms the main plot of a woman's life" (1867 [2013]: 83). If the conclusion of the "main plot of a woman's life" cannot conform to the traditional definition of "comedy"—a story ending in marital closure—then it is doomed to be "tragedy", defined as the inability to marry. The fourth level on which I read the novel, though, examines the extent to which its revised conclusion gestures towards a different ending for the "plot of a woman's life": one in which remaining unmarried is not tragic.

Sensual Appeals: The (Incomplete) Expurgation of Kate's Sensational Body

The description of Kate Chester at the beginning of the second chapter of *Not Wisely*—a blazon of physical details—signals the centrality of the heroine's body to Broughton's representation of female desire. A classic example of the type of piquant beauty, popular between the 1850s and 1870s, that Jeanne Fahnestock calls "the heroine of irregular features",[11] Kate possesses a "turn-up nose" which "def[ies] all rules" (1867 [2013]: 49) as well as other unconventional attractions that signal her vulnerability to sexual arousal. Like her green eyes, her lips suggest "an immensity of latent, undeveloped passion" (1867 [2013]: 49), and her auburn hair is a hue associated with sensual women in both Pre-Raphaelite paintings and sensation fiction.[12] Most striking—and innovative—is the unabashed celebration of Kate's shapely form:

> Now for Kate's figure. I do not think it was exactly of the cut of the Venus de Medici, but, for all that, it always seemed to me rather ensnaring to the fancy, in its partridge-like plumpness, soft undulating contours, and pretty roundnesses; so removed from scragginess, and free from angles. Many *women* affirmed that it was too full, too developed for a girl of twenty. The Misses M'Scrag, whose admirers might have sat with comfort in the shade cast by their collar-bones, were particularly stiff on this point; but no *man* was ever yet heard to give in his adhesion to this feminine fiat. Anyhow

> the light did seem to fall lovingly, as in the case of "The Gardener's Daughter",[13] on "the bounteous wave of such a breast as never pencil drew", and on the waist—no marvel of waspish tenuity, but naturally healthily firm and shapely. (1867 [2013]: 49–50)

Despite its disturbing voyeurism, the perspective of the male narrator—self-identified as one of Kate's many admirers—enables a feminist critique of the Victorian ideal of "ladylike anorexia."[14] As in that moment in *The Woman in White* when Walter Hartright realises that the "natural circle" of Marian Halcombe's waist is "delightfully undeformed by stays" (1860 [1996]: 31), it apparently takes a male point of view to resist the "feminine fiat" of the anorexic ideal embodied (or, more accurately, disembodied) by the bony Misses M'Scrag. (Kate herself has so far internalised this ideal as to apostrophise her arm in a later scene as "'[u]gly great fat thing'" [1867 [2013]: 90].) Claiming that Kate's "naturally" and "healthily" curvaceous waist was "no marvel of waspish tenuity", Broughton deploys a rhetoric similar to that of Victorian attacks on tight-lacing, which characterised corsets as unnatural and unhealthy. Although some Victorian calls for dress reform reflected the conservative belief that women should be asexually maternal— for instance, corsets were blamed for emphasizing women's curves as well as damaging their reproductive organs—feminists also assailed the corset as an emblem of restrictive gender ideologies.[15] It is not surprising that, unlike the voluptuous and unconventional Kate, her boringly conventional sister Margaret possesses a "17-inch wasp-waist" that "displayed very unmistakably that want of development which is so grievous and common a fault among English girls": as the narrator proclaims, "I have heard people say that Margaret's figure was more refined than Kate's. If that be the case, a skeleton's was more refined still" (1867 [2013]: 55).

Indeed, the *Spectator* reviewer who called Broughton a "novelist of revolt" explicitly linked the "full" bodies of her first two heroines, Kate Chester and Nell Lestrange of *Cometh Up as a Flower*, to their hunger for freedom:

> In each story the central figure is the same—a girl of a full and noble nature, round as to her lines mental and bodily, with full bust and an exuberant mental life, despising conventionality and contemning the usual cut-and-dry formulas for living, ensnared, but not stained, by a burning passion for a man who cannot, or does not, become her husband[.] (19 October 1867, in *NW*, 1867 [2013]: 437)

* * *

Like the *Spectator* reviewer, Geraldine Jewsbury recognises the link between Broughton's depiction of a full-figured heroine and the young author's representation of female desire. Yet, while Broughton's narrator gushes happily about Kate's "soft undulating contours, and pretty roundnesses", Jewsbury's report on *Not Wisely* for Richard Bentley identifies this soft roundness as evidence of the novel's problematic sensuality:

> [A]s a picture of strong unregulated sensual passion it is life like enough—but the story—it is nothing but a series of love scenes (if <u>love</u> it can be called) & the point of interest turns upon the man being a "big Titan" with "brawny athlete arms" "superb broad shoulders" & "cavernous gleaming eyes"—a thorough blackguard contrasting with the heroine who is "little" "round" "soft" with ["]soft white shoulders" "soft white arms" "seagreen eyes" a witching power & face— who the aforesaid "Titan" "crushes" & "kisses" & "devours" & "holds in [his] iron grasp." (*BA* 2 July 1866, in *NW*, 1867 [2013]: 378)

A perceptive, if hostile, reader, Jewsbury identifies in this summary the tactile as well as gendered nature of the novel's opposition between "soft" femininity and "iron"-hard masculinity. Whereas Kate is "soft and downy ... like a kitten" (1867 [2013]: 77), Dare, an athlete with muscles "rising in knotted cords" (1867 [2013]: 67), is hyperbolically phallic; as Kate's awe-struck brother exclaims "'Why, he is about as broad as this room, and as hard as iron'" (1867 [2013]: 61). As Sally Mitchell notes, in fact, in the serial Kate responds to one of Dare's signature "iron" embraces with a sensation resembling orgasm: "the strain that fulfilled the wild longing, the burning dreams of weeks, was quite painful" (1981: 89; *DUM,* in 1867 [2013]: 397).

Indicating how Kate experiences desire through fantasy, the phrase "burning dreams" has autoerotic overtones, inviting a largely female readership to participate in an expertly deferred drama of erotic tension. Even Jewsbury admitted that the narrative possessed "force", though she ascribed this power to "high coloured epithets & sensual appeals to the feelings—*sentiment* there is *none*" (*BA* 3 July, 1866, in *NW,* 1867 [2013]: 379).[16] Reporting on its serial version, Jewsbury would have encountered some of the novel's more notable "sensual appeals" to its audience. For instance, when Kate's brother praises Dare's athletic body in the passage cited above—"'he's about as broad as this room, and as hard as iron'"— the *DUM* version includes a line inviting the reader to join the scene's female characters in imagining this phallic body unclothed: "'If you could but see the muscle on his back', he said, rapturously, turning to his sisters" (*DUM,* in *NW,* 1867 [2013]: 388).

Unsurprisingly, the paean to Dare's naked back was one of the passages removed in the serial revision, as was the line evoking orgasm. In addition to pruning particularly explicit references to sexuality, Broughton pared the use of slang in her revisions, substituting, for instance, the exclamation "'Ahem!'" (1867 [2013]: 78) for the original "'Hookey Walker!'" (*DUM,* in *NW,* 1867 [2013]: 390). While such emendations might seem more stylistic than ideological, Broughton's coupling the words "coarseness" and "slanginess" in a letter to Bentley promising to revise the serial text—"I will do my best to expunge it of coarseness & slanginess" (BA [summer of 1867], in *NW,* 1867 [2013]: 381)—indicates the link between these categories during the Victorian era. In her antifeminist diatribe of 1868, "The Girl of the Period", Eliza Lynn Linton assailed the late-Victorian young woman—a being she compared to a whore—for "talking slang as glibly as a man, and by preference leading the conversation to doubtful subjects" (1868 [1995]: 175). A later chapter will return to the parallels between Broughton's slangy heroines and the "Girl of the Period." For now, I will note the relevance to *Not Wisely* of Linton's link between the modern girl's knowledge of slang and her knowledge of sexuality ("doubtful subjects")—both types of knowledge symptomatic of an increased female rebellion against parental control. As Linton says, the "Girl of the Period" is "far too fast" to reverence the "slow old morals" of the days in which "fathers and mothers had some authority" (1868 [1995]: 173).

This context allows us to appreciate how, in muting Kate's use of slang, Broughton downplays her heroine's resistance to familial authority. For example, in the serial version Kate is more disrespectful than in the triple-decker to her guardian, Reverend Piggott, an obese hypochondriac too self-absorbed to exert much control over his niece; Kate's muttered exclamation when he does scold her on one occasion—"'Oh, come, shut up!'" (*DUM* Aug '65 132; in *NW,* 1867 [2013]: 387)—disappears in the novel's volume format. Broughton also downplays both the informality of Kate's discourse and her disrespect of masculine authority in the scene in which her cousin George tries to stop her from exploring the Crystal Palace unchaperoned. In the serial, George is horrified by the notion of her "'sauntering about at public places, quite by yourself'", but Kate rudely "blaze[s] out" at his "assumption of authority," informing him that he has no "'right'" to police her movements before stalking off (*DUM* in *NW,* 1867 [2013]: 411). When Broughton rewrites this scene, which, in the triple-decker, occurs at the end of Volume II, she still allows Kate to get her way, but makes her wheedle George out of playing the "protecting elder brother" (1867 [2013]: 263) rather than rudely repulse his efforts to control her.

* * *

Did Broughton, then, dramatically dilute her subversive portrayal of female sexuality and rebellion in her revisions of the serialised *Not Wisely*? The earliest feminist re-evaluations of the work tended to assume this was the case; writing in 1981, Sally Mitchell claimed that, in removing the line evoking orgasm from the triple-decker, Broughton "violates her original conception" (1981: 89). Subsequent feminist criticism, however, offers a more nuanced view. Responding to Mitchell's claim in 1995, Helen Debenham points out that "only an extremely naïve reader could remain unaware of [Kate's] physical reaction to Dare's presence" (1996: 14). In fact, though Broughton removes the scene's reference to orgasmic sensations, she retains a steamy description in the same paragraph of the lovers' first kiss: "their lips met, and were joined in a wedlock so fast, so long enduring, so firm, that it seemed as if they never could be divorced again" (1867 [2013]: 137). Other sensuous details that survive Broughton's editing include her description of the "pretty roundnesses" of Kate's body (1867 [2013]: 50) and such ineradicably sexy details as Dare's "great, soft, black-brown moustache, drooping silkily" (1867 [2013]: 67).

Finally, too, no amount of tweaking Kate's language or bearing can mask such transgressions of feminine propriety as sneaking out of the house by night to meet her lover and lying to her guardian as to her whereabouts. Admitting that it is impossible to whitewash this behaviour, Broughton inserted a defensive passage in the triple-decker in which the narrator begs "Let no one think I am defending this girl, or holding her sentiments up as the pattern of what a young woman's should be ... To describe bad actions is not, as I would meekly submit to indignant virtue, to be an accomplice in them" (1867 [2013]: 147–48).

Muddy and Polluted: When English Girls Go Native

It is hard to read the triple-decker's reference to "indignant virtue" without suspecting that Broughton had Jewsbury in mind. Predictably, however, Broughton's emendations of the serialised *Not Wisely* did not placate "indignant virtue", which was very much on display in Robert Romer's review of the triple-decker in *The Athenæum*. Dismissing the speech in which the lovelorn Kate laments "'O, why will not God let us have what we like'" (1867 [2013]: 89) as "sickening blasphemy with which we must no more pollute these pages" (in Broughton 1867 [2013]: 431), Romer growls "[w]orse than even the immorality of the whole novel are the stupid, misplaced attempts at sermonizing throughout" (2 November 1867, in Broughton, 1867 [2013]: 431).

When he speaks of "sermonizing", Romer is presumably referring to passages in Broughton's novel that sound like something he himself could have written. Tellingly, the speech of Kate's that Romer reviles as "blasphemy"—"'O, why will not God let us have what we like'" (1867 [2013]: 89)—had already been identified as such within the text itself. In both serial and triple-decker versions of the novel, the narrator greets Kate's declaration that, could she have Dare to herself for just one month, she would "die and live in tortures for all the countless ages of eternity" (1867 [2013]: 90) with the sententious comment "Frantic passion, utterly uncurbed, made this girl blasphemous—this girl, who, if she could have had her own wild will, would have been altogether wrecked for time and for eternity" (1867 [2013]: 90). Even more hellfire-and-brimstone rhetoric is provided by the novel's resident super-ego, the clergyman James Stanley, a "'living skeleton'" (1867 [2013]: 174) reminiscent of a modern-day male anorexic. Notable for his "cuttings and hackings and prunings" of his own appetites (1867

[2013]: 245), including an unrequited attraction to Kate, Stanley directs her in district visiting following her first failed elopement with Dare, and later convinces her to abandon her attempt to become Dare's mistress following the lovers' accidental reunion at the Crystal Palace. On the latter occasion, Stanley, speaking "with the solemn severity of one of God's ministers" (1867 [2013]: 297), browbeats Kate into renouncing Dare with guilt-tripping rhetoric that includes imagining her dead mother's anguish at her fallen daughter's inability to join her in Heaven.

It is tempting to read such "sermonizing", as Romer calls it, as Broughton's attempt to forestall moral outrage at the edgier aspects of her work. Certainly, the distance between James Stanley's rhetoric and Broughton's own taste is underscored by her dismissive reference to him, in a letter to George Bentley in 1870, as "the wishy washy good parson" (BA, 13 February 1870, in *NW, 1867* [2013]: 383), whom she offers to leave out of her proposed rewrite of the novel. One reason Broughton gave Bentley for her loathing of *Not Wisely* "as it at present stands" is precisely its didacticism, or "*canting*": "it is crude vulgar and in parts *canting*, all in the highest degree" (BA, [late December? 1871], in *NW, 1867* [2013]: 384). That Broughton referred to *Not Wisely* as "crude" and "vulgar", as well as "*canting*", however, points to an ambivalence about the more daring features of her own project, including the sensuality of her heroine. As I stated at the beginning of this chapter, this ambivalence informs the narrative itself, as conservative responses to changing sexual mores vie with its more radical features. This section, then, addresses the extent to which contemporary anxieties about female sexuality and autonomy so thoroughly infuse the novel that they cannot be explained away simply as a way to placate potentially disapproving readers.[17]

One sign that Broughton herself (as opposed to her characters) had qualms about her heroine's sexual daring is that her plot proves George Chester right: he had reason to object to Kate's roaming the Crystal Palace without a chaperone. Though she assures her cousin before setting off that "There were no wolves in grandmothers' guise to lure unsuspecting Red Ridinghoods to their destruction" (1867 [2013]: 265), Kate is wrong. All too soon, she stumbles on the predatory wolf in the person of Dare, who, on this second try, succeeds in persuading her to become his mistress. Broughton's allusion to Red Ridinghood—one of several references to the fairy-tale, as Laurence Talairach-Vielmas points out (2007: 102)—reiterates that story's warning about the dangers awaiting unprotected young women in a world filled with sexual temptation and predation.

Indeed, Kate's playing the role of Red Ridinghood in the Crystal Palace is the culmination of the section of the novel—most of Volume II in the triple-decker— which repeatedly alludes to topical concerns about female sexuality. Positioned between Kate's two attempts at elopement—the first aborted when she discovers that Dare is married, and the second abandoned after Stanley persuades her to renege on her promise to Dare at the Crystal Palace to become his mistress—these chapters associate Kate with a series of late-1860s anxieties about female bodies and desires. Bringing Kate into contact with the lower classes in this section of the novel, Broughton plays upon that aspect of the sensation controversy that Susan Bernstein calls "anxiety of assimilation" (1994: 225)—the fear, expressed by the genre's critics, that exposure of female readers to sexual knowledge would dissolve the barriers separating the middle-class woman from the lower-class woman, especially the prostitute.

As a district visitor in London's slums, Kate tries to forget Dare after discovering he is married, an occupation which involves distributing tracts, and with them, bourgeois values of piety and cleanliness. Yet, as Seth Koven says of actual Victorian women who did social work, "slumming" brought them in contact with illicit or "'dirty' desires", thus "flout[ing] bourgeois class and gender expectations" even as they themselves attempted to instil such expectations in the poor (2004: 198).[18] Kate's "slumming" destabilises her class identity all the more because of her unconventional sexual history. The "reeking" slums which she traverses (1867 [2013]: 199) suggest her own vulnerability to sexual pollution, literalizing the narrator's comparison of erotic passion to a "stinking stagnant pond" (1867 [2013]: 296). The excremental overtones of these images of "reeking" and "stinking"—Victorian slums were notorious for being steeped in raw sewage—recall Kate's association with the nether regions of Victorian symbolic geography earlier in the novel. Falling in love with Dare after meeting him at a seaside resort, she sneaks out through the "back door" of the house for clandestine night-time trysts (1867 [2013]: 109). Since, as Leonore Davidoff argues, the "back passages" of the house, normally the realm of servants, were metaphors in the period for the lower regions of the body (1983: 27), Kate was linked, even prior to her excursions in the "back slums and alleys" (1867 [2013]: 198) of the East End, with a series of related abjections: the lower body, the lower classes, excrement, and sexual urges. Moreover, in moving between a bourgeois residence and the slums, Kate threatens to become a conduit of disease; as her cousin scolds when she announces her mission of distributing tracts, "'You'll only be catching some of those horrid nasty diseases that those kind of people are always having'" (1867 [2013]: 187–88).

An episode that underscores the instability of Kate's class and gender identity is also the novel's most explicit reference, prior to the Crystal Palace scene, to the Red Ridinghood story. Red-cloaked and carrying a tract-filled basket, Kate—who laughingly comments at the outset of her mission on her resemblance to the fairy-tale protagonist (1867 [2013]: 197)—is terrified when, after she gets lost on her way home, a loafing "bargee", or barge worker, jokingly calls out to her "'a ha-penny for your crinoline, miss'" (1867 [2013]: 212). Dropping her basket, Kate runs blindly until she collides with James Stanley, who assures her that she was never actually in danger. Despite this reassurance, the scene raises the spectre of sexual assault, with the bargee's offer of money for Kate's crinoline evoking prostitution as well. Such potential dangers awaiting the newly-mobile Victorian girl recall the comment relayed to Kate by one of her cousins: "'Pa says it is not at all right for such a pretty girl as you to be walking about, all by yourself; and that if you were his daughter, he'd as soon think of cutting your throat, as letting you go about those back streets all alone'" (1867 [2013]: 188).

Still, in this scene the crimson-clad Kate is not only the sexually vulnerable Red Ridinghood: she is also the Scarlet Woman. It is significant that the bargee mentions Kate's crinoline, as this controversial fashion was criticised for, among other things, the indecency with which its hoop skirt could swing upward to expose the wearer's legs.[19] Presumably Kate treats spectators to an eyeful as she races on her wild "Mazeppan course" (1867 [2013]: 213)—a reference to a poem by Byron that, appropriately enough, alludes both to sexual transgression and nudity: having seduced a married woman, the eponymous speaker describes his wild ride on the untamed stallion to whose back he has been bound, naked, by the irate husband. Careening into James Stanley in her own mad race through the streets, the crimson-clad Kate symbolically infects him with sexual temptation. Secretly in love with her, Stanley had, hitherto, struggled to quell the passion he sees as a "gin and a trap" (1867 [2013]: 219) distracting him from his celibate commitment to slum ministry; after Kate runs into him, however, he is increasingly tormented by fantasies of marrying her. Commenting on how Stanley touches letters from the girl as gingerly as if "cholera, typhus, and small-pox lurked in every fold" (1867 [2013]: 247), Pamela Gilbert labels Kate "a species of Typhoid Mary" who "'carries' the sexual fever wherever she goes" (1997: 119). It is not surprising that, near the novel's end, Stanley literally succumbs to fever, dying in an epidemic that originates in the slums as spring arrives with appropriately feminised imagery, "bearing malaria in its wet bosom" (1867 [2013]: 307).

Figuratively representing sexual contagion, Kate recalls the urban prostitute, whose potentially infectious body, as demonstrated by the 1860s Contagious Diseases Acts, was a locus of cultural anxiety. But Kate evokes another figure for female sexual threat who, by the late-Victorian period, was increasingly associated with the city: the flirt. In his analysis of flirting in nineteenth-century literature, Richard Kaye draws on the work of George Simmel, a German social theorist who conducted several studies of flirting in the early twentieth century. According to Simmel, the detachment of flirting from actual courtship—the transformation of coquetry from prelude to marriage to often aimless social pastime—was fostered by nineteenth-century urbanization and its breakdown of communal bonds. Reflecting a similar shift from rural community to urban anomie, Victorian fiction, Kaye argues, increasingly represents flirting as a "social menace" (2002: 151) that derails, rather than fosters, domesticity and familial bonds. Like Henry James's Daisy Miller, the incorrigible flirt is a *femme fatale* who distracts men from their proper function as fathers and husbands. Though Kaye does not pursue this link, in the late-Victorian period the figure of the "virtuoso flirt" (2002: 153) becomes intertwined with the stereotype of the "fast" Girl of the Period with whom, as Eliza Lynn Linton opines, men "flirt" but "do not marry" (1868 [1995]: 175). It is striking, indeed, to what extent Broughton associates Kate's obsessive coquetry with her relocation to an urban landscape following her first failed elopement. Even as she launches her career of district-visiting, she hones her already considerable skills at enticing men. "Kate could flirt still, then? Most decidedly, and practised the accomplishment more; was a far greater proficient in it than ever she had used to be in former happy days" (1867 [2013]: 186). Deriving sadistic "pleasure in seeing man after man play needle to her magnet", Kate chooses as favoured victim the infatuated George Chester, "[h]er little coquetries and honeyed looks… snaring him with a false delusion" (1867 [2013]: 186, 249). Depicting Kate as so promiscuous a coquette that she would even "flirt with the undertaker who came to measure her for her coffin" (1867 [2013]:194), the narrative reinforces her association with sexual energies antithetical to domesticity. To find a proper helpmeet, George Chester is compelled to turn to Kate's sister Margaret, whom he later marries.

* * *

Uniting these images of Kate as sexual threat is the Victorian ideologeme of "going native". Identified by Patrick Brantlinger as a defining theme of "imperial Gothic", this ideologeme registers British concerns about cultural degeneration by showing British characters transforming into versions of the colonial subjects they are meant to govern (1988: 230). Like many *femme fatales* in Victorian fiction, Kate is orientalised, represented, by virtue of her overpowering eroticism, as a racial Other in spite of her apparent membership in the English middle class. Labelled a "southern-souled girl" (1867 [2013]: 151)—and thus contrasting her overt sensuality to the asexual chastity of the "northern" or English ideal—Kate is also likened to "a houri" (1867 [2013]: 131), one of the female spirits who supposedly reward faithful males in the Islamic paradise. Significantly, in the scene prior to the one in which she expresses orgasmic delight in the conservatory of exotic hothouse flowers (themselves a symbolic harem), the narrator calls Kate a "Circassian" (1867 [2013]: 132), a term applied to white women of the Caucasus sold in slavery to Eastern traders. A common signifier in nineteenth-century orientalist discourses for female objectification, Circassian women were portrayed in numerous paintings undergoing the inspection of male slave traders or prospective male owners,[20] as is Kate when, in the scene before she goes to the conservatory with Dare, she stands before him "on approval, like a Circassian slave at the market of Constantinople" while he "feast[s]" on her appearance (1867

[2013]: 132). An exchange between Kate and Dare later in this scene emphasises her symbolic racial Otherness. When she refuses to obey his sultan-like command to wear a sun hat—"'or you'll be burnt all manner of colours'",—by proclaiming that "'I don't care if I'm burnt as black as a coal,'" Dare fondly imagines "'[w]hat a dear little negro you would make'" (1867 [2013]: 132–33).

The ideologeme of English cultural decline that undergirds the "going native" topos is especially pronounced in the scene at the Crystal Palace in which Kate consents to become Dare's mistress. That Kate should consent to become a fallen woman in this particular setting is ironic, given the Palace's celebration of British empire. An engineering extravaganza of iron and glass originally constructed to showcase British industrial achievement at the 1851 exhibition in Hyde Park, the Palace was expanded, upon its relocation to Sydenham, to contain such features as a series of "courts" (Egyptian, Greek, Roman, etc.) organised around the art and architecture of famous historical epochs. Coupled with displays of exotic plants and ethnographic exhibits of "savage" cultures, Sydenham's Victorian theme park constructed a historical narrative situating the British empire as the acme of human civilization. Yet, while on one hand Broughton's transforming this apotheosis of empire into the site of sexual transgression is ironic, on the other hand it is overdetermined. As Jeffrey Auerbach notes in his history of the Crystal Palace, "As early as the 1860s ... the Crystal Palace had, for many writers, come to symbolize not the triumph of progress but its failures" (1999: 206). Broughton introduces the Palace in *Not Wisely* with a satiric reference to the "brittle glass domes of the eighth wonder of the world": "Marvellous pitch of civilisation for us to have attained to ... we must come soon to the highest pinnacle we are to reach, one thinks sometimes, and then begin to retrograde" (1867 [2013]: 259–60).

Given this association of the Palace with imperial degeneration, it is significant that Kate traverses its grounds through a landscape that is both racially and sexually symbolic. Beginning her unchaperoned promenade through the "Exotic Court" (1867 [2013]: 265)— the Tropical Department, a collection of plants from Africa and South America—Kate sits for a time next to the fountain, sculpted by Raffaele Monti, and adorned by four barebreasted sirens, each representing a racial category from the earth's four corners. (Although these categories include Caucasians, Broughton nonetheless emphasises the racial Otherness of the "bronze mermaids", describing them all as having "dark shoulders" [1867 [2013]: 265–66].) Leaving this gendered allegory of colonialism, Kate next enters the Greek Court, whose many casts of famous sculptures included such nudes as the Venus de Medici, to whom the narrator compares Kate in his initial description of her figure (1867 [2013]: 49). Reflecting her own connection with decadence, Kate chooses the Greek Court because it affords an opportunity, as did the hothouse in Volume I, to glut her voracious sensual appetite: "She would go in and feast her eyes till they should be sated and saturated with loveliness" (1867 [2013]: 267).[21]

As Kate's gaze lingers on male nudes whose powerful physique reminds her of Dare, he himself enters the room, accompanied by a married aristocrat with whom he is having an affair. Claiming that the "purple and the tiara of Livia or Agrippina" would have suited the adulterous lady, with her "bold, sensual, snaring face" (1867 [2013]: 269), the narrator links the Greek court to Roman *femme fatales* (Agrippina was the mother of Nero). These classical references underscore one of the novel's more reactionary messages: succumbing to erotic temptation, Kate paves the way for British imperial decline.

"Daughters of Eve": Women and Literary Tradition

The anxieties about female sexuality in *Not Wisely* tend either to clash with the book's more positive representations of female desire, or to emphasise how even these representations verge on the negative. For instance, the implication that Kate is susceptible to sexual contagion underscores the problematic potential of her openness to sensation: rather than indicating, like her uncorseted waist, a "natural[...]" and "health[...]y" appetite (1867 [2013]: 50), her hunger for anything that "spoke to the senses" recalls the voracious consumerism attributed to female readers of sensation fiction by critics of the genre. In its mélange of subversive and conservative messages, *Not Wisely* demonstrates how Victorian women's fiction can be, in the words of Nicola Thompson, "'melting pots of ideological conflict'" (cited in Maunder 2004: xix). What makes the novel a particularly striking example of the ideologically fissured woman's text, however, is the way it complicates its own ambivalence about female sexuality.

As I mentioned earlier, one significant way in which this complication occurs is through intertextuality, and the evidence it provides of the historical link between literature and misogyny. Broughton underscores this link both by having her narrator voluminously quote misogynist lines from literature, and by characterizing him, not as the usual neutral, and ambiguously gendered, third-person narrator, but as one of Kate's frustrated admirers ("She was everything to me, and I was less than nothing to her" [1867 [2013]: 45]). In this context, the narrator's moral strictures on Kate are undercut to some degree by his criticizing her preference for his own rival. As she falls in love with Dare in volume I, for example, the narrator declares sententiously "to my thinking, never was she in more completely evil case ... She had made her selection for ever it seemed—had chosen her home in this great lazar-house of ours" (1867 [2013]: 125). Yet the words "to my thinking" lessen the authority of this pronouncement, reminding us that, given the narrator's own unrequited love, he is unlikely to appreciate Kate's "selection" of any lover other than himself. Similarly, the narrator's claim that Dare was a man "who, as I and all his friends knew ... never had any higher guide than his own giant passions" (1867 [2013]: 97) might not be an objective assessment so much as an envious dig.

Broughton's giving the narrator a personal stake in the story—a choice that dramatizes male ambivalence about female sexuality—might explain why she made the otherwise awkward decision to define him as she does. An acquaintance of the novel's characters (though he never appears in any of the scenes), the narrator lacks the omniscience of the typical third-person narrator; the sole knowledge he could have of the novel's events would be through his own memories and hearsay. That, in fact, he provides detailed accounts of supposedly private moments (such as the love scenes between Kate and Dare) makes no sense unless he were even more voyeuristic than Broughton presumably intended. And yet the narrator's frustrated desire for Kate—a desire coupled with puritanical rebukes of her sexuality—makes him all too appropriate a guide to a tale whose male lead similarly combines erotic obsession with misogyny. Not only does Dare declare in the conservatory scene that he would rather cut Kate's "'little soft throat'" than let her be kissed by any man other than himself (1867 [2013]: 138), but he inveighs elsewhere against "'[w]oman's fickleness'" and perfidy (1867 [2013]: 273), with a viciousness particularly pronounced in the serial version when he shoots her for being a "'false, lying woman'" [*DUM*, in *NW*, 1867 [2013]: 418]). Enamoured of Kate's luscious body like Dare, the narrator also views her through the lenses of literary conventions that either represent female sexuality negatively or reduce women to mere objects of male desire.

The first chapter of *Not Wisely* underscores the link between the male gaze and intertextuality, as the narrator describes, not only his obsession with Kate, but his predilection for transforming her into art. Using the metaphor of a "secret picture-gallery" in "an inner chamber" of his spirit to memorialise women he has loved, the narrator identifies Kate's likeness as the "gem of the collection": "None enters there but myself ... Often I stand before that girl image, and gaze and gaze till my eyes ache and burn, in the intensity of my longing that those lips should unclose but *once* again" (1867 [2013]: 45). Recalling the Duke who in Robert Browning's "My Last Duchess" controls his wife's flirtatious behaviour by first killing her, and then reserving her veiled portrait for his gaze and those of visitors he selects ("none puts by/ The curtain I have drawn for you, but I" [1845 [2000]: ll. 9–10]), the narrator's transformation of Kate into a prized, private artwork reveals his sexual possessiveness.

In a symbolic sense, then, Kate's portrait suggests how women have been "framed", as it were, by male-dominated, and frequently misogynist, literary traditions. Before introducing his "secret picture-gallery", the narrator lists literary and mythological *femmes fatales* who, like Kate, illustrate women's attraction as well as their sexual danger. Evoking the originary female temptress of the Judaeo-Christian tradition, the narrator addresses the novel's female readers as "daughters of Eve" (1867 [2013]: 42), and proceeds to celebrate the enduring fascinations of Helen of Troy, Cleopatra, and the goddess Aphrodite. In particular, the narrator's references in this first chapter to Cleopatra—an Oriental beauty apostrophised as "[f]rail, vain, variable, heartless coquette!" (1867 [2013]: 43)—anticipate the "southern-souled" (1867 [2013]: 151) Kate's virtuoso flirtation with George Chester in the novel's second volume, scenes in which the narrator explicitly compares her to both Shakespeare's and Tennyson's depictions of the Egyptian queen. A virulently misogynist work referenced in the section in which Kate flirts with George is Owen Meredith's *Tannhäuser, or the Battle of the Bards*, which, like the medieval romance on which it is based, depicts the goddess Venus tempting knights to abandon their service to God. Associating Venus's outwardly gorgeous body with moral filth and corruption, *Tannhäuser* labels her the "bloat Queen" whose "bestial revels" make men "slaves of their bodies ... wallowing in the arms/ Of their libidinous goddess" (1861 [1883]: ll. 118, 39, 103–05). James Stanley, who resists Kate's charms, and with them the "manacles and fetters of the flesh" (1867 [2013]: 218) which he believes would bar him from heaven, recalls Meredith's celebration of knights pure enough to avoid or overcome sensual entrapment. Placing these misogynistic allusions in the mouth of a narrator who himself has reason to resent Kate's coquetry, Broughton to some extent deauthorises literary discourses which negatively portray women. Even so, however, our perception of Kate cannot help but be influenced by the repeated comparisons between her and such "heartless" and "variable" flirts as Cleopatra.

Broughton's debt to male precursors is, thus, complex. I have, so far, focused on the problems of depicting female experience through a misogynistic lens. On a more positive level, Broughton's allusions to male predecessors enhance her linguistic authority. Tellingly, of all Broughton's novels, the first two—the ones deemed sensational—are the most allusive, often peppering a single page with multiple quotations. While any author might feel the need to shore up their authority in their early work, in Broughton's case such insecurity can only have been exacerbated by the low status of sensation fiction, and its association with a female audience and readership who had limited educational opportunities. Wielding the encyclopedic erudition acquired in her father's library—an acquaintance claimed she knew Shakespeare virtually by heart[22]—Broughton claims membership in the community of cultivated taste embodied in her male narrator. In this light, the narrator's casual use of Greek and Latin phrases is more a testimony to Broughton's knowledge than to his own. While a man of the narrator's sex and class would be expected to know classical languages, Broughton's knowledge of this material asserts her ability, as a woman writer, to compete with educated men. Male authors also help authorise Broughton's engagement of risqué topics, as several of those Broughton is fond of quoting, such as Byron, had themselves written daringly about sexuality. Borrowing from their work, Broughton draws on their cultural capital to legitimate her own representations of this controversial subject, even though, by doing so, she reproduces their frequently stereotyped portrayals of women.

One of Broughton's most sophisticated responses to literary precursors in *Not Wisely* is to show how women are influenced by their reading. When we first meet Kate as an actual character—not just as a static portrait in the narrator's "picture-gallery"—she is, in fact, finishing a book. Not only does this scene, set at a local beach, introduce Kate as a reader, but it identifies her as a critical reader who questions the relevance of literary celebrations of romance to her own life. The book she has just finished is Whyte-Melville's *The Interpreter* (1858), a Crimean War romance in which the hero dies after his life is ruined by a "coquette whose penitence came too late" (1867 [2013]: 37)—ironically, a narrative that employs the same stereotype of the heartless flirt that the narrator will later use to depict Kate herself. Yet, in this early scene, Kate, who has already met Dare but not yet fallen in love with him, doubts the truth of romantic tales. Asking herself whether love is "such an all-conquering influence (the greatest of human influences) as they make out in books like this", she initially answers in the negative, dismissing literary representations of romance as "'one great imposture'" (1867 [2013]: 51–52). Significantly, she changes her mind upon recalling her favourite romantic heroines:

> "Do Juliet, and Imogene, and Francesca of Rimini, and Fatima talk nonsense? If they do, I would rather have their nonsense than any other people's sense. Yes, yes, after all I do believe they are pretty nearly right. Love must be the one great bliss of this world[.]" (1867 [2013]: 52)

Agreeing that literary representations are "'right'" in their view of the world, Kate accepts as models for her own behaviour the obsessed—and frequently doomed—romantic heroines she mentions in the passage above. In addition to Tennyson's Fatima, a version of the eroticised, Oriental beauty, Kate lists Shakespeare's Juliet, who, like Tennyson's Elaine, is a tragic victim of passion.

Ominously, too, the other tragic heroine Kate mentions, Francesca da Rimini, is a fallen woman—and one who falls, moreover, because she reads. In the Byron poem in which she appears, and which is a particular favourite of Kate's after she falls in love with Dare, Francesca, originally a character in Dante's *Inferno*, whirls endlessly in hell with the man with whom she had intercourse after they read a romantic tale together.

Kate's romance reading thus shapes the way she views her own growing attraction to Dare, causing her to reject the belief she had previously espoused, that romantic fictions provide an "'absurdly false'" picture of love because "'[t]hey represent it as the one main interest in life, instead of being, as it mostly is, a short unimportant little episode'" (1867 [2013]: 52). This dismissive view of romantic love as an "'unimportant little episode'", though, is more often associated with men, as the narrator shows in the passage which serves as an epigraph for this chapter, and in which he claims that the "passion which forms the main plot of a woman's life" is "only a small secondary byplay in a man's" (1867 [2013]: 83). Because domestic and gender ideology defines feminine experience through affective bonds rather than, as in the case of men, through public affairs, Kate is unable finally to see love as a subplot, rather than the "main plot", of a woman's life. Thus, when the narrator asks whether Kate's story will be a "tragedy or a comedy", he indicates the sole generic options afforded women in domestic ideology: if their history does not end with "comedy"— in its original definition of marital closure—it must perforce be defined as a tragedy. Interestingly, then, Broughton's critique of women's reading is not the traditional criticism—and the criticism levelled at sensation fiction—that reading makes them susceptible to sexual passion;[23] rather, she implies that reading, all too often, gives women the misleading idea that marriage is the only path to happiness.

* * *

The tension between radical and conservative attitudes toward sexuality in *Not Wisely* is mirrored by a corresponding tension in the narrative between the legacies of ideologically conflicting predecessor texts. On one hand, Broughton alludes to male-dominated, and often misogynistic, literary traditions; on the other hand, she also refers to nineteenth-century women's texts that contest such traditions and, in doing so, revise or resist traditional representations of women. Anne Thackeray Ritchie's *The Story of Elizabeth* (1863), which purportedly inspired Broughton to write *Not Wisely*, is one such text; although the sexuality of its heroine is not as explicitly described as Kate's, Ritchie's novel was innovative in showcasing an unidealised protagonist who sulks and rebels, at least initially, against conventional femininity.[24] Significantly, too, Broughton alludes to one of the originary texts of post-Enlightenment literary feminism, Germaine de Staël's *Corinne* (1807), the female *künstlerroman* which influenced numerous Victorian women writers including George Eliot and Elizabeth Barrett Browning. Twice comparing the stultifying conversation of Kate's social circle in London to (in the words of one such allusion) "Corinne's account of the after-dinner female *séances* at Lord Edgermond's castle of dulness" (1867 [2013]: 71),[25] Broughton reminds her readers of the literary genealogy that links her rebellious heroine to de Staël's improvisatrice, who flees her stepmother's conventional household to seek an artistic career in Italy.

The nineteenth-century woman's novel that *Not Wisely* most obviously rewrites is *Jane Eyre*. Both novels share essentially the same plot: an unconventional heroine falls in love with a dark Byronic male; she discovers that he is unhappily married; she resists his pleas to become his mistress; after removing herself from temptation she spends a great deal of time with an ascetic clergyman. There are, of course, significant differences between the narratives, most notably, as I shall discuss, in their conclusions, but there is little chance that Broughton was not deliberately modelling her first novel on Charlotte Brontë's most famous work; as I noted in my introduction, Margaret Oliphant noted the influence of *Jane Eyre* on the sensation genre (1867: 258), and in Broughton's quasi-autobiographical last novel, *A Fool in Her Folly* (1920), the heroine, a would-be novelist, announces her ambition to become a "second Charlotte Brontë"(1920a: 11). The most significant link between *Jane Eyre* and *Not Wisely*, however, is that both plots address the conflict between sexual desire and social prohibitions on its expression outside marriage.

Notably, however, Broughton's representation of sexual desire is less conventionally moralistic than Brontë's. Though she suffers greatly in parting from Rochester when he tempts her to become his mistress, Jane persists in her resolution to "'keep the law given by God; sanctioned by man'" (1847 [1996]: 270). In the end, she is rewarded with a marriage to a widowed and chastened Rochester who, moreover, experienced a religious conversion after she left him on moral grounds. Dare, in contrast, remains undomesticated in both versions of *Not Wisely*. While this is most obviously the case in the serial, in which he murders Kate before killing himself, it is also true of the triple-decker. Although Dare's injuries following his carriage accident in Volume III recall Rochester's following the fire at Thornfield, Broughton's male lead resists religious conversion even on his deathbed, claiming, in response to Kate's pleas that he pray for forgiveness, that "'it's no good; it's—too late—too late!'" (1867 [2013]: 369). Furthermore, Broughton refuses to resort to the *deus ex machina* ending that, by killing off the unwanted wife, allows Brontë's lovers to achieve sexual fulfilment without being further tempted to engage in bigamy or extra-marital cohabitation. Avoiding the "providential framework", as Helen Debenham puts it (1996: 15), that smooths the path to legal matrimony for Jane and Rochester, Broughton thus presents her readers with the incontrovertible facts of a marriage in which one partner has outgrown his affection for the other, and an extra-marital attraction which, despite the force of her desire, the heroine is unable to consummate in any socially sanctioned way.

Unhappily Ever After: The Problem of the Ending

Closing off the possibility of *Jane Eyre*'s "Reader, I married him" (1847 [1996]: 382)—the "comedy" of the courtship narrative—*Not Wisely* ends in both serial and triple-decker incarnations with the only other conclusion the narrator could imagine in the romantic "main plot" of a woman's life: "tragedy." Both versions of the novel conclude with Kate's death, although, sticking to her promise to Bentley to rewrite the end of the serial, Broughton discarded its sensational, murder-suicide finale. Instead, following Dare's death in a carriage accident, Kate reaches the verge of "gray beautiless middle age" (1867 [2013]: 375) as an Anglican nun ministering to the urban poor—the vocation she had planned to pursue in the serial before a violent Dare gate-crashes the ball preceding her sister's wedding.

It is hard to disagree with Broughton's assessment to Bentley in 1876 that the conclusion of the serial version has "greater power" than that of the triple-decker. In contrast to the (literal) bang of the serial finale, the triple-decker limps along for a chapter after Dare's accidental death before the moping Kate decides—for the second time, no less—to enter a sisterhood. In addition to sacrificing drama, the altered ending obscures the parallel between Shakespeare's *Othello* and Broughton's novel signalled by her choice of title. Claiming that he has loved "not wisely, but too well" (1603–04 [1998]: 127, V.ii. 340), Shakespeare's hero kills himself after slaying the wife he suspected of adultery, events mirrored in the serial *Not Wisely*'s murder-suicide, which is similarly motivated because Dare considers Kate's refusal to elope with him a type of infidelity.

Readers today may find the original ending particularly compelling because they recognise in it a figure sadly familiar in contemporary life: the abusive boyfriend. Dare's jealousy in the serial (he shoots Kate at a party after railing at her for dancing with other men), as well as his self-righteous conviction that she has only herself to blame for any violence he employs against her, might seem a startlingly modern depiction of a male abuser's psychology. Yet, while twenty-first century readers are likely to sympathise with the stalked and murdered Kate, the ideological charge of the *Dublin University Magazine* ending nevertheless reinforces the novel's conservative messages about female sexuality. Although Kate is allowed to display her hard-won virtue by refusing Dare's offer of her life in exchange for becoming his mistress, the serial ending, with its message that violent delights have violent ends, still reads as a cautionary tale for "fast" girls. In contrast, the triple-decker conclusion, though aesthetically weaker, is arguably less reactionary. In presenting Dare more sympathetically—in reworking the ending, Broughton also played down his violent tendencies in earlier scenes—the triple-decker more sympathetically portrays Kate's transgressive desire. Noting the surge of "wild joy" felt by the Kate of the serial in Dare's presence, even as he prepares to shoot her (*DUM*, in *NW*, 1867 [2013]: 423), the reader of the *Dublin University Magazine* version can dismiss Kate as a Red Ridinghood deluded enough to love the wolf. The reader of the triple-decker, however, is compelled to recognise Kate as a woman whose repressive culture forces her to make wrenching choices.

A comparison of the serial and triple-decker versions of the Crystal Palace scene illustrates this point. In the serial, Dare is a textbook abusive male, threatening Kate with violence—"'You *must* stay with me, I say. I'll kill you if you don't'"—while blaming her "'cursed obstinacy'" for any "'harder means'" he employs to detain her (*DUM*, in *NW*, 1867 [2013]: 415). As Dare's villainy becomes increasingly active—he grips her with his "great arm" so tightly as almost to strangle her (*DUM*, in *NW*, 1867 [2013]: 416, 415)—she becomes increasingly passive, only agreeing to elope when, hearing the voices of her sister and cousins, she fears that her reputation will suffer if she is discovered with a married man:

> "Let me go, let me go", cried Kate, struggling frantically. "You villain! How dare you?"
> "Tiger cat!" said Dare, pale to the lips with rage, and balked passion, while two-edged swords of flame came forth from his devil-lit eyes. "Stop fighting and struggling. Just listen a minute. If you say the monosyllable 'yes.' you shall go this minute; if not, *never.*"
> Light laughter heard. George's manly tones apparently close to entrance. Kate was driven to desperation. "They'll be in, in a second", she whispered, horror-struck. "Oh, I'll say anything! Yes, yes, I'll come." (*DUM*, in *NW*, 1867 [2013]: 415–16)

Deleting this undignified scuffle in the triple-decker, Broughton recasts Kate's decision to elope as considered rather than coerced. Although the Dare of the triple-decker is still, to some extent, a stereotypical seducer—he watches "lynx-eyed" to see if she is swayed by his arguments— he nonetheless allows Kate to leave in submission to her wishes: "he only turned his face to the wall and groaned" (1867 [2013]: 280, 281). After witnessing, however, his genuine "desolation" at her departure ("great scorching tears stood in his eyes"), she changes her mind (1867 [2013]: 281).

The revisions of this scene are important in two ways. First, the revised version grants Kate agency by minimizing Dare's control over her choice; second, the portrayal of both lovers' obvious anguish at being separated makes the reader more likely to sympathise with Dare's arguments in favour of an extra-marital union. Since, as he says to Kate, "'[a]part from each other, you and I are like galvanised dead bodies that have a mechanic motion, but no life'", why should they not live together in a state where they would be "'married in the sight of God'" (1867 [2013]: 275, 279)?

As Kate herself asks earlier in the novel: "'But what opposition is there between love and goodness? ... If it is wicked of us to love one another, why did God put it into our hearts?'" (1867 [2013]: 150)

A similar message is conveyed by the revised ending. In contrast to the serial's cardboard villain, the dying Dare of the triple-decker is a man in whom "passion was dead, and love reigned immortal among the ruins of mortality" (1867 [2013]: 368). Broughton highlights the oppressive role of convention in separating the star-crossed couple, describing Kate's arrival at the wounded Dare's side in terms that elevate natural instincts over cultural laws: "In moments of profound mastering emotion we shake ourselves free from the artificial restraints of society and education, as some strong runner, ere setting forth on a long hard race, casts away the heavy garments that would hinder his flight, and returns to the instinct and impulses of Nature" (1867 [2013]: 367). This implied criticism of a society that prevents the dissolution of incompatible marriages anticipates later novels by Broughton, such as *Cometh Up as a Flower* and *Belinda,* which highlight the predicament of frustrated and unfulfilled wives.

* * *

Of course, whatever its critique of sexual convention, the triple-decker version of *Not Wisely* still presents romance as the "main plot of a woman's life", consigning its heroine, in the absence of marriage, to a fate waspishly described by the *Athenæum* reviewer: "she becomes a Protestant Sister of Mercy, and is wretched ever after" (2 November 1867, exc. in *NW,* 1867 [2013]: 431). Broughton's summary of Kate's life as a nun certainly makes it sound miserable: in a dreary return to her former district-visiting, she labours among the poor with no reward other than "much weariness of body, oftentimes discouragement of soul, and small cold praise" (1867 [2013]: 375). This representation of convents as dumping-grounds for frustrated lovers meshes with depictions elsewhere in *Not Wisely* of religious devotion as masochism. For instance, Broughton classifies James Stanley's pious efforts to subdue his feelings for Kate as (in an allusion to the founder of the Jesuits) "tormenting and bullying and maltreating himself after the Ignatius-Loyola type" (1867 [2013]: 241). Similarly, in the aftermath of the Crystal Palace episode, Kate yearns for the hyperbolically penitential lifestyle modelled by the Bernardine nuns in Hugo's *Les Misérables:* "There had come upon her a new type of austerity ... which, had she been of a different faith, would have made her relish, almost enjoy, the severities and mortifications of such a convent as that of the Perpetual Adoration" (1867 [2013]: 303).[26]

In this context, Kate's decision to enter an Anglican sisterhood may seem the closest she can come as a Protestant to the "system of flagellation, and fasting five days a week, hair-shirt, &" that her "distempered imagination" craves following her near-fall (1867 [2013]: 304). Yet Broughton's allusion to Anglican sisterhoods also gestures toward professional options for women that deemphasise romance as the "main plot of a woman's life." In a revealing conversation, Kate responds to her sister Margaret's objections to her entering an Anglican order:

> "Kate, I always hated those sisterhoods; they have been a curse to numberless families, I am certain; a number of women huddled together, cut off from their lives, and their friends, and all their prospects in life. Why cannot women keep to their right functions of marrying and being happy?"
>
> "Be happy if they can, by all means; people's ideas about happiness differ, you know. We had better not get upon a definition of happiness; and marry also, by all means, if they can have your luck, and get the man they are in love with, otherwise marriage would be a punishment hardly inferior to being tied to a dead body." (1867 [2013]: 351)

Margaret's complaint that Anglican sisterhoods keep women from their "'right function[...] of marrying'" echoes objections to their emergence in the wake of the Oxford movement. In her history of Anglican nuns, Susan Mumm claims that the sisterhoods were controversial not only because they smacked of "Papistry", but, even more subversively, provided an alternative to domesticity: "Sisterhoods generated such outrage precisely because they expanded the boundaries of full-time work for women; sisters worked in public, without apology and without direct male supervision" (1999: 96). Living among the poor out of a strong sense of social purpose—as a nun Kate toils "[e]arly and late" in London's East End (1867 [2013]: 375)—members of more than ninety Anglican women's orders established by 1900 defined professional identities as teachers, nurses, and social workers.[27] Such a destiny compares favourably with Kate's Gothic evocation of marriage as "'being tied to a dead body'"—an image which, although she applies it to a woman's marriage to a man she does not love, would presumably describe the experience of the numerous women of the period who married for financial stability rather than affection.

Independent of domesticity as well as professionally active, the Anglican nun prefigures the New Woman of the fin-de-siècle and her flapper successor—women for whom, as Broughton put it in her 1920 essay "Girls Past and Present", marriage was merely "an unessential accident, which may or may not happen to them, but which in any case cannot materially affect the serious business of their lives, their professional or political activities" (1920b: 38). In the late 1860s, however, Broughton evidently could not imagine deemphasising the romance plot in favour of female-centred professional identity. Though she enters the convent yearning to "'find some work in the world to do'" 1867 [2013]: (374), Kate labours in the slums only because the "main plot" of her life—her romance with Dare—turned out a "tragedy" rather than a marital "comedy."

Even in death, moreover, Kate cannot seem to free herself from literary convention. The last words of the triple-decker, which tell us that Kate passes "'[t]o where, beyond these voices, there is peace'" (1867 [2013]: 375), are a quotation from Tennyson's "Guinevere" section of *Idylls of the King* (l. 692). Comparing Kate's death to Guinevere's, the allusion consigns both women—each of whom became a nun following sexual transgressions—to the time-worn category of penitent *femme fatale*. Nonetheless, in a novel as self-conscious about literary influence as *Not Wisely*, the allusion can also imply another, more liberating meaning. As Kelly Blewett points out, Kate's escape to a place "beyond" the literary and cultural voices that have hitherto defined her mirrors Broughton's own efforts to envision new ways of telling women's stories (2013: 11). In *Cometh Up as a Flower*, the novel she wrote after *Not Wisely*, Broughton would continue to experiment with strategies for representing female desire, while also developing a critique, only incipient in the earlier novel, of the perils of marriage for Victorian women.

CHAPTER TWO

An Interesting Corpse: Desire, Marriage, and Disembodiment in *Cometh Up as a Flower*

> ... [I]t is the female novelist who speaks the most plainly, and whose best characters revel in a kind of innocent indecency, as does the heroine of 'Cometh up as a Flower.' ... Nasty thoughts, ugly suggestions, an imagination which prefers the unclean, is [sic] almost more appalling than the facts of actual depravity ... It is a shame to women so to write; and it is a shame to the women who read and accept as a true representation of themselves and their ways the equivocal talk and fleshly inclinations herein attributed to them.
> – Margaret Oliphant, "Novels" (1867: 274–75)

> Whereupon I fell a-thinking what an interesting young corpse I should make lying in the big four-poster in the red room, with my emaciated hands folded on my bosom, and a deluge of white flowers about me.
> – Nell Lestrange in *Cometh Up as a Flower* (1867 [2004]: 225)

Broughton's first two novels scandalised redoubtable women writers who, whatever their personal unconventionality, defined themselves in the literary establishment as guardians of feminine propriety. Having shocked Geraldine Jewsbury with *Not Wisely, but Too Well*, Broughton outraged Margaret Oliphant with *Cometh Up as a Flower*. In the most famous of her attacks on sensation fiction in *Blackwood's*, in September 1867 Oliphant singled out the recently published *Cometh Up* as emblematic of the genre's moral dangers, particularly when women were the authors. Interestingly, what troubled Oliphant most about Broughton's book was not its depiction of the sexual transgressions (or, in the words of the epigraph above, "actual depravity") with which sensation fiction was associated. Although at one point the heroine and narrator, Nell Lestrange, vainly begs a former suitor to rescue her from a loveless marriage, her proximity to sexual fall in this scene bothered Oliphant less than the girl's articulation elsewhere of "[n]asty thoughts" (1867: 275). Under this heading the critic classifies both Nell's hope that she and her dead sweetheart will not be merely "sexless, passionless essences" in heaven (*CU* 1867 [2004]: 273], and another passage in which she shudders at the vision of marital embraces from the wealthy bridegroom whom she weds for the sake of her bankrupt father (Oliphant, 267). Whether the subject of the heroine's musings was sex in paradise or the hell of unwanted intimacy, Oliphant felt that the invitation to the female reader to join in erotic reverie was "the abomination in the midst of us"—an "indecency", no matter how "innocent" its intention, which threatened the very basis of the British empire: "a woman has one duty of valuable importance to her country and her race which cannot be over-estimated—and that is the duty of being pure. There is perhaps nothing of such vital consequence to a nation" (1867: 268, 274, 275).

In penning this diatribe, Oliphant was doubtless unaware that, because Jewsbury similarly disapproved of Broughton's "sensual appeals" to her readers (BA, 3 July 1866, in *NW*, 1867 [2013]:

379), *Cometh Up* had been published as a tamer alternative to *Not Wisely*—a novel which Oliphant did not mention in *Blackwood's* because it had not yet appeared in expurgated form. If Oliphant thought that visions of passionate reunions in heaven exemplified the trend she so deprecated—girls being encouraged to dream of "flesh and muscles" and "strong arms that seize [them]" (1867: 259)—one only wonders what she would have made of athletic Dare's "iron" embraces or, indeed, of Kate's orgasmic sensations upon being enfolded in them (*DUM*, in *NW* 1867 [2013]: 397). As for Broughton herself, she claimed in a letter to Bentley that *Not Wisely*, "tho' an improper book", had "infinitely more <u>verve</u> and strength" than *Cometh Up* (BA, [summer of 1867], in *NW* 1867 [2013]: 381).

My point here is not to agree that *Cometh Up* lacks verve and strength (it has plenty of both). But I will argue that the novel employs a different strategy for representing female desire than *Not Wisely*—a strategy that, while not adopted in direct response to Jewsbury's report, reads as if it were. Obviously, no strategy for representing a heroine's adulterous desire could mollify critics like Oliphant and Jewsbury (the latter of whom claimed in the *Athenæum* that the anonymously published *Cometh Up* was so "destitute of refinement" that it had to have been written by a man [1867 [2003]: 140). At the same time, it is unsurprising that Richard Bentley and Broughton's uncle J. S. Le Fanu judged *Cometh Up* to have less potential for offending readers than *Not Wisely*.[28] unlike its precursor, Broughton's second novel chooses, paradoxically, to represent transgressive bodily desire through images of disembodiment. In *Not Wisely*, sexual desire is indubitably and defiantly corporeal, as in the description of Kate's uncorseted waist and Dare's crushing embraces. Yet, although we hear in *Cometh Up* that the heroine feels an "odd shiver" on one of her first meetings with the male lead (1867 [2004]: 234), the novel's emphasis is more on the wasting disease from which she dies when her passion is thwarted than it is on the passion itself. This strategy of "disembodied embodiment", as I have called Broughton's method for representing female sexuality in her second novel,[29] is emblematised in one of the passages that offended Oliphant, in which Nell anticipates embracing her lover in heaven. Although the notion of sex in paradise might well shock the conventionally pious, celestial eroticism is necessarily more ethereal than its earthly manifestations. It is telling that, in chapter one, Nell first sees the man with whom she will fall in love, Major M'Gregor, as she day-dreams in a churchyard. Although Nell dismisses her original suspicion that the "figure of a man" entering the graveyard is incorporeal—"[i]f he were a ghost he was a very substantial one" (1867 [2004]: 219)—M'Gregor's solidity is deemphasised by being viewed against a backdrop of death and decay that foreshadows both his and Nell's untimely ends.

Significantly, then, the type of sex most concretely evoked in *Cometh Up* is not the heroine's transgressive fantasies about the male lead, but her horror at the prospect of (as Oliphant put it) "giving her shrinking body to the disagreeable bridegroom" (1867: 267) whose wealth she needs to save her father from bankruptcy. As I will address in the first section of this chapter, this depiction of Nell as an innocent whose natural instincts are thwarted by a corrupt culture is yet another strategy enabling Broughton to depict her nearly-fallen heroine sympathetically. Associating Nell with a Romantic vision of nature, Broughton represents her diabolical sister, Dolly, whose machinations force Nell into a mercenary marriage, as the embodiment of artifice, a representation that recalls Mary Wollstonecraft's argument, in *A Vindication of the Rights of Woman*, that women are "artificial beings" trained in "coquetry" to attract wealthy husbands (1792 [2007]: 25, 19). Yet Dolly is not the only figure in the novel responsible for derailing Nell's romance. The second part of this chapter addresses the role played by Nell's aristocratic father in controlling his daughter's sexuality by replacing the man she desires with a middle-aged father surrogate whom she does not desire. Nell only escapes the loathsome corporeality of this unwanted union by wasting away, a plot in which consumption resembles the self-starvation of anorexia, an ailment first identified as a disorder around the time *Cometh Up* was published. As I explore in my third section, however, even Nell's lover M'Gregor betrays an ominous anxiety about her sexuality, and he becomes, like Dare of *Not Wisely*, a male lead who, though not married to the heroine, anticipates portrayals of controlling husbands in Broughton's later domestic fiction.

This chapter's final section links the depiction of marriage and heterosexual romance in *Cometh Up* to a central issue in this study: Broughton's relation to literary genre and convention. Like *Not Wisely*, *Cometh Up* is packed with literary allusions, though in this case relayed by the narrating heroine rather than by an elite male. Mirroring that heroine's humorous and irreverent personality, these intertextual references are both tongue-in-cheek and metafictional, as in my second epigraph to this chapter, a passage at the beginning of *Cometh Up*, in which Nell envisions herself as a stereotypical tragic heroine: "Whereupon I fell to thinking what an interesting young corpse I should make lying in the big, four-poster in the red room, with my emaciated hands folded on my bosom, and a deluge of white flowers about me" (1867 [2004]: 225). That Nell eventually suffers this very fate reminds us, as does *Not Wisely*, of the limited definitions of "comedy" and "tragedy" dictated by the traditional marriage plot. In this sense, "disembodied embodiment" is not just a strategy for sympathetically representing a passionate heroine: it is evidence of the Victorian woman writer's own generic constraints. Nell's emaciated end points to the challenges of imagining a heroine in a comic plot other than one that portrays marriage as the sole fulfilment of female desire.

The Sad Fate of Flowers: Nature, Culture, and the Construction of Femininity

Structuring *Cometh Up* around a Romantic opposition between nature and culture, Broughton addresses issues central to the sensation fiction controversy, as well as to the larger context of the Victorian Woman Question. "Nature" was a key term in nineteenth-century debates about gender, which questioned whether women had different natures than men, as well as asking to what role women were naturally suited. Those on the conservative side in these debates defined women's nature according to domestic ideology, which portrayed wives and mothers as moral guides while denying that sexual desire was their natural instinct. In the attack on sensationalism in *Blackwood's* that targets *Cometh Up*, Margaret Oliphant asserts that women do not actually experience the "sensuous raptures" (1867: 259) described by women writers:

> What is held up to us as the story of the feminine soul as it really exists underneath its conventional coverings, is a very fleshly and unlovely record … it is women who describe these sensuous raptures … this intense appreciation of flesh and blood, this eagerness of physical sensation, is represented as the *natural* sentiment of English girls[.] (1867: 259; emphasis mine)

If, as Oliphant argues, the "story of the feminine soul" told by female sensationalists does not portray the "natural sentiment of English girls", then it must be a mendacious mirror, offering women images of erotic fantasy that are not, as they purport to be, "the portrait of their own state of mind" (1867: 259). As Susan Bernstein points out, Oliphant's argument "exemplifies realism as ideology" (1994: 231), portraying the belief that women do not normally feel passion as a fact.

Given the reluctance of many of her contemporaries to accept that sexual desire was natural to women (or, at least, to bourgeois women), Broughton's emphasis on her heroine's closeness to nature is significant. Characterizing Nell as a noble savage, socially maladroit but pure of heart, Broughton implies that sexual feeling *is* natural to women, and evokes sympathy for Nell as a victim who, to quote the organic image from the Book of Job that Broughton uses as her title, "cometh forth like a flower, and is cut down" (Job 14: 1–2). In this Romantic narrative, Lestrange Hall, the decaying manor house that Nell inhabits, is a liminal space perched on the boundary between nature and culture that favours the former over the latter. This is not to say that Lestrange is isolated from problematic social values. Both Nell and her father decry the rise of the middle class in unabashedly snobbish terms, as in Sir Adrian's disgusted reference to "'counterjumper[s]'" (1867 [2004]: 224), or those who, like the Lestranges' nouveaux-riches neighbours, the Coxes, have obtained their wealth from trade rather than by birth. (Nell's anti-Semitic remarks about the "greasy Jews" charged with liquidating the family's assets are a particularly noxious example of reactionary sentiment [1867 [2004]: 417). Nonetheless, for Nell, who, like her father, takes an active interest in the estate's farm and livestock, the manor of "dear old Lestrange" (1867 [2004]:265)—surrounded in spring by Edenic flowers—provides a welcome alternative to the growing obsession with money and commodities in the larger culture.

Reflecting the degree to which Nell, as Kirby-Jane Hallum claims, is "at home in the natural world" (2015: 40), her happiest meetings with M'Gregor occur in bucolic settings. They first meet, in fact, when Nell discovers M'Gregor enjoying, like her, a beautiful spring evening in Lestrange's churchyard, an idyllic place of "dew-freshened flowers" and "fragrant earth" that "it would have been a real luxury to be buried in" (1867 [2004]: 218). Indeed, the novel's first words voice Nell's wish to experience this luxury: "'When I die, I'll be buried under that big old ash tree over yonder'" (1867 [2004]: 217). Anticipating her untimely demise, this wish conflates nature and mortality, framing both as an escape from the demands of family and culture (Nell says she would rather undergo her "'dusty transformation'" outdoors than be buried "'between a mouldering grandpapa and a mouldered greatgrandpapa'" in the Lestrange vault [1867 [2004]: 217]). Many of Nell's other encounters with M'Gregor take place in sites similarly associated with "[d]ear mother Nature" (1867 [2004]: 293), including the garden of Lestrange Hall (1867 [2004]: 241), a meadow "all ablaze with buttercups" (1867 [2004]: 251), and a country road surrounded by banks from which she picks a "great bunch" of "big primroses" (1867 [2004]: 257).

Governed as she is by natural instinct, then, the tomboyish Nell—with her untidy "carrotty locks" (1867 [2004]: 227) and shabby clothes—is uncomfortable with the rules of feminine propriety. She is uneasily conscious of these rules, reminding herself in the first chapter as she clambers over the churchyard wall that her sister would call such behaviour "'indelicate and unladylike'" (1867 [2004]: 218). Later I will return to Dolly and her role in Nell's feminine acculturation, but will note here that the emphasis on Nell's natural qualities, such as her "young ingenuousness" (1867 [2004]: 235), makes it easier for the reader to forgive such lapses in propriety as allowing M'Gregor to hold her hand after an acquaintance of only several days.

As this is a first-person narrative, of course, we must not forget that Nell constructs this image of herself as ingénue, reminding us, and perhaps even trying to convince herself, how "[i]nnocent and childish" she was at this point in her life (1867 [2004]: 236). That Nell professes, for example, to believe that she is ugly, even though, at her first ball, men flock to her, strains credibility. Yet the presentation of Nell (and Nell's representation of herself) as Romantic child is crucial to Broughton's strategy for addressing the-ever perilous topic of female sexuality; a heroine too obviously aware of her own attractions could less plausibly claim to be innocent. Only when she has been unwillingly corrupted by culture—compelled to sell herself in marriage for economic reasons—does Nell comment on her own beauty, bitterly noting on her wedding day that, despite her inward misery, she is "very lovely": "'I'm worth my price'" (1867 [2004]: 404). Nell is thus unlike Linton's Girl of the Period, an artificial creature described as having "false red hair and painted skin" (1868 [1995]: 175). Nell is also unlike Kate Chester, who, despite her own associations with nature—for instance her "naturally and healthily shapely" uncorseted waist (*NW* 1867 [2013]: 50)—is an artful flirt who charms men, such as her cousin George, in whom she feels no interest. Significantly, the flowers we see Kate ecstatically enjoying are not wildflowers, but hothouse blooms in the conservatory where she first kisses Dare (1867 [2013]: 134).

If there is a hothouse flower in *Cometh Up*, it is not Nell but her sister Dolly, whose beauty possesses a "subtle Eastern sweetness" and whose "languid" eyes "look out of place anywhere but in a Seraglio" (1867 [2004]: 404, 291). Dolly is also far more like the Girl of the Period than Nell, who professes a belief in romantic love scorned, according to Linton, by the modern young woman, whose "idea of marriage" is "[t]he legal barter of herself for so much money" (1868 [1995]: 174). Similarly single-minded in pursuit of a wealthy husband, Dolly laughs at Nell's declaration that "'Love is worth all the power in the world'", adding instead:

> "[I]s there any old lord between the three seas, so old, so mumbling, so wicked, that I would not joyfully throw myself into his horrid palsied old arms, if he had but money; money! money! money is power; money is a god!" (1867 [2004]: 349).

Ironically, Dolly angles for a wealthy husband by pretending to be the type of "fair young English girl" mourned by Linton as having been superseded by the Girl of the Period (1868 [1995]: 172). Acting like the inmate of a seraglio only when she deems it necessary to snag a wealthy catch, Dolly more commonly—and duplicitously—assumes the role of Angel in the House. Describing her sister's expression in one scene as "nun-like, dove-like, Madonna-like", Nell admits that her sister looks "as if her life must be one long prayer"—though she quickly adds, in a reference to Satanic ritual, "if it was it was a prayer said backwards" (1867 [2004]: 228). Like that quintessential sensation anti-heroine, Lady Audley, Dolly is a con artist who demonstrates that the feminine ideal is a constructed, rather than a natural, identity.

Unsurprisingly, Dolly loathes the natural world, preferring, in her "righteous horror of freckles" (1867 [2004]: 300), which could damage her value in the marriage market, to stay indoors while her sister happily roams outside. If Dolly resembles anything in nature, it is a snake: with "coiled cables of ink-black hair" on her "small snaky head" (1867 [2004]: 349), in fact, she is the serpent in her sister's Romantic Eden. Fearing that her goal of snaring a wealthy husband would be compromised should her sister "'marry[...] a pauper'" and "'drag down'" the bankrupt family's name still further (1867 [2004]: 348), Dolly forges a letter to M'Gregor in her sister's hand, begging him not to write until her father approves the match. This deception pushes Nell—certain that she has been abandoned and desperate to assuage her dying father's financial anxieties—into the arms of Sir Hugh Lancaster, a match that provides Dolly with the reflected glory needed to hook the fabulously wealthy (and nouveau riche) Lord Stockport. In the pursuit of her materialistic goals, then, Dolly not only thwarts Nell's romance, she causes her sister's death: in accordance with medical theories that linked the onset of consumption to emotional turmoil, Broughton portrays Nell's tuberculosis as the result of romantic heartbreak.[30] In this regard, *Cometh Up* is a striking Victorian example of the plot of sisterly enmity that Helena Michie labels "sororophobia."

In *Cometh Up*, the sororophobia of the Dolly plot is a version of the matrophobia that is a classic theme of female Gothic, and which, in narratives such as Ann Radcliffe's *The Mysteries of Udolpho* (1794) or *A Sicilian Romance* (1790), represents the daughter's fear of becoming, like her mother, a victim of male power.[31] In being more obviously villain than victim, and an elder sister rather than an actual mother, Dolly might not initially recall the figure of the monitory mother, who, in female Gothic, warns her daughter through her own fate of the dangers lurking within traditional domesticity. Nonetheless, Nell does receive a warning from her sister's persistent play-acting (which includes charming "old lady callers" by professing a maternal interest in Nell only when they are around [1867 [2004]: 297]). In teaching Nell how to use artifice to snare wealthy men, Dolly exemplifies the destructive legacy of mothers to daughters under patriarchy decried by Wollstonecraft in *A Vindication of the Rights of Woman:*

> Women are told from their infancy, and taught by the example of their mothers, that a little knowledge of human weakness, justly termed cunning, softness of temper, *outward* obedience, and a scrupulous attention to a puerile kind of propriety, will obtain for them the protection of man; and should they be beautiful, every thing else is needless, for, at least, twenty years of their lives. (1792 [2007]: 36)

Calling the type of "propriety" learned by girls "puerile", Wollstonecraft underscores one of her major points about women, that, due to their economic dependence on men, they are unable to act like rational adults but instead exist "in a state of perpetual childhood, unable to stand alone" (1792 [2007]: 25). Chillingly, this "perpetual childhood" is not the innocence of the Romantic child, but the cunning of a grown woman compelled to act like a child—a hybrid creature who, obscenely, tempts men with her nubile body even as she reassures them of her childish malleability. As Wollstonecraft says, women's "artificial weakness ... leads them to play off those contemptible infantine airs that undermine esteem even whilst they excite desire" (1792 [2007]: 27). Dolly— whose very name evokes a female toy—skilfully stages this kind of child pornography, an effort aided by her slim build; as Nell tells us, Dolly was not buxom: "not a fine woman, as they say, at all;

not *beef to the heels*" (1867 [2004]: 329). Exploiting a physique at once prepubescent and provocative, Dolly typically wears plain, tight-fitting clothes, as in the scene where she flirts at a picnic given by Sir Hugh Lancaster: "She looked very girlish and simple now as she sat on the grass ... her slender figure looking even slenderer than its wont even, in her dark tight-fitting [riding] habit, out of which her throat rose, like a lily stem from its sheath" (1867 [2004]: 329). Combining sex appeal with infantilism, Dolly charms Lord Stockport, whom she later marries:

> She is no longer the shrewd, worldly-wise woman of two hours ago, whose sentiments might have been those of a French Marquise of fifty, *temp.* Louis Quinze, but could hardly have belonged to any one younger or less world-polluted. She is transformed into the innocentest, childishest Marguerite ... Dolly's whole infantine soul was immersed in her miniature speculations; her soft cheeks were flushing slyly, and the full pink lips, and the velvet eyes, were saying, with a triumph of simplicity, "I should like always to be your partner, you bring me such good luck." The old game! the old game! (1867 [2004]: 365)

Responding to Nell's growing understanding of the pitfalls of female roles, Lindsey Faber describes *Cometh Up* as a "resistant *bildungsroman*", in which she wages a "battle against the conventional womanhood epitomized by Dolly" (2006: 155). It is disputable, however, who wins the war. As Faber remarks, Nell's "attempts to exaggerate the difference between herself and her sister actually emphasize their later sameness" (2006: 157). Like Dolly, Nell marries for money, even if her reasons are more unselfish than her sister's; like Dolly, too, Nell learns to dissemble, never as successfully as Dolly, but well enough to hide from Sir Hugh her continuing love for M'Gregor and her attempt to elope with him after Dolly's machinations are uncovered. Unlike Dolly, however, who thrives on deception, Nell cannot survive being "transplanted", as she puts it with appropriate flower imagery (1867 [2004]: 417), to Sir Hugh's gloomy house where his mother frequently criticises her unladylike behaviour. As she wastes away from consumption, Nell yearns to be buried in the Edenic graveyard at Lestrange, but, imagining Hugh's next wife spelling out the Latin inscription on her tomb in the "dark old church" attended by his family, suspects that she will not be allowed to loose the shackles of culture even in death (1867 [2004]: 450). Indeed, at the end of the serial version of *Cometh Up,* an unidentified third-person narrator informs the reader that Nell was interred, not in the nature she loved, but in the chilly Lancaster vault: "they could not spare such a fair flower from their Death Garden" (*DUM,* in *CU,* 1867 [2004]: 532).[32]

"Am I Not His Property?": Fathers, Husbands, and Female Flesh

> His arm is round my waist, and he is brushing my eyes and cheeks and brow with his somewhat bristly moustache as often as he feels inclined—for am I not his property? ... For a pair of first-class blue eyes warranted fast colour, for ditto superfine red lips, for so many pounds of prime white flesh, he has paid down a handsome price on the nail[.] (1867 [2004]: 399–400)

Not content with selling herself into what Wollstonecraft called "legal prostitution" (1792 [2007]: 180), Dolly ensures that her sister does the same. Shortly before the visit by Sir Hugh described in the passage above—a visit during which the newly-engaged Nell reflects bitterly on the "handsome price" he has paid for "so many pounds of prime white flesh"—Dolly orders her sobbing younger sister, who has been mourning M'Gregor's apparent abandonment, to make herself presentable: "'you'd better try and bathe the swelling and redness out of your eyes, if we are to get any money out of him. You don't look a choice morsel to bribe any man with as you are now'" (1867 [2004]: 399). Yet the shocking spectacle of one sister acting as procuress of another should not distract from the pivotal role played by Nell's father—and, through him, patriarchal ideologies—in engineering her mercenary marriage.

A charming representation of a father-daughter relationship, Nell's bond with her "dear old dad" (1867 [2004]: 226) nonetheless has disturbing elements. For one thing, Nell defines herself, not only as a favoured daughter, but as a surrogate wife. Confessing that she was glad her mother died when she was a baby because otherwise "I should have been only second in his affections' (1867 [2004]: 239), Nell also claims to care more for her father than M'Gregor: "I liked my father a hundred times better than Dick, and always should" (1867 [2004]: 303). The sinister potential of Sir Adrian's hold on his daughter is signalled early in the novel, as he gloats over the newspaper account of a Confederate victory during the American Civil War. A sign of extreme conservatism in a period in which, as Pamela Gilbert points out, "even many Tories were anti-slavery" ("Introduction", 1867 [2010]: 26), Sir Adrian's sympathy with slave-holders is symbolically appropriate, as it is for his sake that his daughter sells herself in a marriage she labels "worse than Egyptian bondage" (1867 [2004]: 405). Nor is Nell's desire to save her father from financial ruin the sole reason she marries Sir Hugh; the marriage is, in fact, Sir Adrian's dearest wish, as it would burnish the prestige of a status-deprived aristocratic family. Exclaiming that Nell's union with Sir Hugh would add "'ten years'" to his life by "'bringing the old family back into its right position in the county'", Sir Adrian nostalgically rejoices "'Lancasters and Lestranges! ... more like the good old times'" (1867 [2004]: 373, 372).

Influencing his daughter's romantic choices, Sir Adrian thus combines his commitment to elitist class hierarchies with the patriarchal control of female sexuality. When, early in the novel, he haps upon his daughter clandestinely meeting M'Gregor in the garden, Nell informs the reader that:

> My father's notions of propriety were rigidity's self. A woman's virtue in his code of *les convenances* [social conventions], should be a stiff vestment of buckram and whale-bone; he would have liked his daughters' modesty to be inferior only to that of the young lady in "Mr. Midshipman Easy",[33] who affirmed, that to shake hands with a man made a cold shudder run down her back. (1867 [2004]: 303)

Tellingly, Sir Adrian's response to discovering Nell with M'Gregor is to call him "'Brummagem'"—a déclassé upstart—and to tell her that her behaviour is not "'maidenly'" (1867 [2004]: 245); in his view, evidently, class degradation and unrestrained female desire are two sides of the same debased coin. Proceeding to champion Sir Hugh as an appropriate suitor for his daughter, he conveniently forgets—or refuses to remember—his recent glimpse of her holding hands with M'Gregor in the garden. When Nell remarks that she has never claimed to like Sir Hugh, "My father did not heed my interruption" (1867 [2004]: 372). In this context, the Biblical epigraph which Broughton selects for *Cometh Up*—"Is the old man yet alive?" (1867 [2004]: 215)—suggests the toxic influence of patriarchal values on Nell's life. These effects continue even after Sir Adrian dies a day after she marries the man of his choice, as she remains stranded in a position in which, as she puts it, "I could reach my darling's arms only through the billows of sin or the floods of death" (1867 [2004]: 405).

In my introduction to the 2004 edition of *Cometh Up as a Flower*, I discussed Nell's resemblance to the fictional daughters analysed by Paula Marantz Cohen in her study of the late eighteenth- and nineteenth-century domestic novel, *The Daughter's Dilemma*.[34] According to Cohen, such heroines as Richardson's Clarissa anticipate the emergence of anorexia nervosa as an ailment, wasting away as they control appetites that could compromise their status as good—in this case, asexual—daughters.[35] Published almost simultaneously with the clinical definition of anorexia nervosa as a disease in 1874, *Cometh Up* similarly depicts Nell dying, emaciated, after sacrificing her chance of sexual fulfilment for Sir Adrian—an undertaking in which she likens herself to Iphigenia and Jephtha's daughter, virgins sacrificed by their fathers. Sir Adrian's pronouncement as he entrusts Nell to Sir Hugh on her wedding day—"'they say good daughters always make good wives'" (1867 [2004]: 406)—reminds us, however, that Nell is unable to remain a virgin, much as she might prefer that state to physical relations with Sir Hugh. As she thinks to herself during their courtship, as Hugh brushes her face with his "bristly moustache" and exclaims "'Jolly this, isn't it? [...] and it'll be jollier still when we're married'", "*When we're married!* Merciful Heavens! If the prologue is so terrible, *what will the play be?*" (1867 [2004]: 400).

In this context, Nell's consumption, like the willed starvation of anorexia, signals her desire to escape a position in which she is consumed by male appetite. (Her bitter claim that Sir Hugh has purchased the right to "kiss my face off if he chooses" (1867 [2004]: 400)—a horrifying image of the loss of feminine identity—portrays herself as the prey of a voracious male.) It is, indeed, following her engagement to Hugh that Nell first wishes "Oh, why could not I die of consumption, like that girl I took the jelly to yesterday? Why could I not cough myself out of the world, as she was doing so fast?" (1867 [2004]: 395).

At the same time, the depiction of Nell's revulsion at Sir Hugh is the more poignant because he is not a monster. In fact, compared to the horrid husbands who populate Victorian literature— including Mr. Murdstone of *David Copperfield* (1849), Percival Glyde of *The Woman in White* (1860), Grandcourt of *Daniel Deronda* (1876), Gilbert Osmond of *The Portrait of a Lady* (1881), and the diabolical Prince Zouroff of Ouida's *Moths* (1880)—

Hugh is quite likeable. A bumbling, not overly intelligent Tory sportsman, he is nonetheless sensitive enough to the situation of Nell and her father to offer her money without insisting that she marry him in return (an arrangement that she declines on grounds of propriety). Unlike Sir Adrian, who remains unaware of (or unwilling to admit to) Nell's revulsion at her middle-aged suitor, Hugh recognises her lack of enthusiasm for their marriage, and gives her a chance to break the engagement, pointing out that "'it would be better you should speak out, while it's time'" (1867 [2004]: 401). When Nell refuses this offer for her father's sake, however, Sir Hugh is apparently too enamoured of her not to take advantage of her plight. Whereas the typical Gothic husband of Victorian literature—a Grandcourt or Osmond—is too narcissistic to consider his wife's feelings, Hugh, whom Nell describes as both "honest" and "kind" (1867 [2004]: 406, 433, 451), cares about her very much, but exploits the financial imbalance between them anyway. This complicity of a decent man in a corrupt system is arguably more tragic than the sadism of a one-dimensional villain.

"I Could Not Love Thee, Dear, So Much": M'Gregor and the Problem of the Male Lead

Given the circumstances surrounding Nell's acceptance of Hugh, it is hard to consider the bonds of matrimony holy in her case. Even the moralistic Oliphant had trouble disapproving of Nell's desire to elope with M'Gregor after the lovers discover the extent of the machinations employed by Dolly to ensure that her sister married Sir Hugh. Offensive though she found Nell's "uncleanly talk" at other times, Oliphant refrained from calling her conduct "unnatural" in the scene where the young woman begs M'Gregor to rescue her:

> If two young people fall heartily and honestly in love with each other, and are separated by machinations such as abound in novels, but unfortunately are not unknown

in life, and one of them is compelled to marry somebody else, it is not unnatural, it is not revolting, that the true love unextinguished should blaze wildly up, in defiance of all law [.] (1867: 267)

Though Oliphant hastens to add that, nonetheless, the lovers' behaviour is "wrong, sinful, ruinous" (1867: 267), such is her understanding of their plight that the judgement sounds like an afterthought.

Yet Oliphant is not the only one to label Nell's desire to commit adultery "ruinous." Using similar language, M'Gregor himself refuses to be "'the ruin of the only woman I ever loved'" (1867 [2004]: 424), turning down Nell's plea in "impassioned words" that she later compares to famous lines by the Cavalier poet Richard Lovelace: "I could not love thee, dear, so much/ Loved I not honour more" (1867 [2004]: 449). In an earlier scene, M'Gregor had even sympathised with the ire of Nell's father when Sir Adrian surprises the lovers in a clandestine tryst after only several days' acquaintance:

> "I'm not sure that he was not right. I have no doubt he thought I was taking a great liberty—which I was—and trying to get up an underhand—ahem!—ahem!—acquaintance with you, which I was not. I never like doing things underhand." (1867 [2004]: 261)

On one level, of course, M'Gregor's refusal to elope with Nell reflects the limits of what a mid-Victorian writer—particularly a mid-Victorian woman writer—could represent. It would have been impossible for Broughton to publish a book which sympathetically portrays a couple's decision to live together outside wedlock, no matter what the extenuating circumstances. In *Not Wisely,* the necessary breach between the potentially adulterous lovers was made, not by the libertine male lead, but by the ascetic clergyman James Stanley, who browbeats Kate about the sinfulness of her plan to become Dare's mistress until she gives it up. Broughton's choice in *Cometh Up* to have the male lead save the heroine from sexual fall dispenses with the need for a preachy *deus ex machina*. Rather, representing M'Gregor as honourable accords with the narrative strategy I have called disembodied embodiment, whereby Broughton raises the subject of illicit desire only to defer its consummation until after death. In *Not Wisely*, Dare's refusal to be converted on his deathbed affords Kate no hope of a heavenly reunion, but, in the last chapter of *Cometh Up*, Nell joyfully anticipates passing "through the grave and gate of death" to her "beloved" and "see[ing] his hero face immortal *then* in its beauty" (1867 [2004]: 451).

Thus, although both Broughton's first two male leads are dashing soldiers, they are also opposites, their moral differences signalled by contrasting physiognomic codes. Dare—dark and saturnine—is unrepentantly bad, while M'Gregor—blond and likened by Nell to a Viking king[36]—is indisputably good, if blander than his Byronic precursor. An example of what today would be called "vanilla" masculinity, M'Gregor typifies the type of male lead whom both reviewers of Broughton's novels and later scholars have found dissatisfying. Michael Sadleir, for instance, dismisses Broughton's male protagonists as "stiff or merely dull" when not actively "loutish" [1944: 95].[37] Regardless of whether Broughton's male leads are boring—an assessment beginning to be challenged, in any event, by recent scholars[38]—an issue more pertinent to my focus is the potential danger these male characters pose to female autonomy. Viewed in this light, Dare and M'Gregor are alike even amidst their differences: each embodies aspects of patriarchal ideology that would make him a problematic husband were he able to marry the heroine. Given that, after 1867, Broughton turned from sensation fiction to the genre with which she was henceforth to be associated—domestic fiction—Dare and M'Gregor cannot be regarded solely as representative of extra-marital sexuality, but as precursors of the fiancés and husbands who would thereafter populate her work. In this context, Broughton's representation of male leads in her first two novels—and, particularly, her depiction of how such men control women—anticipates her depiction of the power imbalances between the sexes in Victorian marriage in her domestic fiction.

In the serial version of *Not Wisely*, of course, Dare poses the greatest possible danger to female autonomy, in being an outright murderer of the heroine at the novel's end. Though it deletes Kate's murder, the triple-decker *Not Wisely* continues to include evidence of the male lead's proclivity to sexual possessiveness and objectification, qualities which Dare displays in ways that stress his resemblance to an important precursor, Rochester from *Jane Eyre*. A would-be bigamist like Rochester, Dare is, like him, associated with the metaphor of the seraglio which Wollstonecraft, and later writers such as Percy Shelley, deploy as a metaphor for the economic and sexual imprisonment of wives.[39] After becoming engaged to Jane—and before she discovers that he is already married—Rochester loads her with rich clothes and jewels with a condescension she angrily compares to that of a "sultan" admiring the "slave his gold and gems had enriched" (1847 [1996]: 229). In a scene I discussed in the previous chapter—set, like Brontë's, before the heroine discovers that the male lead already has a wife—Dare is similarly sultanic, lasciviously surveying Kate as she stands before him "on approval, like a Circassian slave at the market of Constantinople" (1867 [2013]: 132).

Admittedly, M'Gregor does not treat Nell like a Circassian slave: the threat he embodies to the heroine's autonomy is subtler than that represented by Dare. Whereas Dare objectifies Kate, M'Gregor idealises Nell, placing her on a pedestal of sexual purity when she urges him to rescue her from her loveless marriage. Apostrophizing her in response as his "'little snow-drop'" (1867 [2004]: 425)—innocent and child-like—M'Gregor refuses to acknowledge her sexuality, telling her "'you don't know what you're saying'" even though she defiantly declares that she would rather go to hell with him than to heaven with Sir Hugh (1867 [2004]: 424–25). Claiming that he would "'sooner cut'" Nell's throat than place her on a "'level with the scum of the earth'" (1867 [2004]: 425)—prostitutes—M'Gregor defines the honourable man as one who controls unrestrained female sexuality. M'Gregor's image of cutting Nell's throat is particularly disturbing given that he, like Sir Hugh, served in the British army during a colonial rebellion, the so-called Indian Mutiny of 1857. (M'Gregor, indeed, commends Sir Hugh's success during that conflict in hunting "'black game'" [1867 [2004]: 306]). Recalling narratives about the Mutiny in which white women are killed, either by themselves or by their husbands, to avoid being raped by rebellious natives,[40] M'Gregor's claim that he would rather kill Nell than allow her to become a fallen woman suggests that he regards her desire as akin to racial Otherness. In making this claim, moreover, M'Gregor recalls his apparent opposite, Dare, who, in volume I of *Not Wisely*, tells Kate that he would "'cut your dear little soft throat here, this very minute, if I thought any other man would ever kiss you again as I have done to-day'" (1867 [2013]: 138). Although the two men threaten their lovers to different ends—M'Gregor to protect Nell's virtue, and Dare to assert sole claim to Kate's body—in both cases the rhetoric of violence betrays male anxiety about female sexuality.

A Comedian Without a Comedy; or, The Woes of Genre

In their focus on illicit passion and bleak depiction of marriage, Broughton's sensation novels have a complex relation to conventional generic categories. The question posed by the narrator of *Not Wisely*—whether that tale's portrayal of the love that is the "main plot of a woman's life" will be "tragedy or comedy"—is not easy to answer in regards to Broughton's first two fictions. It is difficult to call either of these novels a comedy: not only does neither tale end according to the traditional definition of comedic closure—marriage—but the heroines of both suffer tragic fates. Yet, so frequently does comedy—in the sense of humour—enliven the pages of the two tales, that it is hard to categorise them purely as tragedies. The "acute modern critic" whom Marie Belloc Lowndes quotes in her preface to Broughton's last novel, *A Fool in Her Folly*, may have had Broughton's wit in mind when he called her "the nearest thing in spirit to Jane Austen that we have had in recent times" ("Foreword," 1920: 3). Since Broughton's earliest novels, however, do not, like Austen's, end with marital bliss, the comic "spirit" that Broughton shares with this female predecessor can seem out of place against the backdrop of a tragic plot. The scene in *Not Wisely* where James Stanley dissuades Kate Chester from becoming Dare's mistress affords a striking example of the collision of Broughton's comic perspective with a sombre storyline. Before shifting to Stanley's bravura sermonising, the scene begins with him stumbling upon Kate as she walks to the railway station in heavy rain, wrestling with a "big umbrella" that "the wind was doing its best to turn inside out" (1867 [2013]: 289). Though providing a welcome contrast to the hellfire-and-brimstone rhetoric with which the dialogue will shortly be awash, this humorous, homely detail of Kate's "unruly umbrella" (1867 [2013]: 289) seems to belong in another kind of story altogether, one not constrained by the conventions of the fallen woman plot.

This is not to say that only comedies can contain humour, or that Broughton cannot write movingly about tragic events. Nonetheless, the frequent disjunction between the humour of her first novels and the lugubrious elements of their plots places Broughton, as it does her irreverent heroines, in the unenviable position of a comedian miscast in a tragedy. In *Cometh Up*, however, Broughton draws attention to this generic predicament through the voice of a female narrator, a strategy not available in *Not Wisely*. In *Not Wisely*, the elite male narrator, himself enamoured of literary images of women, begins the novel with a description of his mental shrine to Kate, uncritically fixing her in the static role of tragic—and dead—heroine. In contrast, the passages in *Cometh Up* where Nell pokes fun at stereotypical image of the doomed woman undercut, from a female perspective, the tragic conventions in which she herself is enmeshed.

For instance, near the end of Volume I, Nell lampoons one version of the lovelorn heroine, the female suicide:

> [S]hould I practise some picturesque form of suicide? should I drown myself in the garden pool, and be found with my long red hair inextricably entangled among the duckweed? or should I choose some sequestered spot in which to "snip my carotid", and be discovered, beautiful but gory, with an explanatory billet in my hand? (1867 [2004]: 313)

Nell's comic evocation of her "long red hair inextricably entangled among the duckweed" sends up the Victorian preoccupation with women committing suicide by drowning, including the numerous paintings of Shakespeare's Ophelia. Indeed, Nell's image of her "long red hair" tangled in the greenery of a "garden pool" evokes John Everett Millais's iconic portrayal of the death of Ophelia (1851–52), in which his red-haired model, Lizzie Siddall, floats down a stream surrounded by lush foliage. Imagining such Pre-Raphaelite tresses entwined with "duckweed", however, Nell transforms the tragic heroine into the subject of farce. Like her earlier daydream of herself as an "interesting" and "emaciated" corpse surrounded by white blooms, Nell pokes fun at the objectification of the female body in tragedies where even suicide is "picturesque" and slashed arteries "beautiful."

Enhancing her parody of tragic conventions, Broughton alludes to a text which itself parodies such conventions, Richard Brinsley Sheridan's *The Critic* (1779). In this play-within-a-play, the dramatist Puff invites the critics Dangle and Sneer to a rehearsal of his work, "The Spanish Armada", Sheridan's send-up of popular historical tragedies. From among the theatrical clichés targeted by Sheridan, Broughton singles out—appropriately, given her own parodic focus—his caricature of the tragic heroine. Nell's reference in chapter 15 to "Tilburina, stark mad in white satin" (1867 [2004]: 302) recalls the scene in *The Critic* in which Puff's heroine, Tilburina, appears onstage after her lover dies, insane and dressed in white satin, a spectacle that prompts the following exchange between Puff and the critic Sneer:

> PUFF. Yes, sir—now she comes in stark mad in white satin.
> SNEER. Why in white satin?
> PUFF. O Lord! sir—when a heroine goes mad, she always goes into white satin. (1779 [1905]: 68 [III.i])

While Broughton's intertextual allusions can serve to critique traditional representations of women, they can also—as they did in *Not Wisely*—show how hard it is to avoid reproducing the problematic gender ideology of earlier representations of women. For instance, when Nell adapts lines from Tennyson's *Idylls of the King* during one of her romantic encounters with M'Gregor—"I lifted up mine eyes,/ And loved him with that love that was my doom" (1867 [2004]: 252)[41]—she writes herself into the role of tragic, lovelorn heroine at which she elsewhere scoffs. Nevertheless, as Broughton's reference to Sheridan demonstrates, in *Cometh Up* intertextuality can take another, important form: metafictionality. In having her female narrator poke fun at conventional images of the tragic heroine, Broughton makes Nell—who at one point actually considers paying the bills by penning a novel "for which emulous publishers should outbid each other" (1867 [2004]: 248)—a figure for the woman writer.[42] Nell's satiric meditations on which "picturesque" version of the suicide plot she should write herself into, for example, comment on the limited narrative options available to the female author. Such self-reflexive moments draw attention to Broughton's own generic dilemma in her sensation fiction, where she is compelled to force a comic heroine who cannot marry her lover into the confines of a tragic plot.

In a scene that comments explicitly on sensationalism, Nell is also a figure for the female reader. In a chapter set after M'Gregor refuses to let her elope with him, Nell describes her thoughts while reading a book that, like one of the most famous sensation novels, *East Lynne,* tells the story of a runaway adulteress:

> It interests me rather, for it is all about a married woman, who ran away from her husband and suffered the extremity of human ills in consequence. I have made several steps of late in morality I flatter myself, but even now, I can hardly imagine that I should have been very miserable if Dick had taken me away with him. (1867 [2004]: 436)

In showing a woman pondering the relevance of literature to her own life, this scene recalls the one at the beginning of *Not Wisely* where Kate Chester questions, after finishing a romantic tale, "'is love such an irresistible power, such an all-conquering influence ... as they make out in books like this?'" (1867 [2013]: 51). Unlike Kate, however, who concludes that "'Love must be the one great bliss in the world, though I know nothing about it'" (1867 [2013]: 52), Nell refuses to accept the version of reality proffered by her reading. That the fictive version of reality Nell resists is moralistic—we hear that the "naughty matron" of her novel dies "of a broken heart and starvation in a Penitentiary" (1867 [2004]: 436)—allows Broughton to satirise the conventions of the purportedly transgressive genre of sensation fiction. In its hyperbolic chastisement of its protagonist, the novel Nell reads resembles such iconic sensation novels as *East Lynne* and *Lady Audley's Secret,* which address the topics of adultery and marital failure only to punish the adulterous anti-heroines who flee unfulfilling marriages. In making Nell a resistant reader of this convention of sensationalism, Broughton again transforms her heroine into a figure for the woman writer who confronts patriarchal literary traditions. Doubting whether "I should have been very miserable if Dick had taken me away with him," Nell leaves the reader of her tale to imagine a narrative as yet too controversial to be published: one in which the adulterous woman flees an unfulfilling marriage with her lover and thrives.

Though this as-yet unwritten story is not Nell's, neither is it quite that of the "naughty matron" of the sensation novel she reads. Though Nell's death from consumption could be read as punishment for her transgressive desire, it can also be read as an escape to a realm where she can finally satisfy her desire. Ambiguous as is the ending of *Cometh Up* in terms of conventional messages, though, it still firmly writes Nell into the role of tragic heroine. With her next novel, *Red as a Rose Is She,* Broughton would move away from sensationalism to a type of love story that ends according to the traditional definition of comedic closure, marriage. At the same time, Broughton's shift from sensationalism did not mean that her novels henceforth avoided tragedy. Not only would her fourth novel, *Good-bye, Sweetheart!,* end with the death of its protagonist, but many of the works that followed *Not Wisely* and *Cometh Up* would invert the generic paradox of these early fictions. Whereas *Not Wisely* and *Cometh Up* combined a comic tone with a tragic ending, even those works that Broughton wrote after 1867 with conventionally "happy" endings are infused with potential, if not actual, tragedy. A marriage plot might be the classic definition of comedy, but, according to Broughton's definition of domestic narrative, the power imbalances between men and women can easily transform that comedy into something very different.

CHAPTER THREE

The Girl of the Period and Her Jealous Fiancé: Sexuality, Power, and the Courtship Plot in *Red as a Rose Is She* and *Good-bye, Sweetheart!*

> "I *hate* her!" he says to himself, fiercely; "she is a vile unprincipled coquette. Thank God, I found her out in time!"
> — St. John Gerard, in *Red as a Rose Is She* (1870 [1899]: 365)

> "'Girl of the Period!' ... after all, the *Saturday* does not overcolour; from all such, 'Good Lord deliver us!'"
> — Paul Le Mesurier, in *Good-bye, Sweetheart!* (1872: 16)

A vibrant girl with a "delicious carmine" complexion (1870 [1899]: 314) pines after her fiancé—who is incensed that she lied about having a previous suitor—breaks their engagement. Pale and gaunt in a grim job as companion to an elderly couple, she nearly dies before reconciling with the lover who discarded her. Another vivacious girl, with a "full, womanly figure", is similarly rejected by her fiancé for flirting; she too becomes "'much thinner'", and finally dies of consumption (1872: 41, 314). These summaries of Broughton's third and fourth novels—*Red as a Rose Is She* (1870) and *Good-bye, Sweetheart!* (1872)—attest to the continuing literal and symbolic centrality of female appetite to her fiction. Recalling *The Spectator*'s description of Kate Chester and Nell Lestrange as girls "of a full and noble nature, round as to [their] lines mental and bodily" (19 October 1867, in *NW*, 1867 [2013]: 437), Esther Craven of *Red as a Rose* and Lenore Herrick of *Good-bye, Sweetheart!* also resemble these earlier heroines in suffering sexual and emotional starvation. Becoming alarmingly thin in the wake of romantic setbacks, Esther and Lenore join Nell in somatically expressing their deprivation, the tubercular Lenore in fact reprising Nell's consumptive end.

Yet, while Esther and Lenore resemble Broughton's earlier heroines, the male leads of *Red as a Rose* and *Good-bye, Sweetheart!* differ from their predecessors in a significant regard. Unlike Dare and M'Gregor, neither St. John Gerard of *Red as a Rose* nor Paul Le Mesurier of *Good-bye, Sweetheart!* is associated with transgressive desire. Although, as I argued in the previous chapter, Broughton's depiction of Dare and M'Gregor hints at the problematic role of husbands in Victorian marriage, both characters are primarily linked to extra-marital sexuality. In contrast, St. John and Paul not only offer marriage to the heroines, but do their best to stamp out wayward female behaviour. Sharing first names with puritanical men in novels by Charlotte Brontë—St. John Rivers of *Jane Eyre* and Paul Emanuel of *Villette*[43]—St. John and Paul zealously and jealously police their fiancées for any sign of immodesty, punitively withdrawing their affection when they suspect potential infidelity. That both men are themselves veteran sowers of wild oats increases, rather than diminishes, the outrage at their fiancées' supposed peccadillos. As the narrator of *Red as a Rose* points out,

"The wilder a man is or has been himself, the more scrupulously fastidious he is about the almost prudish nicety of the women that belong to him" (1870 [1899]: 109).

This chapter explores the plot of the jealous fiancé in *Red as a Rose Is She* and *Good-bye, Sweetheart!*, as well as the significance of its emergence at this point in Broughton's career. Broughton's choice to structure her third and fourth novels around a courtship plot—a version of the domestic novel—retreats at least to some extent from sensationalism, and the controversial adultery (or near-adultery) narratives of her first two books. At the same time, the jealous fiancé plot—in which the male lead is troubled by the heroine's resistance to conventional propriety—allows Broughton to portray power imbalances between the sexes in Victorian domesticity. In this sense, Broughton's version of the courtship narrative undercuts the celebration of romantic love that is the genre's central convention.

The jealous fiancé plot also enables Broughton to engage with the debate about changing gender roles sparked by Eliza Lynn Linton's publication in 1868, the year following Broughton's authorial debut, of "The Girl of the Period", an anti-feminist essay that ignited a controversy identified by Elizabeth Helsinger, Robin Sheets, and William Veeder as a "major cultural moment" in articulating the concerns of the Victorian Woman Question (1983: 1, 117). Explicitly likening the heroines of *Red as a Rose Is She* and *Good-bye, Sweetheart!* to "The Girl of the Period", the male leads in both novels echo Linton's jeremiad about the decline of traditional English womanhood and the rise of a newfound, and problematic, female resistance to patriarchal authority. In one scene, surveying Esther over his own copy of the "*Saturday*"—*The Saturday Review,* which published Linton's essay—St. John of *Red as a Rose* considers the current social climate with trepidation: "Woman's Rights ... the Girl of the Period—they have all been passing through his eye into his brain, and, mixed with Esther Craven, make a fine jumble there" (1870 [1899]: 109). And, when Lenore of *Good-bye, Sweetheart!* disguises herself as a Breton servant to get a good look at her new neighbour Paul, he mutters upon discovering the deception: "'Girl of the Period!' ... after all, the *Saturday* does not overcolour; from all such, 'Good Lord deliver us!'" (1872: 16).

The Girl of the Period debate is relevant, not only to the heroines of *Red as a Rose Is She* and *Good-bye, Sweetheart!*, but to Broughton herself. Horrified by a modern version of femininity, St. John Gerard and Paul Le Mesurier recall the scandalised critics who identified Broughton's early fiction as symptomatic of a new, unsettling female rebellion against traditional domesticity. While Broughton's first two novels occasioned the greatest critical animosity in this regard, attacks on the impropriety of her work continued even after she distanced herself from sensationalism. Indeed, during the first decade of her career, Broughton was viewed by critics—even those who, like the *Spectator* reviewer I referred to in the introduction, admired her—as a kind of literary Girl of the Period herself: defiant of social convention, impatient of male authority, and, even after she had abandoned sensationalism, still worrisomely associated with that genre's sexually suggestive themes.

Before discussing *Red as a Rose Is She* and *Good-bye, Sweetheart!*, then, I will examine the critical reception of Broughton's early fiction—especially those aspects relevant to the Girl of the Period debates—as this material provides a context for her representational choices and strategies in these two works. That some of the criticism I cite refers, not only to Broughton's sensation novels, but to the tales that followed them, underscores the difficulties she continued to face in portraying unconventional and passionate heroines, even those not in imminent danger of sexual fall.

"Outrageous Young Ladies": Girls—and Women Writers—of the Period

Broughton had a strong financial incentive to move away

from sensation fiction. The circulating library system—which compelled her to write bulky triple-decker novels—also enforced standards of propriety by refusing to carry books considered too risqué for the eyes of the stereotypical "Young Person", or teenage female reader. Given that readers relied on the circulating libraries to rent multi-volume books too expensive for individuals to buy, writers whose work was not offered by the libraries lost access to a wide audience, as well as to royalties accrued from the libraries' purchase of novels from the publisher. In Broughton's case, both her sensation novels sold well, but were not advertised in the catalogue of the most prestigious and widely patronised circulating library, Mudie's. Although, as Monica Fryckstedt has discovered, Mudie's secretly bought copies of *Cometh Up as a Flower* to offer to interested buyers, this kind of clandestine patronage could not provide the level of reimbursement gained from advertisement in their catalogue.[44]

Nonetheless, Broughton probably did not abandon the sensation genre for financial reasons alone. That she felt beleaguered by the critical reception of her first two novels is evinced by the defiant dedication she tried (and failed) to have Bentley's append to *Red as a Rose Is She*: "TO MY ENEMIES, ALL AND SUNDRY" (*BA*, Pt. 2: Reel 22, 20 January 1870). As demonstrated by the *Spectator* piece to which I referred in the introduction, not all the reviews of *Not Wisely, but Too Well* and *Cometh Up as a Flower* were hostile. Nonetheless, Robert Romer lambasted *Not Wisely* in *The Athenæum* as "blasphemy" (1867, in *NW*, 1867 [2013]: 431) and Geraldine Jewsbury—angry that Bentley published work by an author of whom she disapproved—declared in her *Athenæum* review of *Cometh Up* that the novel had to have been written, not by a woman, but by a man "destitute of refinement of thought or feeling, and ignorant of all that women are, or ought to be" (1867 [2003]: 138).

Even though Broughton's reviewers in the 1870s could not make the same complaints about her plots as they had of her sensation novels, they continued to sound alarms about class degradation and sexual impropriety in her fiction. In 1873, a reviewer for *The Pall Mall Gazette* sneered that the eponymous heroine of *Nancy* speaks "with the flippancy and smartness of a barmaid" (1873: 1824), the barmaid being a figure, not only for a working-class woman, but for one who is presumably of easy virtue. As we will see in the next chapter, Broughton was, after reading this review, so dejected by the "coarse and indiscriminate abuse with which I am belaboured" that she claimed to have "half a mind never to put pen to paper again" (BA, 28 November 1873, Pt. 2: Reel 22).

Broughton's use of the word "coarse" to describe hostile reviews turns the tables on the reviewers' frequent use of this word, or its synonyms, to describe her own writing. Especially in the first decade of her career, Broughton was frequently criticised in reviews for being "coarse", "crude", or "vulgar", terms which conflated sexually suggestive language with working-class status.[45] One of the main linguistic signifiers of "coarseness" or "vulgarity" was the use of slang. As noted in chapter 1, Broughton pledged Richard Bentley to purge both "coarseness" and "slanginess" from the serial version of *Not Wisely, but Too Well,* and she was apparently sensitive enough to criticism of her use of slang to issue a second edition of *Cometh Up* in 1877, which, while by no means as thorough an overhaul of a serial text as her revisions of *Not Wisely,* replaced such informal terms as "barnacles" with "spectacles" and "'jolly girl'" with "'charming girl'" (*DUM* in *CU,* 1867 [2004]: 523, 524). Throughout the 1870s, however, critics continued not only to carp at Broughton's use of slang, but to link it to the more unconventional aspects of her portrayal of women. As mentioned in the introduction, the *Athenæum* review of *Goodbye, Sweetheart!* labelled Broughton's linguistic choices a feminist usurpation of male power, declaring that, in "affect[ing] the tone and manner of a man", she "throws down the glove as distinctly as does a female orator at a Woman's Rights convention" (1872:

585). According to Linton, after all, one of the defining features of the Girl of the Period is "talking slang as glibly as a man" (1868 [1995]: 112), and the *Athenæum* review labels Broughton's style "simple coarseness, nor is it any sign of strength in a woman that she should write as men talk in the sanctity of the smoking room" (1872: 586). Significantly, only when the language elite men use "in the smoking room" is spoken by women does it become "simple coarseness", or a form of class degradation.

Discomfort with Broughton's "vulgarity" underlies even a sympathetic response to her early work, as shown in a discussion of her fiction by Alfred Austin published in 1874 in *Temple Bar* magazine, the journal which serialised a number of her novels. It might seem strange that Austin would value Broughton's work, given that he wrote several essays for *Temple Bar* inveighing against sensationalism.[46] In his attack on the "sensational school" in 1870, however, he strove to disassociate Broughton from the genre, declaring in a footnote that, "while the exceedingly clever authoress of 'Cometh Up as a Flower' may seem to share some of the peculiarities of this school ... in many respects she is brilliantly distinguished from those writers" (1870: 410). In the appreciation of Broughton's novels that he wrote four years later, Austin asserts that it is not her fault for noticing that a new breed of young woman "is on the increase":

> Miss Broughton's typical heroine is of a sort neither common nor uncommon, but, we suspect, growing more common every day ... It is an age of women's rights and the emancipation of a sex supposed to have been long-enthralled ... If women are to do pretty much as men do, it follows that they are to do pretty much what they please ... Doubtless a select minority of women will avail themselves of their new liberty to deliver lectures, to study medicine, to follow an honourable trade, and to sit on school boards. But the vast majority will employ their time in listening to the whispers

and promptings of love with an indulgence never before permitted them, whilst a certain number will not be too particular in drawing the line between being made love to and making it. (1874: 205)

Unlike Linton, whose "Girl of the Period" essay neglected to address "[t]he volatile issues of 1868, suffrage, higher education, and unemployment" (Helsinger, Sheets, and Veeder 1983: 1, 112), Austin situates the modern girl in the context of feminist movements seeking improved professional opportunities for women (delivering lectures, practicing medicine, pursuing an "honourable trade"). Yet he mentions employment equity only in passing, focusing instead on how modern young women are becoming more sexually aggressive (not "too particular in drawing the line between being made love to and making it"), a trend he sees reflected in Broughton's novels. Austin's diction suggests that he is not altogether pleased with the era's feminist trends, as when, for instance, he claims that women are only "*supposed* to have been long-enthralled" (my emphasis), and describes girls' freedom to read love stories as the result of "indulgence" rather than of liberation.

In its frequent defensiveness, indeed, Austin's attitude towards Broughton's fiction is as ambivalent as his response to feminism. Even as he argues that she is not herself vulgar ("[I]s a novelist vulgar who represents people as they really are?"), he concedes that

> Miss Broughton paints characters that are unruly, rebellious, "fast," and at times even what is called "slangy," ... very outrageous young ladies indeed; young ladies we would rather not have for our sisters, sweethearts, wives, or sisters-in-law, but with whom, nevertheless, we could imagine ourselves spending a not unpleasant quarter of an hour[.] (1874: 204).

Highly qualified praise, these lines recall Linton's assertion that, though men enjoy the "fast" talk of the Girl of the Period—mimicking as it does the courtesan's witty chatter—they prefer the company of more respectable women: "They may amuse themselves with [the Girl of the Period] for an evening, but … when they go into their mothers' drawing-rooms, to see their sisters and their sisters' friends, they want something of quite different flavour" (1868 [1995]: 174–75). Willing to be entertained by "outrageous young ladies" for only a limited time, Austin implies that Broughton's heroines, like Linton's Girl of the Period, resemble fallen women too closely for comfort.

"A Rose in Her Burning Prime": Esther Craven's Unsettling Eroticism

The review of *Red as a Rose Is She* in the London *Times* in 1870—an uncharacteristically positive critical response to her early work—"delighted" Broughton (*BA*, Pt. 2: Reel 22, 8 March 1870). Apparently agreeing with the narrator that the novel was not intended for readers who craved "the flavour of violent immorality" (1870 [1899]: 3), the *Times* reviewer sounds relieved that the protagonist was not "one of those heroines who get into difficulties through the commission of murder or bigamy, or who are constrained by circumstances to fall in love with other people's husbands" (1870: 4 c. 1). Yet, while identifying the tale as being "very far from relying … on the sort of incidents usually recognized as sensational", the reviewer nonetheless recalled that it had been "sensationally" advertised, with placards announcing its periodical instalments in *Temple Bar* replacing the "principal word" of the title with a "flaunting red rose" (1870: 4 c. 1). The contrast between the heady eroticism of this marketing graphic and the reviewer's assurance that the heroine's behaviour lay "within the pale of conventional respectability" captures a paradox within the text itself. Relying, like her novel's advertising campaign, on a metaphor comparing her heroine's blush to a red rose, Broughton depicts Esther as both virginal and seductive. Described near the novel's end as having "the innocentest, freshest, shyest rosebud-face" (1870 [1899]: 446), Esther blushes, at an earlier point in the story, "red as a rose in her burning prime" (1870 [1899]: 172); soon afterward, in an even more striking evocation of female arousal, her cheeks are "flushed with a deeper hue than the crimson lips of a foreign shell" (1870 [1899]: 186).

To some extent, these depictions of Esther's blushes reproduce a tension between sexual innocence and sexual knowledge already present in the source for Broughton's title, Samuel Taylor Coleridge's "The Rime of the Ancient Mariner". Proclaiming "The bride hath paced into the hall,/ Red as a rose Is she" (1817 [2006]: 581, ll. 33–34), the poem's narrator conveys what Ruth Bernard Yeazell, in a study of eighteenth- and nineteenth-century courtship literature, describes as the "ambiguity" of the blush, or its dual signification of modesty and, as Yeazell puts it, "modesty's other face", female desire (1991: 75, 74). In Coleridge's poem, the bride is as yet virginal, but her blush nonetheless suggests her anticipation of the wedding night. In Broughton's third novel, however, the ambiguity of the blush is heightened by the historical anxieties about female sexuality to which the text responds, including the sensation controversy and the debate occasioned by Linton's "The Girl of the Period". In this sense, *Red as a Rose Is She* is a novel about reading—or, more precisely, about misreading, as the male lead mistakenly concludes that the heroine is, like the *femme fatale* of a sensation novel, willing to prostitute herself to snare a wealthy husband.

For its readers, then, the novel has a different plot than St. John thinks it does. Privy to the events that precede her visit to his house, the reader is aware that Esther's worst failing is—as suggested by her last name, "Craven"—timidity. Too kind-hearted to turn down an unwanted suitor, Robert Brandon, without giving him any hope, she allows him to think that she might eventually change her mind about not wanting to marry him—

an indeterminate response that he and his family, to her horror, take as an assent to his proposal. Unaware of this backstory, St. John has a more sensational interpretation of Esther's relationship to the other man. Hearing a rumour, after he himself becomes engaged to her, that she was, in fact, already affianced to Brandon, he concludes that she resolved to jilt her less well-heeled suitor after meeting a richer man. Having already been reminded by Esther of "The Girl of the Period" in the passage I cited at the beginning of this chapter, St. John readily believes that she shares the mercenary mindset that Linton attributes to that figure: "The legal barter of herself for so much money, representing so much dash, so much luxury and pleasure—that is her idea of marriage" (1868 [1995]: 174).

Significantly, the most erotic descriptions of Esther's blushes occur in scenes that address her ambiguous relationship with Robert Brandon. The passage I cited earlier, in which she blushes "red as a rose in her burning prime", depicts her reaction after St. John asked why Brandon's name was inscribed in her prayer book, and she claims never to have met him; her cheeks are likened to "the crimson lips of a foreign shell" when she is angry at herself for not being brave enough to tell either one of her suitors about her situation with the other. Esther's blushes, in other words, enhance her sexual attraction at moments which could be retrospectively read by St. John, after hearing the rumour about her engagement to Brandon, as proof that she is ashamed of her mercenary behaviour and anxious that it will be discovered.

Fittingly, in a narrative structured around the male lead's misreading of the heroine's motives, the reader often sees St. John looking questioningly at Esther, simultaneously entranced by her beauty and suspicious of her character. In a type of visual intertextuality, Broughton stages one such scene so that St. John gazes, not only at Esther, but at an iconic image of femininity before which she is standing: "The same sunbeam that brings out with such clearness Monna [sic] Lisa's faint, weird smile, takes in also within its compass Esther's small, swart head, round the back of which coils a great, loose, careless twist of burnished hair, like a black snake" (1870 [1899]: 87–88). Like Walter Pater's famous discussion of Mona Lisa, three years after the volume publication of *Red as a Rose Is She*, in which he compares "la Gioconda" to a "vampire" and mentions her in tandem with the Borgias and the "lust of Rome" (1873 [2000]: 1642), Broughton's description of Da Vinci's portrait focuses on its evocation of an enigmatic, potentially sinister female sexuality. Positioning Esther in front of this painting—and having the reader see St. John looking at both—Broughton demonstrates, as she does by quoting literary works, the role of art in shaping cultural perceptions of women. In this scene, the overtones of sexual danger are heightened by an allusion to racial Otherness, the braid twined "like a black snake" on Esther's "swart" head. (Underscoring this racial symbolism, a blonde rival for St. John's affections sneeringly calls Esther one of "'those black women'" [1870 [1899]: 400].)

The scene where St. John surveys Esther over his copy of *The Saturday Review*—another moment when the reader sees her through his eyes—conveys how unsettling he finds her sexuality:

> St. John has been rather unlucky in his experiences of women hitherto. He has got rather into the habit of thinking that all good women must be stupid, and that all pleasant women must be bad. Esther is not stupid. Is she bad, then? Those glances of hers, they give a man odd sensations about the midriff; they inspire in him a greedy, covetous desire for more of them; but are they such as Una would have given her Red Cross Knight?[47] Are they such as a man would like to see his wife bestow on his men friends? (1870 [1899]: 109)

Noting St. John's erotic response to Esther (her glances "give a man odd sensations about the midriff"), this passage conveys as well his discomfort with her obvious attraction to him: "[t]hose glances of hers ... Are they such as a man would like to see his wife bestow on his men friends?" Although himself associated with the male gaze, St. John finds the concept of a corresponding female gaze disconcerting, as a woman's amorous glances at a man suggest that she is not merely the object of male desire, but a subject with desires of her own. Tellingly, St. John's concern about Esther's potential infidelity—his fear that, as his wife, she might look at his "male friends" as she does at him—introduces the topic of adultery in a novel supposedly free of sensationalism. As St. John says when he breaks off their engagement after discovering that Esther lied about her relationship with Brandon, "'a woman who has deceived a man once for one object may deceive him a second time for another'" (1870 [1899]: 205).

Before breaking up with her, however, St. John tries to control Esther's sexuality by censoring her reading. In an episode reflecting the moral panic over French fiction exacerbated in the 1860s by the sensation controversy, the scandalised St. John discovers Esther immersed in a French novel, which he demands she return to the shelf because it "'is a book that no modest woman ought to read'" (1870 [1899]: 137).[48] Unsurprisingly, given the reception of her own sensation fiction, Broughton has scant sympathy for St. John's moralistic viewpoint, and has her narrator comment dryly "men are always shocked that women should *read about* the things that *they do*" (1870 [1899]: 136). In a similar critique of the sexual double standard, Esther retorts, in response to St. John's pronouncement that her book is one that "'no modest woman'" should read: "'But ... all modest *men* may, with pleasure and profit for themselves'" (1870 [1899]: 137). (When, indeed, she goes to St. John's study to inform him that she has returned the partially-read novel to the library, she sees, scattered on his table, several "enticing Gallic titles, similar to the one she has just so heroically foregone" [1870 [1899]: 139].) Showcasing St. John's conventional views of female behaviour, the incident contributes to his break with Esther; thinking that she "'had sooner put [her] hand in a lion's mouth'" than offend his "'fastidious, strict ideas of what a woman should be and do and look'" (1870 [1899]: 151), she does not tell him what really happened with Robert Brandon, leaving him to hear a version of the story that reflects badly on her.

As his autocratic (not to mention hypocritical) behaviour in the French novel incident attests, Broughton does not scruple to represent her male lead as flawed. At the same time, that the reader so frequently views the heroine through his eyes attests to the challenges Broughton faced in depicting female sexuality while distancing herself from sensationalism.[49] To portray Esther as she had Kate Chester—as a woman unabashedly aware of her desires and attractions—Broughton would risk inviting the accusations of immorality that had greeted her sensation fiction; she might also cause the reader to agree with St. John's characterization of Esther as a "'vile unprincipled coquette'" (1870 [1899]: 365). To forestall the appearance of impropriety on either her part or her heroine's, then, Broughton displays Esther's charms from the vantage point of the male viewer, either St. John himself or the narrator, whose sex is not specified but who, as in the passage below, displays a conventionally masculine fascination with female beauty:

> No one would ever call Esther's a Madonna face. No artist would ever ask her to sit for St. Catherine, or St. Cecilia, or St. Anybody else; hers is essentially *beauté du diable*—one of those little, sparkling, provoking, petulant faces that have a fresh dress of smiles or tears, or dimples or blushes, for every trivial, passing, question; one of those little faces that have been at the bottom of half the mischiefs the world has seen. (1870 [1899]: 78)

Like the metaphors elsewhere likening her blushes to both rosebuds and resplendent blooms, this passage simultaneously eroticises and infantilises Esther. Twice using the adjective "little" to describe her face, the narrator employs other words evocative of childish behaviour such as "dimples" and "mischiefs." Later in the novel, however, St, John's comparison of grown women to children is represented as problematic: even the timid Esther bridles when, explaining why she should not read French fiction, he opines that "'all women are children till they are twenty-one; and you are particularly childish for your age'" (1870 [1899]: 137). That Broughton attributes St. John's sententious outlook to his being "not much fonder of opposition than are most of his masterful sex" (1870 [1899]: 136) suggests that she, too, finds such sexist rhetoric objectionable. Nonetheless, having her narrator echo St. John's paternalistic tone enables Broughton to avoid characterizing her heroine as a *femme fatale*. In the passage above, for example, the juxtaposition of Esther's "*beauté du diable*" with her childlike character represents her attractions, not as genuinely diabolical, but as a force whose power she is not yet mature enough to comprehend.

Broughton further avoids portraying Esther as immodest by placing her, in the novel's most risqué scenes, in a state of diminished consciousness. In the first such scene, St. John, arriving at the door of her room as she is recovering from a headache, finds her "lying careless, restful on her couch", her "laughing, sleeping eyes" shooting "shafts of quick fire" (1870 [1899]: 107) as they meet his. Although the scene is obviously daring—the male lead sees the heroine lying down, her "smooth elbows and shoulders gleaming warm, cream-white, through the colder blue-white of her dress" (1870 [1899]: 107)—Broughton implies that Esther's glances are so inviting because she has been caught in a "careless" moment between sleeping and wakefulness. Still, as if to remove all doubt about her heroine's chastity, Broughton stages a later racy scene with Esther in a state of complete unconsciousness. Visiting the house where Esther, impoverished by her brother's death, labours as companion to an elderly couple, St. John once again enters her bedroom—an especially provocative scenario because he does so at night, when she is wearing only her nightgown. Unlike the earlier scene, however, there is no question of her reciprocating his feelings, because she has fainted from terror after waking him with the news of a male intruder in the house. Before determining that the supposed intruder was only an errant footman, St. John deposits Esther, still in a swoon, on her bed and, feasting his eyes on her beauty from the "tangled riches" of her hair down to her "bare feet" (1870 [1899]: 411), gives her a kiss of which she is necessarily unaware.[50]

Even the reconciliation that precedes St. John and Esther's marriage takes place when she is on the verge of unconsciousness. Apparently on her deathbed from a fever, Esther begs St. John for a farewell kiss before, yet again, swooning. With her penchant for satirizing plots involving women, Broughton transforms the convention of the heroine's tragic demise into bathos, as, upon unexpectedly recovering, Esther gasps "'*I asked him to kiss me, and I did not die!* How horrible!'" (1870 [1899]: 445). So mortified is Esther by the memory of an embrace she deems inappropriate that she blushes "a torrent of red ... even to the roots of her hair" (1870 [1899]: 445). Signalling her readiness for domesticity, Esther's earlier, vividly erotic blushes have now been replaced by one occasioned by a fear of transgressing feminine propriety.

Audiences today are, admittedly, less likely to be pleased than their Victorian forebears by a conclusion that not only stresses the heroine's adherence to sexual convention, but weds her to a censorious, possessive boyfriend. Yet Broughton herself suggests that a happy marriage between Esther and St. John is not wholly plausible. Proposing before their earlier break-up, St. John had, in fact, ominously joked that he might "'very possibly'" turn out to be a second version of his tyrannical father (1870 [1899]: 183), who is happiest, according to his son, either when eating a meal or bullying his wife (1870 [1899]: 165). Perhaps the most discordant note in Broughton's supposedly happy finale, though, is the implication that Esther has no viable economic options other than marriage. As St. John declares to her shortly before the novel's end, "'To be my wife, ill-tempered and jealous as I, no doubt, should often be, would be distinctly a better fate than to be old Blessington's drudge'" (1870 [1899]: 427). Implying that a controlling husband and wage-slavery are a penniless gentlewoman's only options, Broughton takes the bloom off her rosy ending.

Rebel Without a Cause: Lenore Herrick and the Tragedy of the Exceptional Woman

Despite its disturbing undertones, *Red as a Rose Is She* was a highly successful novel. More popular even than *Cometh Up as a Flower*, it sold, as Marilyn Wood notes, "nearly twelve thousand copies" in the seven years following its publication (1993: 30). Yet, although one advertisement predicted that Broughton's next book, *Good-bye, Sweetheart!*, would "be decidedly THE novel of the season",[51] it did not fare nearly so well. To some extent, this discouraging performance could, as Marilyn Wood notes, have been the result of the work's "sombre tone" (1993: 33); while an ending in which the lovelorn heroine dies of tuberculosis had not prevented *Cometh Up as a Flower* from being a best-seller, the similar conclusion of *Good-bye, Sweetheart!* may have disappointed the many fans of *Red as a Rose* who expected the author's next novel to have a cheerier finale. Still, it is also possible that *Good-bye, Sweetheart!* was not popular for the simple reason that its heroine is hard to like. Described as having "that very sweet smile which is, they say, the peculiar attribute of ill-tempered people" (1872: 4), Lenore Herrick is frequently moody, capricious, and confrontational. Probably the least idealised of all Broughton's heroines, she is also the most overtly resistant to the Victorian feminine ideal. Scorning "'the shackles of conventionality'" (1872: 8–9), she declares that she "'*loathe[s]*'" children (168) and has no intention of becoming a domestic angel. She scandalises the male lead, Paul Le Mesurier, with her lack of respect for her father: not only does she refuse to be sorry for a childhood incident in which she bit his hand after he punished her for not knowing her catechism, but she declares his death a "'mercy'" (1872: 42). When the shocked Paul responds that "'Every woman needs some one to keep her in order ... Until she has got a husband—her natural and legitimate master—she ought to have a father'" (1872: 42), Lenore counters "'There is not that man living that could keep me in order; I would break his heart, and his spirit, and every thing breakable about him, first!'" (1872: 43). Paul's disgust at the thought of a "'man in a state of abject submission to his wife'" cannot shake her conviction that the most "'degrading sight on the face of the earth'" is a "'woman in a state of abject subjection to her husband'" (1872: 43–44).

Such arguments between the heroine and male lead over female power and male authority make *Good-bye, Sweetheart!* Broughton's most explicit reference to the Woman Question thus far —and, indeed, her clearest allusion to controversies over gender roles until her novel about the New Woman, *Dear Faustina* (1897). Although it was ostensibly the "coarseness" of the style of *Good-bye, Sweetheart!*, that moved the *Athenæum* reviewer to claim that Broughton "throws down the glove as distinctly as does a female orator at a Woman's Rights convention" (1872: 585), passages like the ones quoted above could themselves remind readers of the emergent feminist movement. *Good-bye, Sweetheart!* was also notable in Broughton's career as the first work to which she signed her name. As she told George Bentley, her main reason for doing so was piracy: "So many people claim my stories I may as well assert my own right to them" (27 Mar 1871; qtd. in Wood 1993: 30). In light of this assertion of her rights, it is fitting that the novel containing her most assertive heroine to date should also be the one in which Broughton discards the cloak of anonymity assumed by women writers to hide their participation in the marketplace.

It is also fitting that the first novel in which Broughton claims public ownership of her art rewrites the nineteenth century's most influential saga of the female artist, Germaine de Staël's *Corinne* (1807).[52] It is unsurprising that the erudite Broughton would have read *Corinne*, and, indeed, twice in *Not Wisely* she alludes to passages in which the eponymous heroine recalls the boredom of domestic life at her stepmother's house.[53] *Good-bye, Sweetheart!* and *Corinne* share the same essential plot: a male lead who prefers conventional women falls in love with a brilliantly unconventional one, but eventually chooses to wed a more docile fiancée, abandoning the heroine to a tragic end. In de Staël's version of the story, the aristocratic Lord Nelvil falls violently in love with the renowned improvisatrice Corinne, but, fearing she is too unorthodox, marries her retiring half-sister instead, leaving the pining artist to die of a lingering illness. In Broughton's revision, Paul Le Mesurier breaks his engagement to Lenore—to whom he had been drawn against his will—when she refuses to obey his orders about dancing with other men; heartbroken, she falls into a consumptive decline, and he marries his angelic cousin.

In the introduction, I referred to *Corinne* as the quintessential nineteenth-century text by and about the female genius. That Broughton should choose to rewrite de Staël's plot at this point in her career is highly significant, reflecting, not only her debt to an illustrious female precursor, but her continuing difficulties in defining her own literary project in generic terms. Unlike *Red as a Rose Is She*—which, while not a particularly rosy portrayal of heterosexual love, is recognizably a courtship novel—*Good-bye, Sweetheart!* is harder to classify. It is not, of course, unknown for authors of domestic fiction sometimes to write stories ending in tragedy rather than in marriage. And it is certainly not uncommon for women writers of status—Romantic feminists such as de Staël, or Victorian women of letters such as George Eliot—to include in their novels tragic female characters, in either lead or supporting roles, who represent the frustrations of the unconventional woman. *Good-bye, Sweetheart!* is, however, unusual in the degree to which its tragic plot blurs increasingly rigid boundaries between the categories of popular and canonical literature. Linking herself to the high-status art of the woman of letters by revising de Staël, Broughton nonetheless pitches *Good-bye, Sweetheart!* to a popular readership. Ironically, however, the plot of her fourth novel is—even more than that of her third—in tension with the genre of romantic fiction that established her popularity. For *Good-bye, Sweetheart!* is not just a tragic version of romance: in its portrayal of a woman whose death is caused by her passion for a man whose control she refuses to accept, the novel could more accurately be described as an anti-romance.

Reflecting its complex relation to, at once, high-status art and popular fiction, *Good-bye, Sweetheart!* revises not only *Corinne*, but *Red as a Rose Is She*. A "darker re-working", as Shirley Jones calls it, of *Red as a Rose* (2004: 218), *Good-bye, Sweetheart!* recasts the plot of the Girl of the Period and her jealous fiancé in the earlier novel not only as a tragedy rather than a courtship novel, but as an out-and-out battle of the sexes. Reflecting this heightened combativeness between the heroine and male lead, Paul Le Mesurier is more openly anti-feminist than St. John Gerard, and Lenore is far more defiant of male control than her timid precursor. In *Red as a Rose*, Esther rebels against St. John only once, when he presses her not to read French fiction—and even then changes her mind, returning the offending volume to the shelves. Even after St. John breaks their engagement, she continues to placate him: fearing, at the Blessingtons' house, that he still thinks her "an insatiable greedy coquette" (1870 [1899]: 372), she denies herself a session of the first fun she has had in ages—skating with another male guest—because St. John so obviously disapproves. In contrast, Lenore, who proclaims "'I have never yet been forbidden to do any thing that I did not instantly strain every nerve to do it'" (1872: 148), is nowhere near so malleable. Although Paul reminds her that a bride's promise to "'obey'" her husband is part of the wedding ceremony, she refuses to bow to male authority (1872: 148). When the jealous Paul "'forbid[s]'" her to dance with an admirer at a ball, in fact, she defies his "'right'" to use that word to her (1872: 252–53), a reference to the concept of individual liberties that implies her feminist sensibilities.

The differences between Esther and Lenore extend to their appearances. Whereas a passage I quoted earlier repeatedly describes Esther as "little", Lenore's attractions—"her full, womanly figure", "proud throat", "strong, white hands", and "large white" arm (1872: 41, 67)—evoke power and grandeur. These regal attributes emphasise Lenore's similarity to de Staël's Corinne, the magnitude of whose extra-domestic ambitions is signalled by a "tall full figure, reminiscent of Greek statuary" (1807 [1987]: 21). Like Corinne, Lenore literally embodies a heterodox version of femininity, as Paul uneasily realises upon meeting her:

> She is the exact opposite of every thing he has hitherto thought good and fair in woman. Her very beauty—large and noble—is the reverse of the small, meek prettiness that has hitherto been his ideal[.] (1872: 110–11).

Lenore's "large and noble" beauty threatens to unsettle, not only Paul's attitudes towards women, but his attempt to define himself as the "'natural and legitimate master'" (1872: 42) of the woman he loves. This potential upsetting of male power is comically suggested by an actual upset when Paul and Lenore's boat capsizes during a romantic outing on the river. When Paul chivalrously offers to carry home the dripping Lenore, she hoots "'Carry me! ... Why, I weigh nine stone eight! I might as well talk of carrying you!'" (1872: 71).

By teasing Paul about his penchant for disembodied women, Lenore indicates, not only her own divergence from the feminine ideal, but her disdain for it. When Paul is displeased by a risqué song she sings on their boat-ride, she asks him the revealing question "'is the ideal woman clothed with flesh?'" (1872: 65). On a literal level, the question is meant to elicit information about the women in Paul's life, and he answers it by mentioning the cousin he greatly admires. Yet Lenore's question also has a symbolic dimension: to query whether the "'ideal woman'" has "'flesh'" is implicitly to challenge the assumption that, to be perfect, a woman must be ethereal. (Paul, in fact, admits that his docile cousin is "'rather *too* thin'" and pale as "'a lily'" [1872: 66].)

The incident that causes Paul to break his engagement to Lenore—her refusing to obey his command to stop dancing with another man—is a dramatic example of his inability to stomach the types of power and appetite embodied by her full figure. It is, of course, scarcely surprising that Lenore's dancing with Charlie Scrope, a man who obviously admires her, should enrage the jealous Paul, who growls "'*I will go shares with no man*'" before forbidding her to continue (1872: 252). Yet the pleasure that Lenore takes in dancing is itself a proclamation of her unabashed sensuality. We hear that she "loves dancing *intensely;* with an intensity, indeed, seldom met with among sad and sober Englishwomen" (1872: 241–42). Implying that her heroine's sensual delights make her the equivalent of a foreigner, Broughton strengthens Lenore's resemblance to the half-Italian Corinne, whose Mediterranean heritage figures the difference between her unconventional version of femininity and that of the British side of her family. That Paul objects, not just to Lenore's dancing with another man, but to her doing so in public, further emphasises her likeness to de Staël's heroine. Angered that Lenore was making herself "'remarkable'" (1872: 248)—in other words, a focus of attention—by dancing with Scrope, Paul displays a discomfort with his fiancée's performance before an audience reminiscent of Lord Nelvil's discomfort with Corinne's public appearances as an improvisatrice—a publicity he finds disturbingly akin to that of a fallen woman.

Yet, although Lenore's dancing is too close to public performance for Paul's comfort, she is not, in fact, an artist. An exceptional woman like Corinne—the *Athenæum* reviewer called her "as out of place among her common-place companions as Achilles in the court of Lycomedes" (1872: 586)—Lenore nonetheless lacks a professional outlet for such talents as her accomplished piano playing. Consequently, even though she identifies herself as a free-spirited "'Bohemian'" (1872: 182), she is a rebel without a cause, a feminist manqué who despises the "'abject subjection'" of married women while shrinking from the prospect of spinsterhood. When, upon meeting her, Paul assumes that she is too independent to want to marry, she angrily asks "'Do you think I mean to be an old maid?'" (1872: 43). Walter Sichel's description of Broughton's work as spanning "the distance between the 'Girl of the Period' and the 'New Woman'" (Wood 1993: 116) captures the frustrating indeterminacy of Lenore's historical position: she is feminist enough to be discontented with domesticity, but as yet unable to imagine herself actively pursuing an extra-domestic vocation.

In one scene, however, Lenore explicitly voices her regret at not having a role in the public sphere. Disdaining the cultivation of domestic "'little every-day virtues'", she announces to her companions that she would have liked to have been Madame Roland or Charlotte Corday: "'Now if it were some *big* thing … I could do it'" (1872: 51). This reference to the French Revolutionary era contrasts the possibility of political power it briefly offered women with the lack of such options during the Victorian period. Lenore's lament, however, at her inability to do some "'*big* thing'" is relevant not only to her situation but to Broughton's, pointing as it does to a loss of epic dimension between her own work and that of the Romantic-era de Staël. Not only was de Staël herself a politically engaged woman—her views famously angered Napoleon—but her work, an influence on such prominent women of letters as Elizabeth Barrett Browning and George Eliot, is a classic exposition of a theme that would continue to be important for women artists: the tension between career and domesticity. Romantic love dooms de Staël's heroine, as it does Broughton's, but, while Corinne's story is about both love and art, Lenore's is about love alone. Unable to escape the romance plot, Lenore thus resembles Broughton herself, whose role in the marketplace is defined as a purveyor of romance even though her novels increasingly note its pitfalls for women.

Still, if Broughton was unable to imagine the plot of a popular novel in which the heroine's story did not centre on romance, in *Good-bye, Sweetheart!* she imagines a version of that plot in which the heroine becomes a recognizably proto-feminist figure, the hysterical woman. By the end of the nineteenth century, Sigmund Freud and Josef Breuer's groundbreaking *Studies of Hysteria* (1895) would portray the hysteric, such as Anna O., as a woman whose illness was occasioned by frustrations with conventional domesticity.[54] (Anna O. was in reality Bertha Pappenheim, who, following her recovery, became a socialist and feminist.) Appearing in a novel published twenty-three years before Freud and Breuer's study, Lenore Herrick is, in many ways, a precursor of the Freudian hysteric, whose somatic symptoms can be traced to such psychic stresses as sexual repression. In Lenore's case, sexual desire is not so much repressed as incapable of being fulfilled if she is to preserve her independence: were she to marry Paul, the man she passionately loves, she would, as I have said elsewhere "have to renounce those aspects of her character that make her passionate to begin with" (Heller 2011: 71). Faced with this dilemma, Lenore immediately, and dramatically, exhibits a symptom commonly associated with hysteria. Having begged Paul's rival Scrope to marry her after Paul breaks their engagement—a childish attempt at revenge on her erstwhile fiancé—she falls, before the ceremony, into a faint that lasts several days, and which resembles the catatonic fits experienced by women diagnosed with hysteria.

The most obvious somatic symptom of Lenore's psychic impasse, however, is consumption. Like Nell's tubercular decline in *Cometh Up as a Flower*, Lenore's consumption is linked to romantic heartbreak—a link that, as Basil Meyer has argued, reflects Victorian medical theories that tuberculosis could be caused by severe emotional shock (2003: 289).[55] Like Nell's version of consumption, too, Lenore's resembles the self-willed starvation of anorexia, in that both heroines waste away following the frustration of their deepest desires. Whereas Nell does not become ill until several years after M'Gregor's death, though, Lenore begins to exhibit tubercular symptoms, including "loss of flesh" (1872: 350), soon after Paul's desertion and her abortive attempt at marriage to Scrope. Her sister Jemima's comment after Paul's abandonment—"'Anyone ... more resolute to die than you, I have seldom had the pleasure of meeting'" (1872: 317)—suggests, indeed, that we should read Lenore's death as a form of self-destruction. It is also telling that Lenore's death should result from a malady that evokes the particular version of hysteria—anorexia nervosa—first identified as a disease around the time *Good-bye, Sweetheart!* was published.[56] Susan Bordo has called anorexia "both protest and retreat in the same gesture" (1993: 174), at once a capitulation to cultural ideals of thinness and a dramatization of those ideals' deadly influence on women. Paring down the "large and noble" form whose passions Paul found so hard to control, Lenore's emaciation has a similar couble meaning, at once registering her anger at Paul and taming the sensuality he thought transgressive.

While reflecting a specifically Victorian medical context of hysteria and anorexia, Lenore's "loss of flesh" also recalls Corinne's wasting, final illness. Even here, however, de Staël's heroine has an advantage on Broughton's. Characteristically dramatic, Corinne transforms her declining health into a spectacle that shames the man who, as she says "'*has done me too much harm*'" (1807 [1987]: 403); upon seeing a portrait of her now-ravaged form captioned "a pena si può dir: questa fu rosa" ("scarcely can one say: she was a rose"; 1807 [1987]: 405)[57], the remorseful Lord Nelvil is consumed by a grief that will verge on madness after he attends Corinne's deathbed. Lenore, however, has no such opportunity to encourage her former lover to feel guilty. While she encounters him briefly during her illness, prompting him to note "'surely you are thinner than you used to be'" (1872: 359), her final wish to see him before she dies is never fulfilled. Instead, she expires as soon as

Scrope, the messenger she sent to fetch Paul, explains that he was unable to bring him back "'because it was his wedding-day when I got there'" (1872: 437).

Although Lenore herself never marries, it is appropriate that her story ends with the mention of a "'wedding-day.'" In the fiction that Broughton wrote in the 1870s after completing *Good-bye, Sweetheart!,* she moved from the courtship plot to chronicling women's experiences as wives. Further exploring the subject addressed in her courtship novels—the power imbalances between the sexes in heterosexual romance—these marriage plots also manage, without actually crossing over into sensation fiction, to revisit the topic of adultery that had made her earliest work so controversial.

CHAPTER FOUR

"*All* Married People Grow to Hate One Another": Marital Breakdown and the Adultery Plot in Broughton's Fiction, 1873–86

> "*All* married people grow to hate one another after a bit", say I comprehensively; "it is only a question of time."
> — Nancy Grey, in *Nancy* (1873 [2005]: 1.79)

In *Red as a Rose Is She* (1870) and *Good-bye, Sweetheart!* (1872), Broughton turned from the plot of potential adultery in her early sensation fiction to the courtship narrative. Following these first two novels of the 1870s, however, Broughton returned to the adultery theme. The eponymous heroines of *Nancy* (1873) and *Belinda* (1883) do not in fact betray their considerably older husbands—though Belinda comes closest—but the possibility of female infidelity propels both narratives. Although *Joan* (1876) and *Doctor Cupid* (1886) are versions of the courtship genre, they too incorporate adultery plots: in the second half of *Joan*, the heroine's former suitor begs her to elope so he can escape an unhappy marriage, and the protagonist of *Doctor Cupid* falls in love with a man in a long-term relationship with a married woman. Even "The Man with the Nose" (1873), a supernatural tale in which a young bride is abducted by a hypnotic stranger, can be read as a version of the adultery plot.

At least to some extent, Broughton returned to the adultery plot in response to market forces. Despite critical censure of their impropriety, the popularity of her novels was bolstered by her reputation for racy stories. In fact, following the tepid reception of her tamest narrative of the 1870s and 1880s—the Austenian courtship tale *Second Thoughts* (1880)—she wrote to her publisher Bentley that she envisioned returning to an idea for a novel she had initially thought "too risqué", but "since the public like it hot & strong, I am not the person to disoblige them" (*BA*, Letter to George Bentley, 22 June 1880, Pt. 2, Reel 2). Indeed, Broughton's next novel, *Belinda,* ends with a wife nearly eloping with a former lover.

In this chapter I will examine the ever-more elaborate strategies Broughton used in the 1870s and 1880s to make her novels "hot & strong" without too outrageously transgressing the boundaries for depicting extra-marital female sexuality. Her most astonishing feat in this regard is *Nancy,* a tale in which an admirer bombards the married heroine with amorous advances of whose meaning she is apparently unaware. At the same time, I will also be interested in how Broughton's fiction between 1873 and 1886 continues to address the issue raised in the early 1870s by the plot of the jealous fiancé: the problematic nature of marriage for women. One of the more striking aspects of the works discussed in this chapter is the way their tales of potential adultery are, in a broader sense, narratives of marital breakdown. Although Broughton does not explicitly mention divorce, her fiction of the 1870s and 1880s can be compared to the other nineteenth-century works that Anne Humpherys (2007) has discussed— including *Jane Eyre* (1847), *East Lynne* (1861), and *Jude the*

Obscure (1895)—which depict the lack of options for dissolving incompatible marriages faced by couples even after the 1857 Matrimonial Causes Act. As Broughton poignantly shows, the relative indissolubility of marriage affected both husbands and wives, yet the power imbalances inherent in Victorian marriage made this problem particularly intractable for women. Revising *Middlemarch, Belinda*—with its tale of a young wife trapped in a loveless union with a grim scholar—is probably the most vivid example in Broughton's oeuvre of domestic Gothic in which marriage is the tomb of female autonomy and desire.

The fictions of the 1870s and 1880s thus emphasise and expand upon the double paradox of Broughton's work: representing female desire while apparently expunging the record of its existence, these narratives also celebrate romantic love only to expose ever more insistently its dangers for women. A notable example of this second paradox is the last novel I shall discuss in this chapter, *Doctor Cupid*, which evokes in its title the romantic ideology it deftly deconstructs in ways that anticipate Broughton's more innovative revisions of the romance plot after 1890.

The Case of the Vanishing Bride: Marriage and Mesmerism in "The Man with the Nose"

In 2004, Nina Auerbach expressed her surprise that Broughton's supernatural fiction has been "oddly ignored" despite doing "everything feminist critics want women's ghost stories to do."[58] As an example of how Broughton's collection *Tales for Christmas Eve* (1873) reveals "the horror and pain lurking in ordinary female experience", Auerbach singles out "The Man with the Nose" as the "most nightmarish haunted honeymoon" narrative she has ever read (2004: 281). Depicting a honeymoon, a transitional state between courtship and marriage, "The Man with the Nose" is a useful bridge between the novels explored in the last chapter—Broughton's courtship narratives of the early 1870s—and the later fiction portraying marriage discussed in this chapter. Raising, albeit in ghostly form, the topic of adultery that would inform *Nancy* and *Belinda*, "The Man with the Nose" also harks back to *Red as a Rose Is She* and *Good-bye, Sweetheart!* in making its male lead, and narrator, a newlywed version of the jealous fiancé who, like his precursors in the earlier novels, frets about the heroine's potentially transgressive sexuality.

So subtly crafted is this remarkable story, however, that it might be hard for a first-time reader to notice the narrator's anxiety about the fidelity of his young wife, Elizabeth, until the tragic denouement. The tale's power derives from the contrast between its initially light tone—the newlyweds' banter sparkles with Broughton's trademark wit—and Elizabeth's growing fear that the couple is being stalked by a man whose distinguishing feature is a prominent nose. Even after himself glimpsing this figure—and hearing that others have seen him as well—the narrator attributes his wife's fears to an overactive imagination, and, despite her urgent pleas that he stay, leaves her in Switzerland while he attends the deathbed of a wealthy uncle. Upon returning several weeks later, however, he learns that, shortly after his own departure, his wife left the pension accompanied by a man with "'a most peculiar nose'" (1872 [1981]: 141). In the frantic, and ultimately futile, search for the missing woman that follows, the only sighting is an account by peasants of seeing, on the day of the abduction, a carriage whose sole occupants were "a dark gentleman, with the peculiar physiognomy which has been so often described" and "a lady lying apparently in a state of utter insensibility" (1872 [1981]: 142–43).

Generically, Broughton's "dark gentleman" is descended from the legendary figure of the demon lover or incubus. A notable nineteenth-century example of the theme—which may well have influenced Broughton—is her uncle J. S. Le Fanu's "Schalken the Painter" (1851), the tale of a young woman married off to a wealthy suitor who turns out, apparently, to be a corpse. Fleeing the ghastly intimacy of this union, the terrified bride briefly takes refuge in her father's house, gasping "'the dead and the living can never be one; God has forbidden it'" (1851 [1964]: 42) before, like Broughton's Elizabeth, vanishing forever in an apparent abduction. In "Schalken", as in "The Man with the Nose", the demon lover embodies a terrifying version of male sexuality; Le Fanu describes the face of the corpse-like Vanderhausen as "sensual, malignant, and even satanic" (1851 [1964]: 38), and one need not consult Sigmund Freud to identify the phallic symbolism of the prominent nose of Broughton's sinister stranger. Moreover, given the stereotypical association of large noses with ethnic and religious outsiders, most notably Jews, Broughton's aquiline "dark gentleman" evokes images of sexually dangerous racial Others. Recalling what Patrick Brantlinger calls "sexual atrocity" narratives—British tales written in the aftermath of the Indian Mutiny in which rebellious natives defile English womanhood (Brantlinger, 209)—the man with the nose even manages to penetrate the English couple's marriage-chamber; one night the terrified Elizabeth wakes her husband to say that she has just seen the sinister stranger in their hotel room, "'between the window and the bed'" (1872 [1981]: 134).

Representing the demon lover as an Other and intruder, "The Man with the Nose" appears to locate problematic sexuality outside the English domestic unit. Yet, like such other Victorian narratives of racial and sexual anxiety as *The Moonstone* (1868) or *She* (1886), Broughton's story blurs clearly-defined binaries between English and Other, as well as between "pure" and "impure" womanhood. Recalling Esther Craven in *Red as a Rose Is She*, Elizabeth, the bride in "The Man with the Nose", is simultaneously childlike and erotic. Addressing her as "'child'" and "'little one'" (1872 [1981]: 137, 133), the narrator repeatedly describes her in diminutive terms, as when he claims that, upon trying on a bonnet, she evokes "a delicious picture of a child playing at being grown up" (1872 [1981]: 132), or when he remembers the "dear little babyish notes she used to send me during our engagement" (1872

[1981]: 140). At the same time, there is a decided sexual charge to this infantilisation, as when the narrator remembers the last time he saw Elizabeth, "her small and wistful face looking out from among the thick fair fleece of her long hair" (1872 [1981]: 140). Revealingly, too, the narrator is quick to assume that Elizabeth has been unfaithful. The most obvious example of this is when, near the story's end, he rages when told she left the Swiss pension with a gentleman: "'So this is it! With that pure child-face, with that divine ignorance—only three weeks married—this is the trick she has played me!'" (1872 [1981]: 141). Yet even earlier the narrator betrayed jealousy. At the beginning of the story, as the affianced couple debate where to go for their honeymoon, the narrator responds to the tale's first ominous note—Elizabeth's admission that she is afraid of going to the Lake District because "'[s]omething dreadful happened to me there'"—by crying, "in a jealous heat and hurry", "'what the mischief *did* you do, and why have not you told me about it before?'" (1872 [1981]: 129). Kissing his hand "in timid deprecation" of this anger, Elizabeth replies that she did not "'*do* much'", but, rather, had a "'nervous fever'" (1872 [1981]: 129).

A substitute for the hidden romantic history of which the narrator suspected her, Elizabeth's "'nervous fever'" defines her not as a transgressive woman but as a hysterical one. Evoking this latter stereotype, the narrator refers to Elizabeth having "so nervous a temperament" and describes her reaction to one sighting of the mysterious stranger as "hysterical sobbing" (1872 [1981]: 131, 137); in general, he treats her fears of the man with the nose as a neurotic delusion. Yet the story of Elizabeth's first attack of "'nervous fever'" may, indeed, have been occasioned by sexual transgression, albeit unconscious on her part. When the narrator asks her why she avoids the Lake District, she answers that, while vacationing there as a girl, she went to see a "'mesmeriser'", who selected her from the audience as a medium:

> "[A]fter that I do not remember anything—I believe I did all sorts of extraordinary things that he told me—sang and danced, and made a fool of myself—but when I came home I was very ill, very—I lay in bed for five whole weeks, and—and was off my head, and said odd and wicked things that you would not have expected me to say—that dreadful bed! shall I ever forget it?" (1872 [1981]: 130)

Compelled to perform in public without her volition, Elizabeth anticipates the Englishwoman who, in George du Maurier's *fin-de-siècle* novel *Trilby* (1894), becomes a famous singer under the hypnotic control of the hook-nosed Svengali—an explicitly Jewish version of Broughton's man with the nose. Yet, as Alison Winter argues in her study of nineteenth-century mesmerism, anxieties about men mesmerising female subjects were not solely occasioned by fears of men violating innocent women. Rather, there were also concerns that the female mesmeric subject willingly participated in sexually inappropriate behaviour. Citing a case in which a French girl purportedly lost her virginity to a mesmerist, Winter notes that one English doctor refused to believe that the young woman was truly unconscious; instead, he claimed that mesmerism was a "ruse" that enabled "'nervous and impressionable females'" to enter into temptation without admitting they were doing so (Winter, 1998: 101). As Winter says, such theories assumed that mesmerism allowed young women to "succumb to the (pretended) power of the mesmerist, but in reality ... to place themselves in the (real) 'power' of an unscrupulous lover" (1998: 101).

Winter's discussion illuminates Broughton's portrayal of Elizabeth, a "nervous" young woman whom the mesmerist selected as a subject because "'he said I should be such a good medium ... —and—and —I let him'" (1872 [1981]: 130). Elizabeth's use of the verb "'let'" suggests the degree to which she was, or felt she was, complicit in doing the mesmerist's will. This perception of her ambiguous agency also informs Elizabeth's memories of the experience:

> "[S]ometimes, in the dead black of the night, when God seems a long way off, and the devil near, it comes back to me so strongly—I feel, do not you know, as if he were *there* somewhere in the room, and I *must* get up and follow him." (1872 [1981]: 130)

When, on her honeymoon, Elizabeth wakes up her husband to say she has seen the man with the nose in their hotel room, she draws the parallel between her past and present experience of a mesmeric male:

> "He was standing as still as stone—I never saw any live thing so still—*looking* at me; he never called or beckoned, or moved a finger, but his eyes *commanded* me to come to him, as the eyes of the mesmeriser at Penrith did ... I *hated* it", she cries, excitedly; "I loathed it—abhorred it. I was ice-cold with fear and horror, but—I *felt* myself going to him ... I *longed* to stay with you, though I was *mad* with fright, yet I felt myself pulling strongly away from you—going to him[.]" (1872 [1981]: 134; emphasis in original)

Significantly, Elizabeth confesses to ambivalence. On one hand, she longs to reject the mesmerist's command; on the other, she cannot resist following it. In this sense, the man with the nose can be read as an externalisation of, as Melissa Purdue puts it, "unspoken desires" (2020: 187) that transgress the bounds of conventional wifely behaviour. The "'odd and wicked things'" that Elizabeth says on her sickbed after encountering the mesmerist at Penrith declare what she really wants—but refuses to admit wanting—were she able to shed her inhibitions.

Interpreted in this way, "The Man with the Nose" is a tale

of adultery rather than of abduction. Still, like all great Gothic villains, the man with the nose evokes more than one meaning. Simultaneously a figure for the demonic sexuality of the male Other and for the bourgeois woman's repressed desires, he can also be seen as the embodiment of the theme that haunts so many of Broughton's fictions, the fear that marriage will constrain female autonomy. As if embodying the bride's vow to obey her husband, the man with the nose commands Elizabeth to do his will and tolerates no dissent. Furthermore, reading the man with the nose as an image for the domination of women within marriage, and their resistance to that domination, is not incompatible with reading him as a figure for female desire. In *Not Wisely, but Too Well*, for instance, Kate's wayward passion both transgresses feminine ideals and places her in thrall to Dare's controlling masculinity. A similar duality—a simultaneous representation of female desire and control of the female body—occurs in "The Man with the Nose" when the newlyweds, during a boat ride on the Rhine, see a young woman eating "ravenously":

> There are few actions more disgusting than eating *can* be made. A handsome girl close to us—her immaturity evidenced by the two long tails of black hair down her back—is thrusting her knife halfway down her throat.
> "Come on deck again," says Elizabeth, disgusted and frightened at this last sight. (1872 [1981]: 135)

Elizabeth's emotions in this scene convey a revulsion at female appetite as well as a terror at the danger in which it places the female body. That Elizabeth glimpses the phallic knife "thrusting" down the girl's throat underscores the story's association of the honeymoon—the period of a bride's initiation into heterosexuality and marriage—with danger for women. Viewed in this light, one of the narrator's earlier comments foreshadows the tale's marital Gothic; as he says, all the bride needs to do during the typical wedding ceremony is to stand, "prettily passive", with "a veil to gently shroud her features"—an image that equates marriage for women with the loss of identity, if not actual death (1872 [1981]: 131).

Nancy: The Perils of an Improbably Obtuse Heroine

Published the year after the initial appearance of "The Man with the Nose" in *Temple Bar*, *Nancy* does not, like the supernatural tale, limit itself to depicting a honeymoon. Yet a honeymoon—described over no fewer than four chapters of volume I—plays a crucial role in the narrative, introducing, like "The Man with the Nose", a potential intruder on a newlywed couple's relationship. Honeymooning in Europe (and pursuing an itinerary similar to that of the newlyweds in "The Man with the Nose"), the eponymous nineteen-year-old heroine and her forty-seven-year old husband, Sir Roger Tempest, encounter a handsome young man, Frank Musgrave, whose estates border Sir Roger's. Apparently surprised that Nancy would wed a man who attended school with her father, Musgrave is assiduous in his attendance on her, even accompanying her on shopping and sight-seeing expeditions while Sir Roger rests at the hotel. When the newlyweds bid Musgrave farewell before returning to England, Nancy exclaims, puzzled: "'He looked as if he were going to *weep*, did not he? and what on earth about?'" (1873 [2005]: 1.170)

Presumably Nancy is the only one in any doubt about the answer to this question. Her inability to fathom the cause of Musgrave's discomfiture—especially in light of his strong hints about his feelings—places the reader of Nancy's first-person narrative in the position not only of knowing more than the heroine, but of wondering how she could possibly be so dense. The reader's bewilderment, if not outright incredulity, as to Nancy's misunderstanding of the situation can only grow once Musgrave himself returns to England and pays her numerous visits during the prolonged absence of her husband on a business trip to the West

Indies. Though Nancy is amazed when Musgrave bluntly reveals his regard, the reader, in the words of a snide reviewer in *The Pall Mall Gazette*, "will sympathise much more with the astonishment of the suitor" (1873: 1824). The review quotes from the passage in which Musgrave refuses at first to believe that Nancy could be unaware of his motives:

> "It is *impossible!*" he says, roughly. "Whatever else you are, you are no fool; and a woman would have had to be blinder than any mole not to see whither I—yes, and *you*, too—have been tending! If you meant to be *surprised* all along when it came to this, why did you make yourself common talk for the neighbourhood with me? Why did you press me, with such unconventional eagerness, to visit you? Why did you reproach me if I missed one day?" (1873 [2005]: 2.51)

Unimpressed by Nancy's virtuous rejection of Musgrave's adulterous suit, the *Pall Mall Gazette* reviewer claims that the sole reason she remains "uncorrupted and incorruptible" is her "sheer and incredible obtuseness" (1873: 1824).

Though hostile, the *Pall Mall Gazette* review nonetheless pinpoints the problem with *Nancy*'s plot. The sexual innocence that the narrator of "The Man with the Nose" calls "divine ignorance" might, in Nancy's case, be labelled utter stupidity. And yet none of Broughton's novels more vividly bear witness to the difficulties faced by an English woman writer of the period in depicting marital incompatibility. Broughton's response to the *Pall Mall Gazette* review in a letter to George Bentley expresses her frustration:

> The Pall Mall is most unfair. Is it not singular that "Nancy", so much the purest in tone and so much the most inoffensive of my stories, should be more violently reviled than any of its predecessors? I positively dread the "Saturday". I cannot get

used to the coarse and indiscriminate abuse with which I am belaboured ... Tell me honestly whether the sale of the book is seriously affected, or whether it will weather the storm. I am sick of the whole thing, and have half a mind never to put pen to paper again. (BA, 28 November 1873, Pt. 2, Reel 22)

Signed "in great depression and discomfiture", this "cri de coeur", as Marilyn Wood calls it (1993: 42), poignantly expresses Broughton's sensitivity to negative reviews of her work, especially to repeated accusations of vulgarity. *The Pall Mall Gazette* reviewer, for example, levels the familiar charge of coarseness when they claim that the heroine speaks "with the flippancy and smartness of a barmaid" (1873: 1824), giving as an example of this "not over-refined" humour Nancy's claim that the existence of her five siblings evinces the "foolhardy fertility of British householders" (1873 [2005]: 1.8). Yet *The Pall Mall Gazette*'s simultaneous attacks on the impropriety of Broughton's language and the naïveté of her heroine hint at the intractable dilemma of her situation as an author. Like the reviewer of *Goodbye, Sweetheart!* in *The Athenæum*, the *Pall Mall Gazette* reviewer reads the risqué elements of *Nancy* as evidence that Broughton is only too well acquainted with masculine slang: "the author of 'Nancy' ... seems to have modelled her style upon that of the young gentleman who represents fashionable fastness on the boards of a music-hall" (1873: 1824). Yet the same reviewer scoffs at Nancy's inability to comprehend sexual innuendo. No wonder Broughton was exasperated: if she had portrayed Nancy as aware of, or worse yet, eager for, Musgrave's efforts at seduction, the book would probably have never been published, much less reach a mainstream readership; when she insists on her heroine's naïveté, however, hostile reviewers label her plot incredible while accusing her of indelicacy anyway.

Broughton's "cri de coeur" to Bentley notwithstanding, critical response to Nancy was by no means uniformly negative. Despite its author's fears that savage reviews would damage sales of the novel, *Nancy* proved popular—even inspiring a play—and earned praise from some critics for being Broughton's strongest work to date. *Nancy*'s commercial success, however, may be added evidence of the limitations Broughton faced in depicting female passion, as her strategy of rendering her heroine "inoffensive" by making her a sexual ignoramus was apparently effective in securing an audience. In certain ways *Nancy*'s plot can be read as a tamer, more conventional version of *Cometh Up as a Flower*. In both novels young women (both Nell and Nancy are nineteen) marry far older men, but Nancy, unlike Nell, falls passionately in love with her older husband and repels the amorous overtures of a more caddish version of M'Gregor. Also unlike Nell—who ignited Oliphant's ire by shivering at Sir Hugh's touch and imagining a sexual reunion with her lover in paradise—Nancy seems breezily unaware of the physical dimensions of marriage. When she accepts Sir Roger's proposal after only knowing him several weeks, Nancy brushes aside his fear that she might feel imprisoned in a loveless marriage with an older man by declaring "'People can help falling in love ... If I belonged to you of course I should never think of any one else in that way'" (1873 [2005]: 1.93). And she apparently—but rather improbably—never does.

The couple's sexual relations remain, however, the elephant in the room, a blank space in the narrative that calls attention to its own erasure. It is, of course, unlikely that a Victorian woman writer (at least before the *fin-de-siècle*) would provide details of her heroine's sexual initiation during her honeymoon. Nonetheless, coded references to such relations do exist, as in Eliot's portrait in *Middlemarch* of the distraught Dorothea in Rome during her wedding tour with Casaubon. As we have seen, "The Man with the Nose" contains a number of references to sexuality, including the newlyweds sharing a bed and the phallic symbolism of the man with the nose. The absence of any such references in the prolonged account of Nancy's honeymoon — save for the extra-marital temptation afforded by the handsome Musgrave—leaves it unclear whether her marriage has yet been consummated; so worried had the considerate Sir Roger been about Nancy's distaste for his age prior to the wedding that it is possible to imagine him deferring sexual relations. At the same time, Nancy's sexual ignorance is such that she seems scarcely to notice, let alone care about, what is lacking in her marriage. Thus, her complaint at one point during her honeymoon that "'I *hate* being married'" (1873 [2005]:1.123) apparently records her boredom at long, dusty train-rides rather than secret sexual disappointment or anxiety.

Yet Broughton nonetheless inserts several pointed references in the novel to marital sexuality. When Nancy and Sir Roger are married the priest, a "clergyman of the old school", "spare[d] us not a word of the ritual. Truly in no squeamish age was the marriage service composed!" (1873 [2005]: 1.111). To get a sense of what Nancy is talking about, one only need consult the Anglican marriage service from the 1662 *Book of Common Prayer*, which would have still been in use during the Victorian period. (*Cometh Up as a Flower* alludes to it as well.) The 1662 "Form of Solemnization of Matrimony" begins with the declaration that marriage was not ordained "to satisfy men's carnal lusts and appetites, like brute beasts" but rather for "the procreation of children" and as "a remedy against sin, and to avoid fornication; that such persons as have not the gift of continency might marry, and keep themselves undefiled" ("Form"). The subject of procreation comes up later in the novel, and is clearly defined in terms of women's responsibility to bear children who carry on the male name. When Nancy tries to persuade Sir Roger not to travel to the West Indies to salvage the fortunes of the property he owns there and he asks "'Do you think it would be quite *honest*—quite fair to those that will come after us?'":

"*Those that will come after us!*" cry I, scornfully, making a face ... "And who are they, pray? Some sixteenth cousin of yours, I suppose?"

"Nancy", he says, gravely, but in a tone whose gentleness takes all harshness from the words, "you are talking nonsense, and you know as well as I do that you are!"

Then I know that I may as well be silent. (1873 [2005]: 1.220–21)

The problems surrounding marital relations between the naïve Nancy and the worldly-wise Sir Roger are exacerbated by the gap in their ages. Since Sir Roger is the romantic lead, Broughton emphasises his vigour and virility; despite having "iron-gray" hair, he is "tall and stalwart" with "vigorous shoulders" and eyes "blue as steel" (1.22, 20, 21). In a description that recalls that Dare Stamer's sexy moustache, Sir Roger even sports a "thick and silky beard that falls on his broad breast" (1873 [2005]: 1.22). At the same time, the relationship between Sir Roger and Nancy—who, when they meet him, looks upon him as a "*vieux papa*" (1873 [2005]: 1.24)—hints at incest. Finding him considerably kinder than her own father—whose favourite hobby is finding fault with his children—Nancy exclaims soon after meeting her husband-to-be "'*How* I wish that *you* were my father instead!'" (1873 [2005]: 1.68). Taken aback by Sir Roger's marriage proposal, she blurts out "'I had as much idea of marrying you, as of marrying *father!*'" (1873 [2005]: 1.94). Her brother Bobby claims that, on her honeymoon, she "'will be taken for a good little girl making a tour with her grand-papa!'" (1873 [2005]: 1.104). When Sir Roger suspects, upon his return from the West Indies, that his young wife has fallen in love with Musgrave, he blames himself for subjecting her to temptation, lamenting the "'*monstrous* ... *unnatural* disparity'" in their ages: "'what possessed me to *marry* you? Why did not I *adopt* you instead? It would have been a hundred times more seemly!'" (1873 [2005]: 2.122)

Yet, despite Sir Roger's characterization of the age difference between him and his wife as "'*monstrous*'" and "'*unnatural*'", it was not unusual for husbands to be at least somewhat older than their wives during the Victorian era. In her study of "January-May" marriages in nineteenth-century fiction, Esther Godfrey cites the historian Pat Jalland, who claims that upper-middle-class women were often "significantly younger" than their husbands, and that, moreover, a "twenty-five year difference [Nancy's and Sir Roger's is twenty-nine years] was not uncommon between spouses" (Godfrey 2009: 149–50).[59] While the reason for this difference was—at least for the middle classes—largely economic, as men had to work for extended periods to accumulate the necessary capital to marry, the coupling of a young woman with an older man also reinforced gender ideology that defined men as paternal and women as childlike, and in need of guidance. In her study *The Daughter's Dilemma*, which I mentioned in chapter two, Paula Marantz Cohen identifies the figure of the daughter, rather the wife, as emblematising "the nineteenth century ideal of femininity" (1991: 22). Conflating the figures of daughter and wife in Nancy, Broughton emphasises the child-like innocence of her married heroine, thus apparently neutralizing the disruption a fully awakened female sexuality could pose to the marriage. Nevertheless, the combination of wife and daughter in one character suggests that it is impossible to present young girls as wholly asexual. Indeed, Sir Roger's suspicion that Nancy has fallen in love with a younger man implies that even the most child-like wife's desire can be hard to contain. As Broughton's portraits of Esther Craven in *Red as a Rose Is She* and Elizabeth in "The Man with the Nose" demonstrate, even the childish woman can be sexually aroused.

In this sense, the January-May coupling, which emphasises hierarchies of power between the sexes, becomes the vehicle through which Broughton explores the problematic nature of marriage itself for women, including the economic disadvantages they suffer relative to men. Though she does not marry for the pressing monetary reasons that propel Nell to wed Sir Hugh, Nancy nonetheless realises that Sir Roger has connections that would enable him to advance her brothers' professional prospects; when her elder sister Barbara asks why she is considering marriage to a much older man, Nancy replies "'It would be such a fine thing for all the family: I could give all the boys such a shove'" (1873 [2005]: 1.80). Moreover, as a former general in the Indian army who, according to Musgrave, has sent many "'Russians and Chinamen and Sikhs to glory'" (1873 [2005]: 1.150), Sir Roger is associated not only with economic privilege but imperial power, actively participating in the colonial economy by owning property in the West Indies. When, indeed, Sir Roger travels alone to Antigua shortly after his marriage to manage his estate, one of Nancy's brothers teases: "'perhaps he has got another wife out there—a *black* one—and he thinks it is *her* turn now'" (1873 [2005]: 1.238)—a comment that emphasises the racial, as well as class and gender, dynamics inherent in Sir Roger's position.

Figuring power imbalances in Victorian marriage, the January-May marriage plot in *Nancy* also functions as a trope for marital incompatibility. In the first positive review she received from the journal, *The Athenæum* praised Broughton's "clever treatment" in *Nancy* of "married life between two people, both good and true, who hardly suit each other" (1873: 592). More recently, in an article about Broughton's revision of sensationalism in *Nancy,* Tamara Wagner characterises the work as "an important marriage novel that unsentimentally delineates the stark realities and uncomfortable truths of an at least initially loveless marriage" (2013: 211). Viewed in this light, we can see *Nancy* as a narrative that explores the dangers of marital miscommunication and lack of candour. Upon returning from the West Indies, Sir Roger is informed by a neighbour, Mrs. Huntley, that she saw Nancy running in tears from an interview with Musgrave in the woods; when Sir Roger questions his wife about this, Nancy is ashamed to tell him about the advances Musgrave made on this occasion and lies—unconvincingly—about the interview ever taking place, an obvious deception that only fuels her husband's suspicions. Meanwhile, Nancy herself suspects that Sir Roger is dallying with the officious Mrs. Huntley, a beautiful woman who, Musgrave untruthfully tells her, was once his fiancée. Only at the novel's end does each spouse dispel the other's misconceptions, Nancy confessing the encounter with Musgrave, while assuring Sir Roger that she had been disgusted by his overtures. Though *The Pall Mall Gazette* complained that "the plot of the book is a tangle of misunderstandings between the lady and her husband which a moment's plain speaking would have unravelled" (1873: 1824), one of the novel's greatest strengths is its compelling portrait of marital dysfunction. "Our bodies indeed are nigh each other, but our souls are sundered", Nancy poignantly declares (1873 [2005]: 2.155), and Sir Roger, commenting on the couple's estrangement, eloquently regrets the indissolubility of marriage:

> "Husband and wife we are!" he says, with a slow depression of tone, "and as long as God's and man's laws stand, husband and wife we must remain! ... We have made a mistake, perhaps ... The inscrutable God alone knows why He permits his creatures to mar all their seventy years by one short false step" (1873 [2005]: 2.125–26)

In another type of novel, a less sympathetic husband would hunt for evidence of his wife's infidelity and use it to divorce her on grounds of adultery, virtually the only means of escape from marriage, and one that, even after reforms in divorce law brought about by the Matrimonial Causes Act of 1857, remained limited largely to wealthy men. (Under the provisions of the Act, wives could only divorce if they proved both adultery and cruelty.) By depicting, as *The Athenæum* put it, two "good and true" partners who "hardly suit each other", Broughton draws attention to the lack of options for dissolving a marriage on the grounds of incompatibility alone. As Nancy points out "with a harsh laugh" when her husband laments that they cannot be released from their vows, "'Cheer up! One of us may *die!* who knows?'" (1873 [2005]: 2.128). In a sensation novel, of course, such a marital impasse could lead to the trial of one spouse for murdering the other.

In general, *Nancy* calls attention to plot options it does not explore. Nancy could have been involved with Musgrave; Sir Roger could have had an affair with the beautiful Mrs. Huntley or (as Nancy's brother suspected) kept a native mistress at his colonial estates. It is certainly much easier for other characters to believe the stories that turn out not to be true than the ones that are. When Nancy's brother Algy smiles knowingly when she tells him about the time spent with Musgrave on her honeymoon, she becomes upset:

> "Algy! ... You did not mean it, *really?* You do not think I—I—I—*neglected* the General, do you?—you do not think I—I—*liked* to be away from him?"
>
> "My lady!" replies he, teasingly. "I *think* nothing! I only know what your ladyship was good enough to tell me!" (1873 [2005]: 1.188)

Of course, Algy's reference to what his sister does—and does not—tell him suggests another possibility enabled by Broughton's use of a first-person narrator: consciously or unconsciously, Nancy is covering up her real feelings for Musgrave.

So compelling is Broughton's portrayal of a failed marriage that the happy ending seems perfunctory. The couple resolve their problems at the grave of Nancy's saintly sister Barbara, a site both appropriate and ironic. On one hand, the grave of the novel's resident Angel in the House is a fitting place to bury marital discord; on the other hand, Barbara's own history makes her an unlikely patron saint of romance. Before Nancy discovered Musgrave's feelings for her, she tried to match-make between him and Barbara, who did, in fact, fall in love with him; after Nancy rejects his advances, Musgrave proposes to Barbara, who joyfully accepts him with no inkling that he presumably only wishes to wed her to be within sight of Nancy. Catching a fever after nursing her brother Algy, who had been dancing attendance on the beautiful, and morally suspect, Mrs. Huntley, the selfless Barbara dies, secure in her illusion that Musgrave is devoted to her alone. In this context, her death can be read as a narrative ploy to spare her the pain of marriage to a cad who still lusts after her sister. Barbara's death also points to the limitations of the domestic ideal, which trains women to efface themselves for men who, like Musgrave, can be unworthy of their devotion. Given the self-immolation inherent in the role, it is hardly surprising that the Angel in the House should end up, not only figuratively disembodied, but literally dead.

Further unsettling the happy ending, the final line of *Nancy* is fraught with ambiguity. After claiming that "now we are happy", Nancy exclaims "Only I wish that Roger were not nine-and-twenty years older than I!" (1873 [2005]: 2.301–02). While presumably registering her concern that one so dear as her husband will likely die before her, Nancy's regret about the disparity in their ages reminds the reader of a problem that had supposedly been resolved. Celebrating the renewal of a marriage, the novel ends by expressing anxiety about its inevitable dissolution.

Belinda: **Marital Gothic and the Case for Adultery**

Just as *Good-bye, Sweetheart!* can be read, in Shirley Jones's words, as a "darker re-working" of *Red as a Rose Is She* (2004: 218), *Belinda* is a strikingly more negative portrayal of the January-May marriage than *Nancy*. The still-handsome and virile Sir Roger Tempest is replaced in the later work by the decrepit pedant, Professor James Forth, whom the heroine marries after she (mistakenly) assumes that a younger suitor has abandoned her. Marilyn Wood notes that the unflattering portrait of Professor

Forth was modelled on the renowned scholar Mark Pattison, with whom Broughton had a falling-out during her residency in Oxford (1993: 58–59), yet it would be misleading to imply that a personal grudge alone inspired *Belinda*. If the novel's plot is the story that Broughton thought "too risqué" before the lukewarm reception of *Second Thoughts* inspired her to return to it, then the genesis of *Belinda* predates the quarrel with Pattison. Moreover, Broughton's depiction of a nightmarish January-May marriage expands upon the problems of such unions suggested, but not fully articulated, by the rosier *Nancy*. In this sense, *Belinda* implicitly makes an even more compelling argument than the earlier novel for the legal dissolution of failed marriages, as well as for the heroine's right to pursue the sexual fulfilment she cannot find with her husband.

Here, again, it is useful to turn to Esther Godfrey's analysis of January-May marriages in fiction—in this case, to her discussion of age disparity between man and wife as Gothic. As Godfrey claims, late nineteenth-century representations of older husbands feeding, either literally or figuratively, on the vital power of their younger wives—representations that include Hardy's *Jude the Obscure* as well as more obviously Gothic texts, such as vampire tales—are animated by converging anxieties about "aging, sex, and death" (2009: 114). This portrayal of cross-generational unions as a "Gothic horror show", Godfrey argues, was in part fuelled by an increased medical focus on "the aged body as diseased", as well as by "a growing association of aberrant sexualities with aging" (2009: 116, 120). In *Belinda* the aging male body is both ugly and ridiculous: "'slouching along on his great flat feet'" (1883 [1984]: 4), his "sparse, colourless hair thriftily drawn across the baldening crown" (1883 [1984]: 168), Professor Forth is "pinched" and "bloodless" (1883 [1984]: 290). In one memorable image the Professor and Belinda, now married, are reflected together in a mirror that mercilessly contrasts his shrivelled form with her glowing youth (she is in her early twenties).

Yet if *Jude the Obscure* portrays sex between the young Sue

Bridehead and the older Phillotson as the "ultimate horror" (Godfrey 2009: 422), Professor Forth's body is notable not so much for monstrous sexuality as for obvious impotence. It is even clearer than it is in *Nancy* that the intergenerational marriage is sexless; at one point Belinda reflects that she "shiver[s]" at the professor's "accidental touch" (1883 [1984]: 365), implying that he only touches her without meaning to. There is not the least sign of affection or even friendship between husband and wife; the couple agree before the wedding that Belinda's sole wifely function is to be the professor's amanuensis.

Just as Broughton had plundered a description of Maggie's arm from Eliot's *The Mill on the Floss* in *Cometh Up as a Flower*,[60] the representation of Belinda as her scholarly husband's unhappy assistant owes an obvious debt to *Middlemarch*. The *Times* review noted the similarity between the novels' plots, claiming, however, that "The Rev. Mr. Casaubon, for pure, unmitigated tyranny towards his wife, is not a patch upon James Forth, "Professor of Etruscan" in the University of Oxbridge", who makes Belinda "toil like a galley-slave" over the proofs of his arcane manuscripts ("Recent Novels", 1 January 1884: 2F). Indeed, Broughton's portrait of the professor—who, in addition to his lack of affection for his wife, is stingy and hypochondriacal—is not nearly so nuanced as Eliot's of Casaubon, who is treated somewhat sympathetically. The *Times* viewed the one-dimensional portrayal of Forth as a flaw: "In drawing Professor Forth so outrageously brutal in his demeanour towards Belinda, Miss Broughton disregards the delightful conflict of emotions which might have been aroused if she had drawn him occasionally sympathetic" ("Recent Novels", 1 January 1884: 2F). Admittedly, a more multi-faceted depiction of Forth would add both psychological complexity and realism to Broughton's novel. To the extent that *Belinda* is a Gothic novel, though, it is not so much a realistic work as a depiction of the professor as a terrifying embodiment of male tyranny.

Emphasizing the Gothic nature of the marriage, the ceremony

itself is replete with images of death. For example, her aunt claims that "'it was almost like kissing a dead person'" when she embraces Belinda before the wedding, and, when she and her sister Sarah arrive at the church, the latter exclaims "'We have got to the gallows, it seems!'" (1883 [1984]: 216, 217). In another touch of gallows humour, the clergyman offers his congratulations to the couple "hastily and abstractedly" because he is preoccupied with the funeral he has next to attend (1883 [1984]: 219). Stripped of the usual rituals (the bride is wed in everyday clothes, and eschews a honeymoon), the marriage is the more obviously a "'mere matter of business'", as Belinda calls it when she suggests to Forth the practical benefits of her becoming his live-in secretary (1883 [1984]: 183). Underscoring the economic realities of marriage for many late-Victorian women, Broughton emphasises that these practical benefits extend to Belinda as well as to the Professor; as Belinda's aunt, Mrs. Churchill, points out to Sarah, Forth is bestowing an "'excellent settlement'" on his bride. If, Mrs. Churchill claims, Sarah were to dissuade her sister from marrying, she would "'not be acting at all a friend's part in making her quarrel with her bread-and-butter'" (1883 [1984]: 201).

Buried alive in a loveless marriage—replete with such ghastly touches as the young wife's painful attempts to communicate with her senile mother-in-law—Belinda quickly realises her mistake. This realization is the more agonizing because, as any astute reader will have foreseen, Belinda's erstwhile lover returns after the wedding, still enamoured of her, and filled with remorse for his inexplicable aversion to letter-writing. Recalling M'Gregor's return after Nell has married Sir Hugh in *Cometh Up*, this plot twist places the heroine in a similar dilemma, the choice between duty and desire. Because the professor is a much less likeable character than the bumbling but well-meaning Sir Hugh, though, it is harder for the reader of *Belinda* than for the reader of *Cometh Up* to conclude that a wife should remain in a disastrous marriage. While Sir Hugh genuinely loves his wife—and would be devastated were she to elope with M'Gregor—so lacking is the professor, not only in love, but in basic humanity, that he begrudges the money he has to spend on Belinda's recovery when she becomes ill from overwork: "since she turned out to be so unhealthy, [he] would not be sorry to be rid of her" (1883 [1984]: 406).

Obviously stacking the deck, then, Broughton places her heroine in a position of pure hell from which it is cruel not to release her. After Sarah, reacting to Belinda's clandestine outings with Rivers after his return, claims that her sister is "'going to the devil'" (1883 [1984]: 364), Belinda reflects rebelliously:

> And pray, what is it to go to the devil? Is it to fulfil with nice scrupulosity every tasteless or even nauseous duty of a most dreary life? To sing as she walks her tread-mill? To smile patiently over her oakum-picking? To forego her own hot bright youth, and clip down its rich proportions to the meagre pattern of the dry and crabbed age with which it is mismated? To be a secretary without pay, a drudge without wage, a *souffre douleur* without hope of enlargement, a prisoner the term of whose incarceration lies in the hands of arbitrary death? If this be to go to the devil, then she is not only going there, but has long ago gone. (1883 [1984]: 365)

Anticipating New Woman writers such as Mona Caird,[61] Broughton underscores the resemblance of marriage to wage-slavery: Belinda is "a secretary without pay, a drudge without wage." She is also sexually unfulfilled, having to "forego her own hot bright youth, and clip down its rich proportions." The allusions to the heroine's sexuality—so much more explicit than in Nancy's case—are presumably part of Broughton's effort to make this work racier than *Second Thoughts*. In *Belinda* we are treated to such details as Rivers' "white fixity of passion" as he grips the married Belinda's "wonderful sweet hands" in one scene; several pages later, he enthusiastically "fasten[s] his lips" upon her palms and fingers, a decidedly erotic touch for literature of the period (1883 [1984]: 396, 397, 399). The novel can thus be read as a story of sexual awakening, in which the heroine learns to express a hitherto unarticulated desire. When Belinda first met Rivers, she had regretted her inability to express passion, wondering "How is it that her heart is so burning hot, and her words so icy cold?" (1883 [1984]: 62). "'What an iceberg you are'", Rivers had told her at the time (1883 [1984]: 62), and only his return after her marriage thaws the "'Ice Queen'" (1883 [1984]: 399).

That Broughton deliberately makes the depiction of the heroine's sexuality more overt in *Belinda* than in *Nancy*—where she was equally intent upon erasing its traces—suggests that, within the ten years that separate the novels, cultural tolerance for representations of extra-marital passion had increased, at least as long as the heroine finally eschewed temptation. This Belinda does; after going so far as to agree to elope with Rivers and leaving a note for her husband, she is in a carriage bearing her to the train-station when her conscience overcomes her and she orders the driver to return to the hotel. Though Broughton attributes Belinda's change of heart to her recollection of a line from *Sartor Resartus*—"Love not Pleasure; Love God: This is the Everlasting Yea" (1883 [1984]: 475)—Carlyle's high-Victorian work ethic pales in intensity compared to Belinda's "bitter cry of anguish and revolt" when she decides to elope with Rivers: "'*I will not die without having lived!*'" (1883 [1984]: 459).

In placing her heroine in a position so hyperbolically dreadful that adultery seems the most rational option, Broughton harks back not only to *Cometh Up as a Flower* but to *Joan* (1876), the novel between *Nancy* and *Second Thoughts*. Compelled through genteel poverty to toil as a governess, the high-minded Joan repels the adulterous advances of her erstwhile lover, Anthony Wolferstan, when he visits her employer's house with his wife. Yet his arguments in favour of escaping "'that ghastly comedy, that caricature, that I am pleased to call my marriage'" (1876 [1877]:

422) are more compelling than her own obdurate chastity, which, Broughton implies, might be the product of neurosis rather than of virtue. Joan's overnice sense of honour, in fact, had originally driven Wolferstan into a disastrously misguided marriage; horrified by the revelation that her father was an embezzler, Joan had refused to cast a stain on the Wolferstan name by marrying him, propelling him into a hasty union with Lalage, a wife who airily implies she does not even care whether her husband is faithful or not: "'I think that marriage is the most colossal imposture in existence, so does Anthony. It is the one point on which we agree'" (1876 [1877]: 339).

To the extent that the case for adultery in both *Joan* and *Belinda* is compromised, it is because men are the weak link. Although recent scholars have begun to question the opinion, voiced by the reviewer of *Belinda* in the *Times,* that Broughton's male leads are "never ... as cleverly drawn as her women" (1884: 2F),[62] Wolferstan and Rivers are, alas, not models of psychological complexity. David Rivers of *Belinda* is, indeed, not only an unremarkable Prince Charming but an unreliable one, never offering Belinda a compelling reason why he did not write to her for eighteen months, during which time he was spotted enjoying himself at a London theatre.

What finally saves Belinda from marital Gothic is not another man but a Gothic event in its own right: her husband's death. Returning from her near-elopement, Belinda finds her farewell note unopened, and the professor dead in their hotel room. Rewriting the scene in which Dorothea discovers Casaubon's lifeless form, Broughton replaces Eliot's poignant tone with grotesque Gothic comedy. In the novel's final paragraph Belinda peers into her apparently sleeping husband's face:

> The next instant a sharp shriek rings through the hotel, and when frightened visitors and chamber-maids, hurrying from all quarters, reach the room, they find Mrs. Forth lying

stretched on the floor beside her husband, as inanimate as he. Only that in time they bring *her* round again. As for him, he has for ever vindicated his character from the imputation of being a *malade imaginaire,* and the Professorship of Etruscan in the University of Oxbridge is vacant! (1883 [1984]: 478)

What, then, happens to Belinda when she does come "round again"? Broughton is deliberately silent on this score; similarly, she had ended *Joan* with a newspaper notice of Lalage Wolferstan's death, implying—but not specifying—that, after a decent interval, Joan would finally wed Lalage's widower. Yet Belinda's fate is even more unclear than that of Joan. Though she revives from her death-like swoon, Belinda may be too traumatised to return to her former tempter. Or she might eventually wed Rivers, or wed someone else, or even do something altogether different with her reclaimed life than pursue romance. Anticipating the ambiguous conclusions of many of her later, single-volume novels, the open ending of *Belinda* may finally be more satisfying than a finale that, once again, confines the heroine in wedlock.

Coda: Doctoring Cupid, or the Incurable Ills of Romance

Recalling Jane Austen's *Sense and Sensibility* (1811)—a novel Broughton adored[63]—*Doctor Cupid* (1886) relates the romantic history of two sisters: Peggy, who, like Elinor Dashwood, is a paragon of good sense, and the younger, impractical Prue, who, like Elinor's sister Marianne, falls in love with an unsuitable man. Yet arguably the novel's most memorable female character is Lady Betty Harborough, a heavily rouged aristocrat who smokes cigarettes, displays shameless décolleté, and sings risqué songs at dinner parties—a version, perhaps, of what Nancy might have become had she spiced up her dull routine by accepting Musgrave's seductions. For the married Lady Betty has, for the last five years, been inseparable from the civil servant John Talbot, an intimacy ascribed by everyone except Betty's obtuse husband to "lawless passion" (1886: 310). Tiring of "his lady's" demands (1886: 69), and falling in love with the conventional Peggy, John yearns to be free of Betty, though he feels too guilty to break off the relationship himself. In three striking scenes scattered throughout the novel, Lady Betty exhibits the various miseries of her situation. In the first, dishevelled and distraught, rouge "partially washed ... off her cheeks" by tears (1886: 159), she breaks off her affair in a transient fit of religiosity provoked by her son's serious illness. In the second scene, after her son has recovered, she bursts in on John, who has since become Peggy's fiancé, to demand—unsuccessfully—that he give her up. As it turns out, Peggy spots Betty throwing herself into John's unwilling arms, and, assuming that he still loves her, breaks with him herself. Finally, in a third scene near the novel's end, Betty visits Peggy to explain that she, not John, initiated the embrace, a confession that reunites Peggy with him for good. By this time Lady Betty has become a mere "ruin" of her former beauty, a "forlorn and God-struck creature" (1886: 307) following the death of her son from a second illness. We hear that Peggy and John go on to marry and have children, but we never discover what happens to Lady Betty, who, having lost both her lover and her adored child, presumably remains in an unfulfilling marriage.

I end this chapter with Lady Betty—unhappily married and in love with another man—because she embodies the linked themes of marital disfunction and transgressive desire that animate Broughton's fiction of the 1870s and 1880s. At the same time, Lady Betty also emblematises the frustrations Broughton continued to face in frankly depicting these issues, despite the greater latitude allowed racy themes by the late 1880s. Although she is the novel's most vividly imagined female character, Lady Betty still cannot be its heroine since she (unlike Belinda or Nancy) has actually succumbed to sexual temptation—or at least appeared to do so. Ironically, the same strictures that prevented Broughton from making Lady Betty the female protagonist also prevent her from explicitly acknowledging the transgression that bars her from this position. Despite overwhelming evidence to the contrary, Broughton retreats from confirming the sexual nature of Betty's and John's relationship, having Betty claim at one point "'*We* know that there is no harm in our friendship ... but nobody else knows it. The world is always only too pleased to think the worst'" (1886: 86). Yet this sanitised account does not mesh with the description of John's attendance on Betty as a series of "unhandsome shifts and expedients ... one long shuffle and evasion" (1886: 52), and his gloomy realization that, in planning "risky rendezvous" with another man's wife, he has "sacrificed his career" and "abandoned the hope of home's sanctities" (1886: 46). As Eliza Lynn Linton declared in an assessment of Broughton's fiction in *Temple Bar*: "If John Talbot was not Lady Betty's lover he was nothing" (1887: 208). Despite her reactionary views on women's roles, Linton was a staunch critic of literary bowdlerisation, joining, in 1890, with Thomas Hardy in a forum on "Candour in English Fiction" in *The New Review* to protest the restrictions on openly depicting sexuality. In a similar vein, her comments on the disingenuous portrayal of Lady Betty read between the lines of Broughton's narrative to clarify what the author presumably wanted to, but dared not, make explicit:

> In truth, whatever Miss Broughton may say to the contrary, John Talbot was not only Lady Betty's lover, but he was the father of her child. A French author would not have fenced with this situation as Miss Broughton has felt herself obliged to do ... If Miss Broughton had carried out her plan as it ought to have been carried out, she would have had a whole pack of angry critics, zealous for propriety, at her heels; so, perhaps, in view of the strange spasmodic kind of virtue which sometimes sweeps over our land and is at other times so strangely absent, she has done well to fail in artistic perfectness for the sake of appeasing Mrs. Gruncy.[64] (1887: 208)

Denied not only the role of protagonist but even that of the incontrovertibly fallen woman, Lady Betty haunts the text like the ghost of female desire, her unruly body eventually worn down to a "pinched" wraith of its formerly vibrant self (1886: 307).

The sad fate of Lady Betty also casts an unflattering light on John Talbot—and, by extension, on the promise of heterosexual romance as a solution to women's problems. Indecisive about breaking off his relationship with Betty but, finally, only too glad to be rid of her, John Talbot is, even for Broughton, an unusually spineless male lead. Yet if Broughton grants Peggy's love story at least a nominally happy ending, she dooms Prue's by revising, not only Austen's portrayal of Marianne, but the celebration of romantic fulfilment that typically ends Austen's narratives. In *Sense and Sensibility*, Marianne unwisely falls in love with the playboy Willoughby, who has seduced Colonel Brandon's ward and callously discards Marianne herself in order to marry for money; Marianne eventually finds domestic contentment with the unglamorous, but steady, Brandon. In Broughton's version of this plot, however, Prue suffers, not because she pursues a potentially dangerous passion, but because she clings to an illusory ideal of marriage. Though she compromises her reputation in visiting the handsome dilettante Freddy Ducane without a chaperone, Prue gladly obeys the dictates of convention and becomes his fiancée— all the while refusing to notice, let alone complain about, his marked reluctance to follow through with the wedding. Dying of consumption after Freddy delays the ceremony to tour the world with a wealthy heiress, Prue is at once the victim of masculine selfishness and feminine gullibility. At the same time, as Eliza Lynn Linton notes in comparing her with Barbara of *Nancy*, death is an escape from what would surely have been an unhappy marriage: "like poor sweet Barbara, [Prue] is well out of it not to be his wife. In each instance death is preferable to the disillusionment which would have come" (1887: 207). Ironically undercutting the romantic ideology inherent in the book's title, as well as in Peggy and John's happily-ever-after ending, the final paragraph of *Doctor Cupid* describes how Freddy Ducane continues to exploit Prue by transforming her death into a source of poetic inspiration:

> About six months after the death of Prue Lambton, the attention of the readers of one of the graver monthlies was arrested by the appearance in its pages of a short ode, the melody of whose versification, the delicate aroma of its fancy, the quaint beauty of its imagery, and the truth and freshness of its feeling, called to their minds the best of the Elizabethan lyrics. It was anonymous, and was addressed 'To Prue in Heaven." (1886: 319)

CHAPTER FIVE

"*A* New Woman, Not *the* New Woman!": Liminal Women and Ambiguous Endings in Broughton's Single-Volume Novels

> "And now I am starting afresh—a new woman in a brand-new world."
> "A New Woman?"—dryly. "I hope not."
> "*A* new woman, not *the* New Woman!"
> – Jane Etheredge, in *The Game and the Candle* (1899: 78)

Broughton's last triple-decker, appropriately entitled *Alas!* (1890), sold poorly, a performance she ascribed to its "innate dullness", and which provoked her to follow through on a long-cherished resolution to "forswear the three volume novel" (BA, 17 November 1890, qtd. in Wood, 1993: 74). Indeed, even before 1894—the year in which changes announced by circulating libraries led to the collapse of the triple-decker system of publication—Broughton switched to single-volume publication, first with *A Widower Indeed* (1891), co-authored with the American writer

Elizabeth Bisland, and then, in 1892, with *Mrs. Bligh*. Necessarily enhancing the narrative economy of her tales, the shortened format proved an elegant showcase for the wry wit that caused contemporaries to liken Broughton to Jane Austen. Significantly, too, liberation from the triple-decker's cumbersome structure allowed Broughton to experiment with new ways of depicting—and, to an intriguing extent, decentring—the romance narrative which, as she had said in *Not Wisely, but Too Well*, had so long in life and literature constituted "the main plot of a woman's life" (1867 [2013]: 83).

How the single-volume novel helped Broughton tell women's stories in new ways—the subject of this chapter—is amply demonstrated by a comparison of her final triple-decker novel with the single-volume *Mrs. Bligh*. The contrast between the two books is the more striking because *Alas!* exemplifies precisely those features which, by the 1890s, caused the triple-decker format to be associated with the prudery and ponderousness of, as Richard Menke puts it, "a caricatured mid-Victorian middle class" (2013). Not only is *Alas!* of more than usual *longueur*, it is singularly timid in its depiction of sexuality. Perhaps hoping to avoid offending reviewers with another adulterous Lady Betty, Broughton structured her novel around an anti-climactically mild version of female sexual transgression. Near the glacial close of the third volume, the reader learns that the secret that has caused Elizabeth Marchand and her parents to flee in shame from country to country—a secret supposedly so dreadful that, upon hearing it, a suitor is felled by an attack of brain fever—turns out to be, simply, that she eloped with a painter who died of heart failure on the way to the altar. While such a tale might have been more shocking in the heyday of sensation fiction, by the cusp of the *fin-de-siècle* it was surely less so, and the contrived union of the barely-fallen Elizabeth and an admirer (not the one with brain fever) makes for a perfunctory happy ending.

In contrast, the single-volume *Mrs. Bligh*, in addition to being naturally more cohesive, concludes with a provocative, protomodernist evasion of marital closure. After the widowed Mrs. Bligh fears she has lost to a younger rival the man with whom she is secretly in love, the noted sculptor Sir Robert Coke, he returns to her apartment after breaking his engagement, settling on a stool by her feet and sighing "'Dear little friend, how pleasant it is to be here again!'" (1892: 358). While at least one reviewer apparently took this line—the last in the novel—as confirmation that the pair will finally wed,[65] Broughton never actually shows a romantic scene, much less a proposal, between the two. They may end up married, but they may instead (as Sir Robert implies) return to their prior footing as friends whose companionship is spiced with erotic tension. Such a relationship seems preferable to the novel's marriages: Mrs. Bligh is the widow of a querulous invalid who apparently turned violent on occasion, and one of her friends is married to a narcissist—ominously nicknamed "'Czar'"—whose inveterate philandering does not prevent his loyal family from catering to his every whim. Sir Robert himself is clueless enough about Mrs. Bligh's feelings, not to mention condescending in his definition of her as his "little" friend, to make the reader wonder whether, as the survivor of one failed marriage, she either would or should enter that institution a second time.

Like *Mrs. Bligh,* other single-volume novels by Broughton end inconclusively, sometimes suggesting, but not confirming, that the heroine's future will include marriage, sometimes leaving the fate of major characters even more indeterminate or suggesting tragic, rather than happy, outcomes. That many of Broughton's late fictions end ambiguously is not to say that she abandons traditional romantic closure altogether: *Lavinia* (1902), for instance, ends with its eponymous heroine and her lover, a Boer War veteran, in the steamiest embrace in Broughton's fiction since Kate and Dare's hothouse clinch in *Not Wisely*, and *Mamma* (1908) rewards with marriage a spinster daughter who had long been the slave of her manipulative mother. Yet even these conventionally romantic endings have ironic undercurrents. There are enough unhappy couples and aborted romances in *Mamma* to trouble any simple celebration of romantic bliss, and the lovers in *Lavinia* are only free to marry over the (literally) dead body of the man to whom the heroine had unwillingly been engaged, a Wildean aesthete who defied late-Victorian masculine ideals.[66]

Whether open-ended or not, then, Broughton's later works continue the critical representation of marriage and conventional gender roles in her earlier fictions, while also, as in the depiction of dissident masculinity in *Lavinia,* reflecting changing and debated definitions of both masculinity and femininity at the *fin-de-siècle*. In this chapter, I will focus on novels with ambiguous endings because they represent a particularly innovative way of representing the seismic shifts in sexual mores of the late Victorian and Edwardian periods, signalling by the inconclusiveness of their conclusions the uncertainty surrounding the fate of women in a period marked by shifting perceptions of their role. At the same time, the novels I address—*Dear Faustina* (1897), *Between Two Stools* (1912), and *Concerning a Vow* (1914)—are notable not only for their ambiguous endings, but for another type of ambiguity: the ambivalence with which they portray gender role change. As I mentioned in my introduction, Broughton's response to turn-of-the-century feminism was complex. Although her fictional critique of marriage and restrictions on female sexuality helped pave the way for a rising generation of openly feminist writers, including Sarah Grand and Mona Caird, Broughton did not share the political and sexual radicalism of the younger generation, and could, indeed, be hostile to it, as evinced by several of the works I discuss in this chapter. *Concerning a Vow* (1914), for instance, contains an unflattering allusion to "Militant Suffragettism" in the heroine's encounter, on a train, with a group of adherents "on their way to some female orgy of sex-revolt" (1914: 193). Nowhere is Broughton's antipathy to feminism more evident, however, than in *Dear Faustina* (1897), which, in the tradition of Eliza Lynn

Linton's *The Rebel of the Family* (1880) and Henry James's *The Bostonians* (1886), portrays the New Woman as a lesbian intent on seducing a girlish acolyte. It would, however, be misleading to characterise Broughton's response to late-Victorian feminism as purely reactionary. Among her friends during the last three decades of her life were feminist writers, including Marie Belloc Lowndes, probably her closest friend, and Mary Cholmondeley, whom Broughton mentored and whose *Red Pottage* (1895) is one of the premier New Woman novels.[67] As I have mentioned, in her posthumously published essay "Girls Past and Present" (1920), Broughton herself seemed more pleased than otherwise that marriage had become "to many of the girls of to-day an unessential accident, which may or may not happen to them, but which in any case cannot materially affect the serious business of their lives, their professional or political activities" (1920b: 38).

Broughton's ambivalent response to feminism recalls Walter Sichel's comment in 1917 that she spanned "the distance between the 'Girl of the Period' and the 'New Woman'" (Wood 1993: 116). This formulation—which locates Broughton in a liminal space, neither conventionally Victorian nor avowedly feminist—is also useful for categorising many of the heroines of her late fiction who, even though they hail from a younger generation than Broughton herself, inhabit a similar limbo between Victorianism and modernity. The epigraph I use for this chapter conveys this indeterminate ideological position: Jane Etheredge, heroine of *The Game and the Candle* (1899), denies being the "'*the* New Woman'", but nonetheless identifies herself as "'a new woman in a brand-new world'" (1899: 78). In this chapter I will use the term "liminal woman" to refer to heroines, and other female characters, who, like Jane, move away from Victorian gender roles towards some new, and as-yet incompletely articulated, version of femininity. While the fates of the liminal women who are the heroines of the novels I examine are, finally, open-ended, the conclusion of only one—*Dear Faustina*—suggests possibilities as happy as those available to the protagonist of *Mrs. Bligh*. Not all of Broughton's liminal women find themselves on the threshold of a "'brand-new world'" of expanded potential.

"Not a Spot on Earth Where She Is Not a Superfluity": The Liminal Woman in *Dear Faustina*

> With daily deepening gloom she realizes that she has cast herself out of her own sphere, without having gained a footing in any other. There is not a spot on earth where she is not a superfluity.
> – *Dear Faustina* 1897: 372

The most topical commentary in Broughton's fiction on changing gender roles, *Dear Faustina* is also her most sustained attack on the New Woman. As such, one might not expect this novel to sympathise with a woman in transition from Victorian femininity. As the passage above suggests, however, Broughton poignantly captures the frustration felt by her liminal heroine, Althea Vane, who "has cast herself out of her own sphere, without having gained a footing in any other." Abandoning the Bohemian flat she shared with her feminist friend, Faustina, after unmasking her as a self-serving hypocrite, Althea feels irretrievably alienated from the idle feminine lifestyle she had previously known, and to which she unhappily returns. In this regard, the novel emblematises Broughton's conflicted reaction to changing women's roles. Reactionary as is her satire of the New Woman (whose Faust-inspired name suggests the danger of the temptation she represents for female followers), Broughton nonetheless paints in Althea a sensitive portrait of a young woman searching for a purpose outside the conventions of upper-class female existence. At the novel's ending—a classic example of Broughton's evasion of romantic closure—the proto-feminist strand will, I argue, edge out the anti-feminist one, emphasising the heroine's escape from Victorian domesticity rather than her reintegration within it.

So negative is the novel's portrayal of the New Woman, however, that it is easy to overlook the work's more progressive aspects. In the novel's first scene, even before being properly introduced to the odious Faustina, we encounter a heavy-handed anti-New Woman stereotype in Althea's widowed mother, who grandiloquently announces to her children that she is leaving them in order to become the leader of a "'band of women thinkers and workers'" devoted to the feminist and socialist agenda of "'redressing ... the balance'" between "'man and woman'", "'rich and poor'", "'the treader-down and the trodden'" (1897: 16). Recalling late-Victorian critiques of feminists as unsexed women who abandon their maternal vocation, Mrs. Vane jettisons not only her responsibilities to her children—as one son says, she has "'chucked us all'" (1897: 25)—but feminine identity itself:

> Were it not for a slight condescension in the matter of petticoats, it would not be obvious to a stranger that it is not a slender man who is preparing to address the little group, so austerely masculine is the just-grey-touched thick short hair parted on one side, the coat, the tie, the waistcoat. This widow might at a pinch, and behind a table which would conceal the degradation of the female skirt, well pass for a little widower. (1897: 13–14)

Pseudo-masculine, Mrs. Vane recalls George Egerton's description of the New Woman as a "desexualised half-man", a term triumphantly adopted by Hugh Stutfield to lambast feminists in his vitriolic essay "Tommyrotics" (1895, in Ledger and Luckhurst, 2000: 124).

Significantly, although Mrs. Vane professes to have always had "'aims and aspirations'" unsuited to the "'clogging, petty impediments of domestic life'" (1897: 15, 19–20), she embarks on her feminist career only after meeting Faustina, a journalist and social activist whose lifestyle Mrs. Vane emulates down to adopting "short hair parted on one side" (1897: 7). Thus Althea's mother, rather than Althea herself, is the first of Faustina's victims in the Vane family: only when Faustina has inspired the mother to abandon her responsibilities to her daughter can she assume the ostensible role of maternal surrogate for Althea, while actually pursuing a sexual agenda. Broughton leaves little doubt as to the erotic nature of Faustina's attraction to Althea. Addressing the girl by pet names in "that tone of passionate caressingness which used to belong to Love, but which female friendship has lately stolen from his quiver" (1897: 2)—a tone which at another point is described as that with which "a man in love ... was wont to part from his mistress" (96–97)—Faustina indulges in such physical intimacies as resting her head against Althea's knee (1897: 81). Enthralled in turn, Althea bestows her own share of embraces and gifts on Faustina with a paperknife inscribed "Auf Ewig", or "Ever Yours" (1897: 352).

Patricia Murphy and Lisa Hager have situated Broughton's depiction of Faustina as, in Hager's words, a "lesbian sexual predator" (2007: 462) in the context of late-Victorian anxieties about female sexuality and power, including the emergent discipline of sexology which, in the work of Richard von Krafft-Ebing and Havelock Ellis, defined the female "invert" as a perversion of heteronormative order. Both Murphy and Hager point to the *fin-de-siècle* discursive conflation of the lesbian and the New Woman; Havelock Ellis explicitly linked an increase in female homosexuality with women's forming alliances in "the modern movement of emancipation" (cited in Murphy 2000: 64), and late-Victorian representations of lesbianism, as Murphy says, tend to portray the feminist as a "concupiscent Sapphic villainess" (2000: 62). The novel which Murphy uses as a quintessential example of this ideologeme—a novel whose plot, as she points out, "strikingly parallels" that of *Dear Faustina* (2000: 62)—is

Eliza Lynn Linton's *The Rebel of the Family* (1880), itself probably an influence on the similarly-themed Henry James novel *The Bostonians* (1886).

It is indeed useful to compare Broughton's Faustina with Linton's portrayal, in *Rebel of the Family*, of the suffrage activist Bell Blount, a figure identified by Deborah T. Meem as "the first fully realised 'modern' lesbian woman in English literature" and a "milestone in the literary representation—and the popular understanding—of lesbianism during the last third of the nineteenth century" (1880 [2002]: 11, 13). Bell, who cohabits with a follower she calls her "'little wife'" (1880 [2002]: 55), anticipates Faustina in seducing young acolytes whom she discards once she tires of them: just as we see Faustina first luring Althea to live with her, and then throwing her over for a new follower, we see Bell courting Linton's heroine, Perdita Winstanley, who, though she does not finally take the place of Bell's current (and jealous) "'little wife'", is nonetheless powerfully attracted by Bell's charisma. In addition to being sexual predators of naïve young women, Linton's Bell and Broughton's Faustina are also both hypocrites. Despite noisy protestations against inequality in regards to gender, Bell turns out to be an incorrigible snob, doing everything she can to sabotage Perdita's romance with the apothecary Leslie Crawford, not only because she wants Perdita for herself, but because she disdains cross-class relationships (1880 [2002]: 288–89). In a similar disjunction between rhetoric and practice, the supposedly muckraking journalist Faustina refuses to write an article exposing conditions at one egregiously unsafe factory for fear of offending the newspaper's editor, who holds shares in the industry and who, she fears, would fire her (1897: 154). By the end of both *Rebel* and *Dear Faustina,* the formerly naïve protagonist repudiates the lustful and hypocritical feminist to ally herself with an unimpeachably heterosexual male: Perdita Winstanley weds her manly tradesman, who had long warned her against consorting with unsexed women like Bell Blount, and

Althea, who has become increasingly attracted to the settlement worker John Drake, accepts his invitation to direct a needlepoint cooperative which he is organising.

From this summary of the anti-feminist elements it shares with *Rebel, Dear Faustina* might seem, like Linton's novel, a classic example of the plot that Meem, drawing on Ann Ardis, calls a "boomerang", one that returns an initially "rebellious New Woman" to "respectability and conformity" (2002: 14).[68] This ideological "boomerang" is narratively defined through the romance plot, as the unconventional young woman's return to heteronormativity is accomplished through marriage. *Dear Faustina,* however, is more complicated than the "sexological female inversion rescue narrative" (Hager, 2007: 461) exemplified by *The Rebel of the Family.* For one thing, Linton ends her novel with Perdita happily and indubitably wed to Leslie Crawford; in contrast, *Dear Faustina,* like *Mrs. Bligh,* ends before the heroine and the apparent male love interest have exchanged one word of romantic love, let alone a proposal. Although Drake assures Althea that he will be "'close at hand'" in case she needs advice in managing the cooperative—"'I live at the Men's Settlement'" (1897: 398)—he will still be separated from the Women's Settlement where she will reside. A marriage that abolishes the boundaries between these living arrangements may, of course, ensue, particularly given that, in the novel's last scene, we are assured that the two will continue to share a common goal: "Both are silent for awhile, a delightful dawning sense of the unity of interest that is for the future to connect their lives giving their spirits the sort of hush that comes with the real dawn" (1897: 398–99). At the same time, it is notable that it is left to the reader, if desired, to assume that the intersection of Althea and Drake's futures will take the form of marriage; what Broughton herself emphasises is the companionate working relationship between the two and their shared sense of social purpose.

Nor is this purpose necessarily, as Hager sees it, a "model of paternalistic reform" in which Althea's instruction of working-class women in needlework, a "very traditional sort of decorative women's work", remakes the labouring class in a bourgeois image (2007: 471–72). Rather than inevitably representing a conservative version of femininity, needlework and sewing played an important, and often radical, role in women's artistic and economic culture in late-Victorian Britain. For example, in the 1880s social activists W. J. Walker and Frances Peak helped found dress-making cooperatives as an alternative to the substandard wages and working conditions of women in the textile industries and sweatshop labour, a strategy also championed by the Fabian Socialists Beatrice Potter Webb and her husband Sidney Webb (Kortsch, 2009: 125). (Significantly, the women whose cooperative Althea will direct in *Dear Faustina* had been fired from factory jobs for testifying to government inspectors about poor conditions.) Embroidery was also a prized branch of the turn of the century Arts and Crafts Movement, and many women associated with its practice and instruction, such as the Glasgow artisans Jessie Newbery and Ann Macbeth, were ardent suffragettes. In directing Drake's proposed needlework cooperative—a division of a settlement house for "'*all* women'" which includes a Lady Principal and other educational programs (1897: 394)—Althea would engage in a form of activism associated with progressive politics; her position, which would include teaching embroidery and sewing as well as finding sellers for finished wares, would also make her a working woman and provide an outlet for her own creative talents with the needle. Under these circumstances, it is no wonder that Ann Ardis claims that Althea finally "chooses for herself a life more defiant of bourgeois ideology than either her mother's or Faustina's" (1990: 123).

By ending *Dear Faustina,* then, after Althea has accepted her position in the cooperative, and before any explicit mention of romance between her and Drake, Broughton underscores her heroine's entry into a professional rather than a domestic sphere—a professional sphere which, moreover, is associated with the very types of female community that the "female inversion rescue narrative" is meant to close down. In generic terms *Dear Faustina*, with its plot of feminist social work, resembles a specific type of inversion narrative that Hager calls the "lesbian slum novel" (2007: 461); exemplified by such tales as Vernon Lee's *Miss Brown* (1884) and L. T. Meade's *A Princess of the Gutters* (1895), this subgenre suggests the dangers of feminists enticing bourgeois acolytes, through work in slum communities, to blur the boundaries of both normative gender and class identities. Yet, for all that Althea has been rescued from Faustina's lesbian slum work—and it is notable in this regard that Faustina comes from a lower-class background than she—at the end of *Dear Faustina* Althea is still associated with cross-class female community. In fact, Althea's settlement work has distinct echoes of the Anglican sisterhood that Kate Chester enters at the end of *Not Wisely, but Too Well*, similarly representing a space where the "slumming" female activist can bond with co-workers and disadvantaged women outside heteronormative domesticity.

Broughton's refusal to represent Althea's marriage at the end of *Dear Faustina* can, I think, be understood in light of her ambivalence about that institution. It is worth noting, indeed, that even a work so stridently anti-feminist as *The Rebel of the Family* is scarcely the unambiguous paean to heterosexuality that Linton apparently intended it to be. Linton's career as a reactionary pundit, which she only embarked upon after an earlier stint as a Wollstonecraftian feminist and political radical did not succeed commercially, was riven by ideological conflicts and contradictions, not least of which was her own erotic attraction to women and discomfort with the mercenary aspects of Victorian marriage.[69] As we have seen, this discomfort with the economic inequalities of marriage for women is marked in Broughton's fiction—and, unlike Linton, Broughton never aspired to advocate for women's choosing, as Leslie Crawford sententiously puts it in *Rebel*, "'the quiet restrictions of home'" over "'the excitement of liberty'" (2002: 397). It was Broughton, after all, who disgustedly refers in "Girls Past and Present" to the Victorian "nuptial yoke" and celebrates post-World War I young women's liberation from domesticity to pursue professional identities (1920b: 141). It is Broughton, too, whose elderly narrator in her last novel *A Fool in Her Folly* (1920) sadly comments on how the custom taken for granted in the modern era, that "a couple of girls should find an affinity in each other … and 'forsaking all other,' betake themselves to a joint flat, to maintain which their own industries should furnish the means", was a notion which in her own youth "would have consigned the holder of it to Bedlam" (1920a: 8–9). Describing the modern form of independent female community—young women sharing a flat—in terms that, especially combined with the parody of the marriage vow ("'forsaking all other'"), recall the living arrangements of the lesbian Faustina, Broughton's narrator wistfully and unequivocally views this arrangement as preferable to marriage.

In *Dear Faustina* itself, marriage is satirised in the depiction of the union of Althea's older sister, Clare, and her fatuous husband William Boteler. A dense young man reminiscent of *Not Wisely's* George Chester, William is annoyingly paternalistic. When his wife becomes pregnant, he insists that she lean on him while walking and props her feet with "needless" footstools when she sits, a "tiresome solicitude" that is not only condescending but self-importantly advertises "to each chance comer" his impending paternity (1897: 369). Interestingly, William welcomes the disillusioned Althea back from her stay with Faustina with a phrase from an Eliza Lynn Linton essay attacking feminists: "'I thought we should end by rescuing you from the shrieking sisterhood'" (1897: 340).[70] Although, of course, Faustina has been represented as someone from whom Althea should have been rescued, putting a dismissive reference to "'the shrieking sisterhood'" in William's mouth dilutes the authority of Linton's anti-feminism, allying it with a character who is not only stodgily conventional but, on a more sinister level, a sexual predator. As his pregnant wife remains either oblivious or unconcerned, William is disturbingly physical in his attentions to Althea and Clare's teenage sister, who also lives in his house: indeed, he has his arm "chronically twined round Fanny's waist" (1897: 334). While it is not clear whether William goes beyond these obtrusive displays of affection, his matter-of-fact sexual possessiveness recalls "Czar" in *Mrs. Bligh,* the philandering paterfamilias who, on the stair landing, attempts to grope and kiss a pretty house-guest (1892: 95).

Given this depiction of domesticity, it is easy to sympathise with Althea's desire to escape the claustrophobic, upper-class female existence symbolised by the Boteler household. This final third of the novel—its most feminist section—includes several scenes which emphasise Althea's frustration with the Botelers' ignorance of grim social realities, and her own yearning to return to a life in which she helps ameliorate them. When William buys Fanny a set of wooden toys and invites Althea to share the laughter at their antics, she tells her horrified audience that the fumes of carbon-bisulfide used in the factories where they are made are "'so noxious that workers have been known to go mad, and throw themselves out of the window'" (1897: 375–76). As John Drake had previously alerted her to the dangers of hazardous chemicals in the workplace—he told her how the dust of chromate of potash "'eats through the gristle of the nostrils, and destroys the palate or roof of the mouth'" (1897: 147)—Althea is eager to expose and remedy these conditions; William Boteler, however, merely resents her having spoiled his fun. In the aftermath of the quarrel that Althea has with William in consequence, she laments "'I shall never do anything with my life'" (1897: 378).

The scene that follows this lament—the last in the novel—is noteworthy, not only because John Drake arrives to ask Althea to join the needlework cooperative, but because Broughton strongly implies that the young woman is right to reject the stultifying way of life of upper-class women. When John is ushered into Althea's presence, he finds her at the otherwise deserted tea-table:

Her head, beautifully dressed by Clare's maid in the latest mode, hangs over the back of her bamboo chair; her feet, in pale silk stockings and broidered shoes, rest on the rung of a vacated seat near her; and her faint-coloured gown, thin and expensive, drifts about her as the light wind gently pulls at it. A more exquisite picture of opulent idleness it would be difficult to see, or one more unlike that working woman which she had been so proud to call herself. (1897: 379)

A languid, objectified female form, Althea recalls the model of Sir Frederick Leighton's famous "Flaming June" (1895), with her similarly filmy garments. The "opulent idleness" of Althea's pose, moreover—joined with such details as the "bamboo chair" against which she leans her head—is quasi-Orientalist, suggesting that Althea has, in joining the Boteler household, become merely another member of a seraglio. Althea herself emphasises the "kept" nature of her existence, informing Drake that even her clothes belong not to herself but to her sisters, and that the lifestyle in which she is situated—"'lying in a wicker chair doing nothing'" (1897: 389)—in no way reflects her true identity. Indeed, announcing Althea's return to being "that working woman which she had been so proud to call herself", the novel's final lines emphasise her decision to distance herself from domesticity. After happily claiming that she will "'renounce'" the gorgeous but constraining ornaments of "high civilization" represented by Clare's gown and Fanny's shoes, Althea mentions marriage not to anticipate her own wedding but, instead, to reject the institution as represented by William:

> "The gown is Clare's; the shoes are Fanny's—I renounce them all!"
> "What are you renouncing?" cries William, appearing round an unexpected corner, with his wife still leaning on his unnecessary arm, and looking curiously at Althea's

unknown companion, while he adds, in a fine vein of flat pleasantry: "What are you renouncing—your godfathers and godmothers? Is not it rather late in the day to do that?"

She turns upon him with a radiant smile.

"Not my godfathers and godmothers—but my brother-in-law!" (1897: 399–400)

Looking Backward: Hysterical Women and Victorian Femininity in *Between Two Stools* and *Concerning a Vow*

Despite being written on the cusp of World War I, a period of greater freedom for women than the 1890s, *Between Two Stools* and *Concerning a Vow* conclude with more unhappy versions of the ambiguous ending than *Dear Faustina*. To some extent, this distinction reflects the differing generic classifications of the three novels. More overtly politicised than the others, *Dear Faustina* ends on a utopian note that hints at a new range of opportunities for late-Victorian young women. In contrast, *Between Two Stools* and *Concerning a Vow* focus on private experience, which in both cases consists of tangled romantic situations less likely to lead to untroubled resolutions. Despite not being as overtly topical as *Dear Faustina*, however, *Between Two Stools* and *Concerning a Vow* also address, though more pessimistically than the earlier novel, the liminal woman's attempt to move beyond Victorian gender ideology. Indeed, both novels share the same basic narrative, wherein the male lead is involved with two female characters who represent different relations to the Victorian past: one rebels against its restrictions on female sexuality more obviously than the other, who is, in many ways, old-fashioned. The male lead is involved with the more dissident woman in a transgressive romance that causes both participants mental pain, while the more conventional female character—who is the man's friend—cherishes romantic feelings for him which she refuses to voice. Both novels conclude without clarifying the male lead's romantic fate, though in *Concerning a Vow* he seems more likely to marry the self-effacing friend than in *Between Two Stools*. Neither novel, however, depicts its two major female characters successfully discarding the Victorian feminine ideal.

Despite its portrayal of the lingering influence of Victorianism, however, *Between Two Stools*—the first of these novels I will discuss—reflects an obvious shift from Victorian mores in its matter-of-fact depiction of adultery. To appreciate the difference made by the passage of time, one need only compare the portrayal of a decade-long liaison between a wife and her lover in *Between Two Stools*, to Broughton's earlier versions of the adultery plot, such as *Cometh Up as a Flower* and *Belinda*, which do not in fact portray actual adultery. Even in *Doctor Cupid*, a novel which anticipates *Between Two Stools* in portraying a long-term illicit romance, Broughton had felt compelled to fudge the question of whether John and Lady Betty have sexual relations. In contrast, in *Between Two Stools* there is little doubt that Elizabeth Delany and Bill Doughty are intimate. Not only do they declare that they consider themselves married to each other, but they kiss, hug, and, we hear, meet whenever possible at a London hotel. In another reflection of changing times, in *Between Two Stools* the adulterous wife has been moved from Lady Betty's position of secondary character to centre stage. Moreover, by representing the gentle Elizabeth as, in the words of one reviewer, "a young woman bound hand and foot to the sofa of a tyrannical and acrimonious invalid husband" (*Times Literary Supplement* 21 March 1912: 118b), Broughton places the adulterous woman in a situation calculated to elicit the reader's sympathy. In this sense, Elizabeth has more in common with the lovable protagonist of *Mrs. Bligh* than with the defiantly outrageous Lady Betty: Elizabeth's husband, Jack, who has suffered an incapacitating spinal injury, is, as Anne Bligh's deceased spouse had been, a cantankerous man unable to have sexual relations with his wife. (Broughton takes care to note that Elizabeth sleeps in a separate bedroom [1912: 27].) So patient is Elizabeth with her irritable husband that she is viewed by friends and acquaintances as "'one of the saints of God'" and an example of "Griseldahood" to rival Chaucer's meek wife (1912: 61, 60). Although both Doughty and Elizabeth are guiltily aware of the irony of these enconiums, what we see of the "Calvary" (1912: 69) of Elizabeth's life reveals admirable grace under trying circumstances.

Indeed, to the extent that Elizabeth is represented critically, it is not for failing to be the Angel in the House but for being too much of one. Although her adultery represents a rebellion against the asexual ideal of Victorian womanhood, in other ways Elizabeth fulfils the demands of that ideal only too well, masking negative emotions in the service of nurturing and pleasing others. Responding to her husband's frequent insults with "the most perfect sweetness", she is incapable of showing anger other than by speaking "in an even lower and softer key than usual" (1912: 36, 49). In many ways she embodies the paradoxes inherent in the Victorian feminine ideal, in which a woman is supposed to be child-like and spiritual on one hand, and a pragmatic household manager on the other. Though "slight" and "girlish" (1912: 209, 19), Elizabeth is nonetheless strong: "Little bit of thistledom as she looked, there was a power of endurance, a wiry force in her little body, which women possessed of many more inches and ounces might have envied" (1912: 270). Her "abstracted spirit-look", moreover, belies the "methodical and practical" nature which enables her to shepherd the family's limited finances (1912: 43). In this context, the elaborate subterfuges to which she is driven to conceal her relationship with Doughty, ostensibly merely a family friend, are not so much a contradiction of the angelic ideal as an illustration of its innate inauthenticity: Elizabeth must constantly pretend to be other than what she is, and not to want the things that she does, in fact, desire. Suffering the inevitable toll of such masquerades, she becomes associated with that ubiquitous Victorian signifier of feminine inner conflict, hysteria. The adjective "hysterical" is used to describe her on several occasions:

on one, for example, she feels a "hysterical spasm in the throat", and on another experiences a "hysterical convulsion" (1912: 194, 210). At one point, convinced that Jack has divined the truth about the affair, she banishes Doughty from the house and urges him to marry a young woman of their acquaintance, Arethusa Browne. Near the novel's end, when Jack has finally died, however, Elizabeth informs Doughty that she now believes that Jack did not know about her affair, attributing her prior conviction that he did to her "'disordered fancy'" (1912: 275), and leaving Doughty to ponder:

> And for what had he been exiled? ... now she was telling him that it was all an imagining—the creation of her own tired brain and overworked nerves, the mere progeny, in fact, of hysteria!
>
> A sudden thought flashed—odiously, irrelevant, and uninvited—across his mind. Arethusa would never be hysterical! (1912: 276)

That he is, by this time, able to compare his mistress unfavourably to Arethusa attests to the serious impact that the former's "overworked nerves" have had on her relationship with Doughty. Banished from his mistress's side, Doughty is thrown into Arethusa's company during a visit to her father's country house. Although he had refused to promise Elizabeth to marry the young woman, Doughty finds himself increasingly attracted to her. As suggested by the "uninvited" thoughts in the passage above, Doughty is reluctant to admit even to himself the degree to which his admiration of Arethusa introduces a critical note into his hitherto uncritical devotion to his mistress. In many ways, Arethusa is a contrast to Elizabeth: a virginal nineteen to Elizabeth's thirty-two (far closer in that period to middle age than now), the young woman is, in marked contrast to the ethereal older one, robust and vital. While Elizabeth's favourite outdoor spot is a symbolically self-contained walled garden, Arethusa delights in roaming the woods. (Her first name, Arethusa—an allusion to a mythic Sicilian nymph associated with a sacred spring—conveys her affinity with nature.) Secretly yearning for children of his own, Doughty is compelled to acknowledge that Arethusa's "superb physique" is suited to fertility (1912: 242). Although the young woman has her own problems—she is at the beck and call of her father and insufferably hypochondriac stepmother—she preserves a "serene good temper" that, unlike Elizabeth's careful façade, seems the spontaneous expression of "*joie de vivre*": "To enjoy and to make other people enjoy. That was Arethusa Browne's creed" (1912: 222, 229, 233). When Doughty sees her upset for the first time, after her stepmother commands her to give away her beloved dog, he impulsively proposes to her and is joyfully accepted.

Yet, while marrying Arethusa could provide a solution to the frustrations of Doughty's relationship with Elizabeth, this turns out not to be the case. Divided into two sections, one entitled "Elizabeth" and the other "Arethusa", the novel suggests a revision of the traditional courtship plot in which the heroine decides between two men: here, a man is confronted with a choice between two women.[71] In Doughty's case, however, the choice leads, not to clarity, but to an exacerbation of the indecision and inner turmoil he experienced during the "ten contraband years" (1912: 8) of his affair with Elizabeth. His impetuous proposal to Arethusa is immediately followed by guilt: feeling he has betrayed Elizabeth, he is also now miserably aware that Arethusa loves him, and that breaking their engagement will cruelly disappoint her. The news that Jack Delany has finally died, leaving Elizabeth free to marry him, only increases Doughty's distress, as does the revelation that, since Elizabeth was mistaken about her husband's knowledge of the affair, his separation from her was, in fact, unnecessary. Determined to do the honourable thing, however, Doughty resolves to follow through on his promise to marry Arethusa, though he is obviously wretched about it.

The novel's ending emphasises Doughty's continuing mental conflict over both Elizabeth and Arethusa. At first, it might seem that his troubles are over: after overhearing a conversation in which someone comments that Jack Delany's death will finally allow Doughty to marry the woman he loved, Arethusa nobly releases him from their engagement:

> By-and-by he felt her hand upon his; and her voice clear, unshaken in its limpid purity, saying with an accent of divine compassion, understanding, and forgiveness, "You poor soul, how you must have suffered! But you will not have to suffer any more." Her hand was in his now, and he bent his bowed head over it in bitter humiliation and reverence.
> "Are you so sure of that?" he asked with a sob. (1912: 287)

This conclusion clarifies the significance of the novel's title, "Between Two Stools", as the saying "to fall between two stools" refers to a situation in which neither of two goals is achieved. Whatever choice Doughty makes following this scene, he is bound to be frustrated. While it is implied that he will return to Elizabeth, he is obviously stricken by the pain he has caused Arethusa, who seems genuinely to love him, and who now has nothing to look forward to but probable spinsterhood in thrall to her selfish family. If Doughty does finally marry Elizabeth, however (and it is not clear that he will), he is by this time uncomfortably aware of her flaws and the ways in which he prefers Arethusa. After Jack's funeral, Doughty not only (as we have seen) inwardly criticises Elizabeth's hysterical tendencies, comparing them unfavourably with Arethusa's serenity, but he also cannot help rebelling against his mistress's sway more generally. Witnessing the distress of Elizabeth's son's tutor—a longtime courtly-love worshipper at her shrine—at having to leave her service, "[t]he odious thought would come buzzing again and again about [Doughty's] brain, of how *very* miserable they became who fell under the spell of the

Beloved Woman!" (1912: 268). As Marilyn Wood perceptively comments, by the novel's last lines Doughty "realises that the perfect wife would now be a fusion of the two women and that his torment must be the knowledge that he will never be truly happy with one" (1993: 110).

Yet it is also possible that, even if one of the women were able to incarnate the qualities that made the other attractive to him, Doughty would never be truly happy with either. Despite their apparent differences, both Elizabeth and Arethusa are enmeshed in still-prevalent Victorian gender ideologies which render them problematic romantic partners: both selflessly serve the demands of capricious invalids, and neither woman is able to voice her desire to the point of urging Doughty to remain with her. When Doughty informs Elizabeth at Jack's funeral that he has just proposed to Arethusa, Elizabeth, though obviously shaken, accedes to the news without protest, as willing to renounce her ties to Doughty for his sake as Arethusa will be in breaking her engagement to him. Broughton apparently admires Arethusa greatly, as indicated by her references to the young woman's "divine compassion" and "limpid purity" in the novel's last lines. In this regard, Arethusa is, finally, a more positively depicted Angel in the House than Elizabeth, who, Broughton implies, derives her attractions from her air of sorrowful inaccessibility (it is not surprising that the "pure pale fineness" of Elizabeth's features is enhanced by her widow's garb [1912: 272]). Still, for all that she is less neurotic than Elizabeth, Arethusa, thanks to the self-denials prompted by her "deep unselfish heart" (1912: 242), is worrisomely lacking in backbone, and Doughty is as exasperated by her inability to stand up to her odious family as he was by Elizabeth's constant efforts to placate her unlikeable teenage daughter.

In *Concerning a Vow*, the novel that followed *Between Two Stools*, Anne Hippisley, Ned Bromley, and Sally Champneys inherit the roles filled by Arethusa Browne, Bill Doughty, and Elizabeth Delany. With her "plain, and rather noble" face (1914: 15), Anne is, like Arethusa, an unglamorous, unmarried daughter whose "hard life" of "unceasing sacrifice and self-suppression" is spent caring for her elderly parents (1914: 345). (The deft portrayal of this mismatched pair—Anne's vacuous father too deaf to understand his wife's constant jibes—is a memorable evocation of marital dysfunction.) Anne falls in love—silently—with Ned, who in turn loves Sally, with whom he will become involved, as Doughty had with Elizabeth, in a transgressive sexual relationship. In Ned and Sally's case, the transgression is not adultery but living together out of wedlock, although the reader, like the book's other characters, only discovers near the novel's end that the couple are not, in fact, married. The reason behind this deception is rooted in events preceding the novel's commencement, and involve Ned's having "'jilt[ed]'" (1914: 13) both Sally and her sister Meg (discarding Sally for her younger sibling, he had—apparently appalled at the mess he had gotten himself into—left her as well). As the novel begins, Meg, seriously ill and lacking the will to live, extracts from her sister a promise that she will never marry their joint deserter. Unwilling to admit she is still deeply in love, Sally initially rejects Ned's pleas for forgiveness following Meg's death; when the pair eventually reconcile, Sally balks at the prospect of breaking her vow to her dying sister. Cohabitation is the sole solution she can think of to the dilemma of wishing to gratify her desire while keeping her promise. For the sake of appearances, though, the couple pretend to elope, living abroad until the demands of Ned's fame—he has authored a wildly successful novel—call them back to England. Only near the novel's conclusion does the truth that they are not married emerge, with tragic results.

If we bracket the melodramatic machinery propelling this plot (Broughton recycled the idea of a deathbed promise from *The Game and the Candle*), it is possible to read Sally and Ned's situation as a reflection of changing sexual mores. Like Elizabeth Delany, Sally rejects Victorian ideals of female passionlessness, daring to satisfy her desire outside traditional wedlock. Yet while Elizabeth, aside from her adultery, conforms to the Angel in the House ideal, Sally more closely resembles the New Woman. Conspicuously lacking such traditionally feminine qualities as gentleness and self-effacement, she is called by her brother a "'violent sort of creature'" (1914: 55) due to her habit of flying into rages. Significantly, too, the headstrong Sally appears in a novel making several allusions to feminism. At one point Anne Hippisley's father mentions that "'all the girls nowadays'" are "'hankering after a life of [their] own'" (1914: 326), and *Concerning a Vow* is the novel I mentioned at the beginning of this chapter, which refers to "Militant Suffragettism" in the form of a band of feminists bound on a train to "some female orgy of sex-revolt" (1914: 215).

Even though Sally does not identify herself as a feminist, she, too, is in several ways linked to "sex-revolt". Not only does she persuade the reluctant Ned to live with her rather than to marry, but she inspires his transformation from a more conventional writer to an avant-garde one. Estranged from Sally following Meg's death, the distraught Ned jettisons the novel he had been serialising—a story described by Anne's mother as "'wholesome'" and "'tender'"—to pen the appropriately entitled *From Hell's Gate,* the book that establishes his fame as a practitioner of the "'New School'" of fiction (1914: 105, 283). That Mrs. Hippisley dismisses this successor to the abandoned tale she had enjoyed as a "'hotch-potch of Morbidity, Irreverence and Ugliness'" (1914: 104) echoes the terminology employed by unsympathetic *fin-de-siècle* reviewers to describe genres, such as naturalism and the New Woman novel, which they saw as symptomatic of degeneration, decadence, and the collapse of traditional gender roles. In this context, it is not surprising that Ned, who at one point goes off to view some "'Cubist'" paintings (1914: 286), becomes associated not only with cutting-edge aesthetics but Bohemian sexuality.

It is notable, however, that Ned—a remarkably weak-willed male lead even for Broughton—is more conventional by far than Sally. Urging her to marry him before succumbing to her pleas to cohabit, Ned is also the one who insists on pretending they are married. As Sally tells him after their secret comes out, "'as you know, it was never my wish to make a mystery of—of it! I never wanted to sail under false colours!'" (1914: 332–33). Once they decide to keep the cohabitation a secret, however, it is Sally who insists that the couple live in "'complete isolation'" (1914: 317) in a rural cottage far from awkward questions about their "'runaway marriage'" (1914: 256). To some extent, Sally's pursuit of privacy can be attributed to an insecurity born of the informal, rather than legally binding, nature of her relationship with Ned; she is jealously eager to limit his access to female fans. And yet her obsessive avoidance of society also suggests a fear of its disapproval should her transgression be discovered, as well as her own shame at having transgressed. When Anne (who, like the reader, is as yet unaware that Sally and Ned are not married) calls Sally a "'very bold woman'" for daring to deprive Ned of access to the London literary scene, Sally evidently construes the term as a slur on her sexual ethics, hotly blushing "crimson" upon hearing it (1914: 317).

Sally's demeanour in this scene, and elsewhere, betrays inner conflict about her sexual self-expression. When first Anne sees her on her return with Ned from the continent, she is "radiantly happy-looking", suggesting erotic fulfilment in the "glory of her confident passion" (1914: 279, 315). In private, Sally does not scruple to display the physicality of her feelings for Ned; in the only scene we see from her perspective rather than filtered through Anne's, Sally "lifted her eager lips to [Ned's] hungry kisses" when he returns to their home after an absence (1914: 329). In the presence of others, however, Sally attempts to check her physical demonstrativeness. In one scene, when Anne is visiting, Sally moves to fling herself into Ned's arms when he enters the room before "decorum slackened her pace and modified the ardour of her greeting" (1914: 284). Always high-strung, following her return with Ned to England Sally becomes increasingly febrile, as in one scene where, her cheeks "flushed", she "restlessly clasp[s] and unclasp[s] her hands" (1914: 316). Different as she is in other ways from Elizabeth of *Between Two Stools,* then, Sally resembles her in suffering the mental strain of long-term secrecy. The stress finally causes her to snap, blurting out the truth of her relationship to Ned to an officious visitor who gleefully spreads the news. When Sally informs the horrified Ned that she has betrayed their secret, he cries despairingly that "'We have been the curse of each other's lives!'" before leaving the house (1914: 336). Overcome, Sally kills herself.

Sally's complex portrayal as a "passionately loving but bad-tempered and exacting woman" (1914: 283) invests her death with Broughton's typical narrative, and ideological, ambiguity. Sally's fate, as well as the hysteria that precipitates it, may be read moralistically as the consequence of sexual laxity and untamed desire. At the same time, Broughton's depiction of Sally's corrosive inner conflict suggests that we can attribute her death at least in part to the intolerable psychic strain experienced by women who defy sexual convention. In this sense, Sally's suicide anticipates the similar end that Virginia Woolf would imagine for the hypothetical Judith Shakespeare in *A Room of One's Own* (1929 [1957]: 50). According to Woolf, Judith Shakespeare kills herself when she is impregnated out of wedlock because:

> Chastity had then, it has even now, a religious importance in a woman's life, and has so wrapped itself round with nerves and instincts that to cut it free and bring it to the light of day demands courage of the rarest. To have lived a free life in London in the sixteenth century would have meant for a woman ... a nervous stress and dilemma which might well have killed her. (1929 [1957]: 51)

In *Anne Hippisley* Broughton also portrays the psychic costs for women that are the legacy of the Victorian feminine ideal. An "'extraordinarily selfless'" person, as Sally calls her (1914: 220), Anne recalls Arethusa Browne in being an Angel in the house who, finally, is more positively represented than the sexually transgressive woman to whom she is a foil. Nonetheless, in her depiction of Anne, Broughton shows, to a greater extent than she had with Arethusa, the psychological repercussions of the Angel role. While we only view Arethusa through Doughty's perspective, we are privy to Anne's thoughts as conveyed through the words of Broughton's third-person narrator. We are thus aware that, though the motherly Anne is "thought to have a good touch in the handling of wounds in her fellow-creatures' souls" (1914: 30), she has no one in whom to confide her own problems, which include, in addition to concealing her growing love for Ned, perpetually hiding anxiety and depression in her parents' presence (she "never allowed herself to be 'low' at home" [1914: 60]). Even though she is not so neurotic as Sally, Anne occasionally buckles under the weight of these combined concealments, as in one scene where she is "seized with a fit of hysterical laughter" (1914: 261) at an only mildly amusing incident at home. To herself, at least, Anne occasionally voices inner rebellion, as when she hears the news of Sally and Ned's purported elopement:

> It was but seldom that Anne Hippisley indulged herself in the bitter luxury of a comparison between her own lot and that of others, but now ... [a]n inward cry of revolt went up from her hungry soul. It is not fair! (1914: 230–31)

The irony of Anne's situation—she had helped Ned repair the rift with Sally—exacerbates the mental pain caused by her subsequent exclusion from his life. When he writes a letter thanking her for her role bringing him and Sally together, Anne tears it up "with a sort of anger against herself and him", feeling "self-contempt" for being contented with, as she sees it, "'[t]he crumbs that fall from the rich man's table'" (1914: 260).

It is significant, then, that Anne rebels, even if only intermittently and inwardly, against the self-effacing role that Ned has defined for her as (in his words) the "'great rock'" who offers sympathy and support without expecting any return (1914: 32). In depicting Anne's rebellion, limited as it is, Broughton thus critically interrogates the ideology of the Victorian Angel; indeed, in this regard we can see *Concerning a Vow* as a revision of that quintessential literary portrayal of the Angel in the House, Charles Dickens's Agnes Wickfield in *David Copperfield* (1850). Anne and Agnes are similar in numerous ways: both are selfless women who silently love a successful male writer who suffers personal tragedy in the premature loss of a beloved, but flawed, romantic partner (in David's case, his immature first wife, Dora). In both narratives, the selfless woman welcomes the male writer home when he returns from a foreign sojourn following his loss (after Dora's death, David wanders the continent for three years, and Ned, after a stint in a madhouse following Sally's suicide, spends five years abroad). In both cases, the male writer belatedly recognises the value of the woman who has been his moral support; on the continent, David realises he is in love with Agnes, while, in the last chapter of *Concerning a Vow,* the returning Ned finds plain Anne "embellished": "Anne … with grief and love lighting lamps in her once inexpressive eyes, seemed sweet and fair to him who so long and dumbly surveyed her" (1914: 350). Whereas David and Agnes end up happily married, however, Broughton, with characteristic open-endedness, gives Ned and Anne no actual romantic dialogue following the above passage, suggesting that the Victorian apotheosis of domesticity is more uncertain than it was in Dickens's day.

To the extent that she evades romantic closure and depicts the angelic woman's inner rebellion, Broughton engages in a feminist rewrite of Dickens's iconic celebration of domestic ideology. It is worth noting, however, that Broughton does not so much invent the depiction of the Angel's inner conflict as expand upon material already present in Dickens's portrayal of Agnes. Though admittedly one of Dickens's most annoyingly perfect heroines, Agnes is not so asexually "legless" as George Orwell thought her (1939): the painful collision of her concealed feelings for David and her inability, as a respectable woman, to voice her desire is particularly pronounced in the scenes in which the widowed David mistakenly thinks she has fallen in love with someone else during his prolonged absence. As Charles Hatten points out, Agnes's increasingly distraught reactions to David's insistence that she reveal the identity of the man she loves suggests that "even the seemingly ideal domestic femininity often conceals an underlying hysteria" (2010: 117). And yet, if Dickens is unexpectedly perceptive in his portrayal of Agnes, Broughton, while recognising the psychic costs of Anne's "hard life ... of self-suppression", is unable to discard the Angel in the House ideal: the passage that I quoted earlier, which describes her welcoming Ned back from exile with "love lighting lamps" in her eyes, portrays Anne, like Agnes, as the embodiment of moral beauty.

The complexity of Broughton's relation to the Victorian past infuses the final lines of *Concerning a Vow*, which simultaneously celebrate Anne's angelic qualities and underscore the inherent inauthenticity of the Victorian feminine ideal. Recalling the words he flung at Sally after she divulged their secret—that they had been "'*the curse of each other's lives!*'"—the prematurely grey-haired Ned asks Anne whether or not he was right in thinking himself a "'*murderer*'" who caused her suicide (1914: 350):

> "You were wrong!" she said, with an accent of the sweetest, tenderest compassion—"they were cruel words, but you did not mean them! They had no connection with—what happened! That was an accident! Of course it was an accident! No one ever doubted that it was an accident!"
>
> It was Anne Hippisley's latest, best lie! (1914: 352)

The word "latest" reminds us that Anne had long been a practitioner of the little white lie, being accustomed to soothe her parents by resorting to "the gift of ready and innocent fibbing which came so easily" to her (1914: 287). Anne's lie to Ned is the "best" of her fibs because it comforts the tormented man, freeing him to find peace in a union with her. Recalling Broughton's description, in the last lines of *Between Two Stools*, of Arethusa's "divine compassion, understanding, and forgiveness" (1914: 287), Anne's "sweetest, tenderest compassion" emphasises her embodiment of ideal Victorian femininity. That the last word of the novel is "lie", however, necessarily troubles this idealisation. For one thing, if Anne's reassurance results in Ned's willingness to marry her—her heart's desire—it is not clear that her angelic behaviour is altogether selfless. The word "lie" is applicable to Ned's situation as well: for him to accept that Sally's death was an "'accident'" would require strenuous denial of what he knows to be the facts of the situation. Whatever her lingering attraction to the Victorian domestic ideal, then, Broughton cannot help but acknowledge that any romance born of such a distortion of reality would be, like the ideology that motivates it, grounded in dishonesty. In this sense, the novel's conservative elements are countered, as they were in *Between Two Stools*, by a continuing interrogation of Victorian gender roles.

AFTERWORD

Broughton's Metafictions in the Feminist Classroom

In her *Athenæum* review of Broughton's *A Fool in Her Folly* (1920)—the posthumously published tale of a failed woman writer to which I referred in my introduction—the modernist writer Katherine Mansfield is supremely dismissive:

> In the sympathetic short preface which Mrs. Belloc Lowndes has written for this, Miss Broughton's last novel, she tells us that Miss Broughton was "curiously humble about her books. It was almost as if she was content to regard her literary gift as a kind of elegant accomplishment ..." Why should this astonish Mrs. Belloc Lowndes? ... for that, after reading "A Fool in Her Folly," is precisely what we feel it to have been—"a kind of elegant accomplishment." (1920: 241)

Judging Broughton's writing as nothing more than she herself purportedly thought it was—an "elegant accomplishment" rather than art—Mansfield rejects the assessment of a critic, cited by Lowndes, that Broughton was "the nearest thing in spirit to Jane Austen that we have had in recent times" (1920: 7). Asserting that "[t]here can be no question of comparison between them," Mansfield concludes that, not only is Broughton undeserving of Austen's canonical status, but *A Fool in Her Folly* is not even a book worthy of mature readers: "It is a girl's book. Girls of all ages, from thirteen to eighty-five, will revel in it. It will not bear looking into" (1920: 241).

Anticipating the critical neglect of Broughton's work through much of the twentieth century, Mansfield's comments convey a characteristically modernist disdain for Victorianism. Identifying *A Fool in Her Folly* as "a story in the Victorian tradition" (1920: 241) that does not reward close analysis, or "looking into", Mansfield implicitly contrasts the superficiality of this antiquated tale with the depth and sophistication of more recent fiction. Her review demonstrates that the generation gap between modern and Victorian women that Broughton describes in "Girls Past and Present" extended to women writers as well: the younger generation of female authors—women writers present, as it were—has trouble understanding the perspective of women writers past. As I argued in my introduction, however, both *A Fool in Her Folly* and Broughton's other tale of a failed female novelist, *A Beginner* (1894), have much in common with Virginia Woolf's parable of the silenced Judith Shakespeare in *A Room of One's Own*. Structured by a trajectory of literary catastrophe, rather than of the success typical of portraits of the artist as a young man, Broughton's reverse *künstlerromans*, as I call them, identify cultural obstacles that cause women to un-become, rather than to become, writers.[72]

Not only, then, do *A Fool in Her Folly* and *A Beginner* "bear looking into", to appropriate Mansfield's phrase, but their metafictionality makes them timely examples of why Broughton's work deserves re-evaluation. The current popular and critical interest in self-conscious authorship, a mode which often includes parodic or metafictional elements, makes Broughton's reverse *künstlerromans*, with their mix of the comic and the serious, especially relatable to modern-day readers. In this afterword, I will argue that one way to reverse the critical neglect of Broughton's work is to introduce her metafictions to a specific group of modern-day readers, students in the feminist classroom. In keeping with the goal of the Key Popular Women Writers Series—to promote the teaching, as well as scholarly analysis, of hitherto neglected female authors—I suggest strategies for integrating Broughton's reverse *künstlerromans* into the contemporary curriculum.[73]

While either or both of these works could work well in a variety of courses featuring women writers, below I imagine teaching *A Fool in Her Folly* and *A Beginner* in a class on the female *künstlerroman* during the late nineteenth and early twentieth centuries. In this course—which would include contextual documents on such topics as the 1860s sensation controversy and the rise of the New Woman writer in the 1890s—Broughton would be a pivotal figure, as her metafictions engage key issues of both the late-Victorian and early modernist periods. Published in the year (1894) when the term "New Woman" was coined, and featuring an author whose critically lambasted first novel addresses such *fin-de-siècle* concerns as heredity,[74] *A Beginner* can usefully be paired with one or more examples of the numerous New Woman narratives that, in Lyn Pykett's words, depict "the conflicts, frustrations, and compromised or thwarted careers ... of the professional woman writer and the aspiring woman artist" (cited in Peterson, 2009: 209). Meanwhile, the semi-autobiographical elements of *A Fool in Her Folly*—its elderly narrator, like Broughton a clergyman's daughter, recounts her disastrous girlhood attempt to write a novel about adultery—refer back to the Victorian sensation controversy, but the tale alludes to modernity as well. Indeed, several of the quotations I have used in this study to illustrate Broughton's appreciation of the freedoms enjoyed by young women of the post-World War I era—freedoms not available to mid- to late-Victorian girls—come from *A Fool in Her Folly*, including the narrator's remark that, in her day, the modern notion that "a couple of girls should ... betake themselves to a joint flat, to maintain which their own industries should furnish the means" would "have consigned the holder of it to Bedlam" (1920a: 8–9).

Although *A Fool in Her Folly*'s reference to sensationalism makes it appropriate to teach in the Victorian section of the syllabus, the novel's reference to the generation gap between Victorian and post-Victorian women makes it suitable for inclusion in the part of the course on modernism. It would, indeed, work well to assign *A Fool in Her Folly* alongside both Mansfield's review of the novel and Virginia Woolf's *A Room of One's Own* and "Professions for Women." Such a juxtaposition would enable students familiar with the sensation controversy to acknowledge in *A Fool in Her Folly* what Mansfield does not: its depiction of the specific obstacles to writing about sexuality faced by mid-Victorian women. At the same time, reading Broughton's novel in tandem with Mansfield's review and Woolf's feminist commentary could also help students understand why a modernist woman writer might not, in fact, applaud a novel that depicts the devastation of a woman's literary career in a comedic way. To a young, experimental female author like Mansfield, a tale whose title implied that a woman writer was a "fool" and her ambitions "folly" would likely be a galling reminder of a not-so distant past in which literary women were routinely denigrated. And a feminist like Woolf, who poignantly envisioned the self-silencing suicide of Judith Shakespeare, might be offended by the farcical tone used by Broughton in her metafictions to describe the heroines' destruction of their own work. In *A Fool in Her Folly,* Charlotte, or Char, Hankey melodramatically flings the shreds of her grandiloquently-entitled novel, *LOVE,* through a train window, while Emma Jocelyn of *A Beginner* burns all two hundred and forty-five copies of the ill-received *Miching Mallecho* in a colossal bonfire.

Paradoxically, though, an aspect of *A Fool in Her Folly* that Mansfield sees as evidence of lack of artistry is apt to be recognised today as proof of the opposite. Complaining that Broughton leaves "*dans le vague*", or unanswered (1920: 242), such questions as whether Char's manuscript is as shocking as her horrified parents think, Mansfield identifies a key enigma of *A Fool in Her*

Folly that characterises *A Beginner* as well: in neither work does Broughton include excerpts from her heroines' novels, leaving her audience in the dark, not only about the aesthetic value of their work, but of the message to be drawn from their failed careers. Yet, while Mansfield considers this lack of information a flaw, present-day readers are more likely to find the absence of a clear-cut moral one of the more sophisticated aspects of Broughton's metafictions, redolent not only of postmodernism but—ironically, given Mansfield's disdain—of modernism itself, a movement that eschewed Victorian didacticism. Instead of being told what to think, we are confronted with a riddle: are we to believe that Char's and Emma's works are, like the unwritten plays of Judith Shakespeare, a loss to literature—a feminist moral—or are we to draw a different, more misogynistic conclusion, that these tales, with their ridiculous titles, are silly novels by lady novelists that would never have been worth reading?

In asking this question, a professor can help students appreciate the complexity of Broughton's metafictions, as one can argue either way. As my remarks below attest, I believe, finally, that there is more evidence than otherwise that Broughton considers the implosion of her heroines' literary careers both unfortunate and unjust. And yet the ambiguity on this issue proves Mansfield right in one regard: Broughton is, indisputably, a Victorian writer. For all that the deliberate silences and parodic humour of her metafictions anticipate postmodern playfulness, the comic send-up of her heroines' aspirations reflects the Victorian ambivalence about female professional authorship noted by Marie Belloc Lowndes. Like the other works by Broughton discussed in this study, her metafictions are ideologically riven, reproducing Victorian anxieties about women's writing even as they critique ways in which these anxieties stifle women's voices.

The first page of *A Fool in Her Folly* invokes late-Victorian anxieties about female authorship. Recounting two childhood memories, Char first recalls the day on which a working-class man informed her, as she walked to church, that her garter was coming off, and then recollects an episode in a similar outdoor setting when "a ruffian of the same class" called "'You're losing your ribbons, my dear'" (1920a: 7). Figuring the degrading publicity she would receive were she to publish her scandalous fiction, these incidents, which show Char shedding her clothes to the amusement of lower-class men, reflect sensation-era fears about the woman writer's loss of a respectable feminine, and bourgeois, identity. Similar anxieties propel a plotline of *A Fool in Her Folly* that could have been penned by Margaret Oliphant to illustrate her point about the corrupting influence of female sensationalism on young girls. Exiled by her family to an aunt's house until she forswears authorship, Char is deluded by her consumption and production of steamy fiction into believing that a handsome, if dissolute, young man is in love with her. Only after spending hours alone with him one night, under the mistaken assumption that he is eager to marry her and find redemption, does she discover that he was, in fact, using their acquaintance as a means of foisting unwanted attentions on her aunt. So horrified is Char to realise that her "unseemly book knowledge" (1920a: 228) led her into a situation where she could have lost her virginity, as well as her reputation, that she destroys her manuscript and rushes home after promising her parents never to write again.

A storyline about the dangerous influence of erotic fiction appears in *A Beginner* as well, when a friend of Emma Jocelyn's is inspired by her novel about adultery to consider launching an affair of her own. Yet, while these cautionary tales about the moral havoc wreaked by women writers are the most conservative features of Broughton's *künstlerromans*, the tales also depict the would-be authors' acquaintance with forbidden knowledge as inspiration for the most promising aspects of their work. In *A Fool in Her Folly*, Char, hearing whispers about the suicide of a pregnant maid, locates in the newspaper the text of the young woman's farewell letter to the lover who abandoned her, and is so moved by its raw emotion that she scraps the clichéd dialogue she had drafted between her own protagonists. That the hitherto sheltered Char has the insight to recognise in the words of a working-class woman the "Truth", as she calls it, of a tragic love (1920a: 41), suggests that she is capable, like Broughton herself, of writing a work of value on the subject. In *A Beginner,* meanwhile, Emma Jocelyn asserts that grappling with moral issues in her novel has not only left her own morality unscathed, but has, indeed, reaffirmed her ethical commitments. Confronting the young man whose scathing review doomed her career—and with whom she thought she might be in love—Emma informs him that, in writing her novel,

> I had put the whole of myself—all that was best and highest of me—into it. If you had had a ray of true appreciation for, or comprehension of, me, you would have found it there. (1894 [2005]: 275).

I will return to the intersection of romance and *künstlerroman* plots in Broughton's metafictions, but for now I use this scene—as I would in the classroom—as evidence of a significant tonal shift in the portrayal of the woman writer in *A Beginner.* Defying a critic whose attack on her work included jibes about her sex, Emma speaks "with inexpressible dignity" (1894 [2005]: 274), a description that contrasts markedly with the light tone Broughton more commonly employs to portray her heroine's experiences as an author.

To provide a context for this, as well as other passages in *A Beginner* and *A Fool in Her Folly* that imply that the careers of aspiring women writers are doomed more by sexism than lack of talent, I suggest pairing Broughton's work with the quintessential New Woman reverse *künstlerroman,* Mary Cholmondeley's *Red Pottage* (1899). Not only is *Red Pottage* thematically similar to Broughton's metafictions, but the two writers had both personal and professional ties. A writer nineteen years younger than Broughton, Cholmondeley was a close friend of the older woman, who, as Linda Peterson notes, served as her "literary mentor" (2009: 210). Assigning students Peterson's article on the relationship between the two women—an article that contains a selection of correspondence between them regarding literary matters[75]—would provide the class with important evidence of Broughton's connection, in the latter part of her career, to openly feminist authors.

Moreover, assigning the three novels in order of publication—*A Beginner* (1894), *Red Pottage* (1899), and *A Fool in Her Folly* (1920)—allows students to consider the possibility that Broughton and Cholmondeley influenced each other's work. The influence of Cholmondeley on Broughton is probably easiest to spot. Published several decades after *Red Pottage*, *A Fool in Her Folly*, like Cholmondeley's novel, depicts the destruction of a woman writer's manuscripts by a horrified clergyman. In *Red Pottage*, the clerical brother of Hester Gresley, stumbling upon the manuscript of her brilliant second novel and judging it a "'profane, wicked book'" (1899 [1985]: 276), burns it before it can be sent to the publisher; in *A Fool in Her Folly*, Char's clergyman father similarly insists on incinerating the first draft of *LOVE*, which he declares "'pestilent balderdash'" (1920a: 81). The parallels between Cholmondeley's and Broughton's novels are further emphasised when Hester and Char both employ the metaphor of literary motherhood to describe their anguish at the destruction of their work, as well as their commitment to an intellectual, rather than domestic, vocation. Reminding her censorious brother that she had nursed his son through a serious illness, Hester asks reproachfully "'I did not let your child die. Why have you killed mine?'" (1899 [1985]: 276); Char, meanwhile, is angered by her parents "murdering" the "offspring of *my* heart and brain—so much dearer, so far more precious, than any mere child of the flesh could ever be" (1920a: 89). Certainly, it would not be surprising if Broughton—whom

Cholmondeley thanked in a letter for the "sympathy and kindly feeling" she "brought to bear upon 'Red Pottage'" (30 October 1899, in Peterson, 2006: 112)—was influenced by her friend's work. Yet there are tantalising similarities between *Red Pottage* and *A Beginner*, published five years previously, that suggest the influence went both ways. The speech in *A Beginner* in which a dignified Emma asserts that she put what was "'best and highest'" of her character into her novel finds an echo in *Red Pottage* when Hester tells a mentor that the book burnt by her brother was "'the better part'" of herself (1899 [1985]: 335). Additionally, the "splendid bonfire" in which Hester's manuscript is destroyed (1899 [1985]: 269) recalls the "bonfire ... blazing and roaring" (1894 [2005]: 277) on which Emma incinerates the copies of her novel.

Nonetheless, the difference between Cholmondeley's and Broughton's versions of this scene is instructive. In Cholmondeley's rendition, the woman writer's work is destroyed by a disapproving reader, while in Broughton's the author destroys her work herself. This focus on the self-silencing of the woman writer, rather than on her silencing by others—a theme conveyed as well by Char's destruction of the second draft of her manuscript —enables Broughton to explore the disabling effect of internalised sexist assumptions on the female author. In her portrayal of this issue, indeed, Broughton anticipates Woolf's insights in *A Room of One's Own*, including the passage, mentioned in my last chapter, in which Woolf ascribes Judith Shakespeare's suicide to her inability to abandon the belief, enshrined by her culture, that chastity was the most important feminine virtue (1929 [1957]: 51). In a passage that similarly addresses the disabling effect of internalised sexual mores on the woman writer, Broughton depicts in *A Beginner* the self-doubt that besieges Emma after reading the review that will scuttle her career, and which decries her novel's "'coarsely expressed passion'" (1894 [2005]: 126):

> Dreadful misgivings assail her, that she, who had always held herself so proudly pure, no less in thought than in action, before whose chaste displeasure all dubious jests and doubtful stories have died, upon whose prudery her cousin Lesbia has so often rallied her, should have been frankly and grossly coarse both in the choice and the treatment of a scabrous subject—assail and batter her self-respect. (1894 [2005]: 131)

In *A Fool in Her Folly*, Broughton illustrates the difficulty experienced by the woman who attempts to jettison outmoded gender ideologies in a manner strikingly reminiscent of the psychomachia Woolf imagines in "Professions for Women." Both writers depict the inhibiting influence on the female author of a figure who embodies domestic ideology, represented in Woolf's case by the stereotypical "Angel in the House", and in Broughton's by Char's mother, a "Haus Engel" (1920a: 21) who, like the "phantom" that haunts Woolf (1931 [1979]: 58), models Victorian propriety. Just as Woolf finds the Angel "com[ing] between me and my paper" when she attempts to write (1931 [1979]: 58), Char, in her first attempt to redraft her novel at her aunt's house, is unable to proceed after picturing her mother's reproach:

> Before me, in the light of the papers, seemed to rise the face of mamma, sadder and severer than I had ever seen it with bodily eyes. The impression was so strong that I flung down the pen[.] (1920a: 187)

Yet, whereas Woolf has no personal affection for the Angel in the House, Char has emotional ties to her mother that she finds impossible to resist. While at her aunt's, she confesses that "the hunger to have my mother's arms once more about me was strong" (1920a: 208), and, when she forswears authorship and returns home, her reunion with the "Haus Engel" is nothing short of ecstatic (1920a: 350).

Although students today may appreciate Broughton's depiction of the psychological pressures on women writers—one of the more overtly feminist features of her metafictions—the conclusions she gives both works could, initially at least, strike them as reactionary: having renounced authorship, Emma and Char marry. In each case, however, this finale more closely resembles one of Broughton's ironic send-ups of the typical happy ending than the thing itself. Char's marriage is the most obviously problematic. Traumatised by her disastrous infatuation, she refuses not only to write any more love stories, but even to read them, and, when she does marry at thirty-one, claims that she could "have employed the phrase of George Whitefield", who, when proposing to "his future wife ... thanked God that there was not the slightest mixture of carnal love in his feeling for her" (1920a: 352). Even if we read Char's abortive romance as a cautionary tale about the danger of erotic fantasies—and hence one of the more conservative elements of *A Fool in Her Folly*—her subsequent renunciation of all sexual fulfilment is troubling. So extreme is her behaviour, finally, that is hard to classify it as anything other than neurotic, evidence of the same inability to contest Victorian mores that costs her a literary career.

As in *A Fool in Her Folly*, in *A Beginner* we only hear of the heroine's marriage on the last page of the novel. Like Char's marriage, too, Emma's is unromantic, as she weds a man in whom she had earlier shown little interest. As Pamela Gilbert notes, this perfunctory deployment of the marriage plot begs to be read more as a young woman's "capitulation to social pressures", than as her discovery of a "domestic vocation" (1997: 129). Even more significantly, the novel's intersection of the plots of failed authorship and failed romance enables Broughton to explore the obstacles ranged against the woman writer in a male-dominated literary establishment. Edgar Hatcheson, who turns out to be the anonymous reviewer of Emma's anonymously-published novel, is her "intellectual guide" (1894 [2005]:270) as well as, increasingly, a potential love interest. A writer of humble background who is gaining visibility as a literary critic, Hatcheson provides Emma with a companion with whom to talk about her love of books, and she reciprocates his friendship by admiring his essays and cheering on his professional successes.

Broughton stages the scene in which Emma and Hatcheson discover each other's concealed identities as author and reviewer with trademark irony: while Hatcheson looks on expectantly, awaiting her usual approbation, Emma opens his new volume of critical essays and spots with horror the offending review. Despite its comic overtones, the scene poignantly conveys the woman writer's pain and anger at being condescended to by a male writer—emotions articulated by Emma, as I mentioned earlier, with "inexpressible dignity." Although it necessarily comes as a shock to her, the revelation of Hatcheson's authorship of the review—which declared that the novel's author must be "'female'" as well as "'foolish'" (1894 [2005]: 125)—confirms Emma's earlier misgivings about his dismissive opinion of women writers; at the dinner party where she meets him, for instance, she "indignantly" responds to his patronising comment "'it is very rare nowadays to meet a lady who has not aired her opinions in print'": "'Why, the very shape of the phrase is contemptuous! Why should not you say simply written, as you would in the case of a man?'" (1894 [2005]: 34–35). Yet, because she erroneously believes that the hostile reviewer of her novel is the cantankerous Miss Grimston—a figure, as critics have noted, probably inspired by Geraldine Jewsbury[76]—Emma largely overlooks the signs of Hatcheson's "contempt...for all female authorship" (1894 [2005]: 70). As evidenced by the dedication of his new volume of essays to Emma—"TO HER/ WHOSE GRACIOUS INFLUENCE/ HAS GIVEN THEM BIRTH" (1894 [2005]: 270)—he, like a tradition of male authors, finds it easier to regard women as silent muses than as creators in their own right.

An important context that the professor teaching *A Beginner* can bring to students' attention is the novel's allusion to the career of John Keats—an allusion which Broughton uses to imply that Romantic ideals of artistic genius available to male writers are not, finally, relevant to the experience of literary women. The story of how a hostile review ruins an author's career, *A Beginner* evokes the version of Keats's life that would have been familiar to Victorians, and which was influenced by Percy Shelley's mythic depiction, in "Adonais", of the poet as a sensitive outsider whose fatal lung disease was triggered by harsh reviews of *Endymion*.[77] Given the modest background he shares with the poet, Edgar Hatcheson might seem a more likely candidate for the role of Keats than Emma; Hatcheson's description of himself as "Cockney born and bred" (1894 [2005]: 71) in fact recalls one of the more vicious attacks on *Endymion,* the fourth instalment of a series of essays by John Gibson Lockhart entitled "On the Cockney School of Poetry." And yet it is Hatcheson who plays Lockhart to Emma's Keats, actually referring to Lockhart's diatribe at several places in his review of her novel.[78] While Lockhart concludes the second instalment of "On the Cockney School of Poetry" by accusing Leigh Hunt—the Radical poet with whom Keats was associated, and of whose politics the conservative Lockhart disapproved—of "prostitut[ing] his talents in a manner that is likely to corrupt milliners and apprentice-boys" (Lockhart 1817), Hatcheson ends his diatribe on *Miching Mallecho* by sneering at the "'milliners and 'prentices'" who will be its readers (1894 [2005]: 126). Ironically, then, the working-class Hatcheson celebrates his successful assimilation into an elite literary establishment—by the time he publishes his new volume, he has been appointed editor of the journal that published his withering review—by ridiculing the work of a woman writer in terms that are classist as well as sexist. Scolding the author of *Miching Mallecho* for daring "'to pose … as a solver of those abstruse and entangled problems which are vexing the best minds of our century'", he declares that "'she—there cannot be a second's doubt as to the sex of the author of this precious performance'" is as fitted for the task as "'a street-sweeper [would be] to head the mathematical tripos'" (1894 [2005]: 124–25).

Thus, although Emma may echo the line that Keats requested be carved on his tombstone—"Here lies one whose name was writ in water"[79]—she will, unlike him, never achieve canonical stature. Early in *A Beginner*, Emma's aunt exclaims after reading her novel "'I have been warming a volcano in my bosom'" (1894 [2005]: 20). The novel's most dramatic conflagration, however, is Emma's own incineration of her inflammatory text.

With this discussion of Broughton's reference to Romantic myths of genius in *A Beginner*, I have come full circle in this study. I began, in my introduction, by addressing the Romantic-era concept of the "woman of genius", and how it both did, and did not, afford women writers in the Victorian era a chance to achieve literary stature. In my fourth chapter, I argued that, in *Good-bye, Sweetheart!*—her revision of that quintessential tale of female genius, Madame de Staël's *Corinne*—Broughton suggests that the popular woman writer of the Victorian era suffered a loss of stature compared to the Romantic-era woman of letters. In her rewriting of Keats's story in *A Beginner*, Broughton explicitly addresses the status of the woman writer in the literary marketplace, depicting it in light of a specifically *fin-de-siècle* context: the increased separation, by the end of the nineteenth century, between popular and canonical literature. While this divide influenced Broughton's entire career, by the turn of the twentieth century, the "growing separation" between "mass and elite culture," as Linda Peterson puts it (2009: 208), made it even harder for women writers of the period to attain the stature of woman of letters than it had for their Victorian precursors.[80] Hatcheson's response to Emma's novel clearly demarcates the gulf between literature produced by the "'best'"—and hence presumably male—"minds of our century" and the "'simple trash'" with which Hatcheson would have unthinkingly classified *Miching Mallecho* had its female author not caught his eye by attempting to "'grasp Jove's thunderbolt'" with her "'feeble hand'" (1894 [2005]: 124, 126). Significantly, Hatcheson's mocking review, published in a prominent London journal he will later edit himself, drowns out the more positive responses to Emma's novel in more obscure, less centrally located magazines, including one that likens her work—as the reviewer in *The Spectator* had once likened Broughton's—to that of George Eliot (1894 [2005]: 92).

Yet, despite her pessimistic depiction of the late-Victorian woman writer's growing association with ephemeral, rather than elite, culture—and despite, as well, her own refusal publicly to represent herself as an author of stature—students may yet come to write a different story about Broughton and her contribution to literature. Indeed, class discussions of the many issues raised by Broughton's fiction—issues of canonicity and the marketplace, of feminism, marriage, and women's complex response to social change—might help students spot a detail in *A Beginner* relevant to their own academic efforts. Although Emma burns every copy of her novel she can find, she does not, like Char in *A Fool in Her Folly*, succeed in obliterating all trace of her attempt at an authorial career. We are told that five copies of *Miching Mallecho* still exist—in libraries (1894 [2005]: 277). Although Broughton may not have considered this detail important, students and other readers of our time could see in the preservation of these five volumes a foreshadowing of feminist efforts to rediscover the work of Broughton and other, hitherto neglected women writers. That a later generation of readers could find in her reverse *künstlerromans* a key to reversing their telos of literary failure is surely an irony that the masterfully ironic Broughton would herself appreciate.

Notes

Introduction

1. See, for example, Debenham, 1996; Gilbert, 1997; and Heller 2006 and 2009. The online conference "Rhoda Broughton: A Centenary Conference", held on 11 September 2021, was organised by Dr. Graziella Stringos, and sponsored by the Victorian Popular Fiction Association.
2. For the passage in the serial cut from the triple-decker, see the entry for p. 137 in Appendix B, "Textual Variants", *Not Wisely, but Too Well*, 1867 [2013]: 397.
3. For more on Broughton's metafictional novels, see Gilbert 1997, pp. 127–39, Heller 2009, and Stringos 2020.
4. See Faber, 2006. Tabitha Sparks not only delivered a paper on metafictionality in *Cometh Up as a Flower* at the Broughton Centenary Conference, but also kindly shared with me the chapter on that novel in her manuscript on Victorian metafictionality, since published as *Victorian Metafiction* (2022).
5. See Debenham, 1996: 10–11 for more on the influence of *The Story of Elizabeth* (1863) on Broughton. Anne Thackeray Ritchie (1837–1919), daughter of William Makepeace Thackeray, was a respected novelist whose domestic fiction was notable for its realistic and sympathetic portrayal of women's lives.
6. Broughton's unidealised portrayal of marriage includes references to domestic violence. Both *Scylla or Charybdis?* (1895), and *A Fool in Her Folly* (1920) mention prolonged physical abuse endured by wives. In *Scylla or Charybdis?*, the widowed mother of the male lead was "'knock[ed] ... about cruelly'" during the lifetime of her mentally ill husband (1895: 23), and, in *A Fool in Her Folly*, we hear that "[t]here was no insult or brutality" which the late husband of Char's Aunt Florinda did not inflict on his wife during twenty years of "married hell" (1920a: 170, 164). The invalid husband of the widowed heroine of *Mrs. Bligh* (1892) "'used to throw things at her head'" (1892: 35), while the bedridden husband of Elizabeth in *Between Two Stools* (1912) subjects his wife to verbal abuse.
7. For the reactionary elements in *Not Wisely, but Too Well* see Talairach-Vielmas, 2007: pp. 89–112, and Gilbert, 1997: 115–27.
8. Marie Belloc Lowndes, a close friend of Broughton's described by Elyssa

Warkentin as a "feminist, popular crime writer, and journalist" ("Introduction", 2015: xiv), was the daughter of Bessie Parkes Belloc, who founded the Woman's Suffrage League with her friend Barbara Boudichon in 1866. For a time, Lowndes herself was vice-president of another organization devoted to suffrage, the Women Writers Suffrage League. For more on Mary Cholmondeley's feminism, see Peterson 2009: 207–23. (I also discuss Cholmondeley's feminism in the Afterword here.) Based on a letter by Broughton in the Jack Mooney collection of Rhoda Broughton to a "Miss Sinclair" (Box II, letter 23, 5 March n.d.), I theorise that Broughton also knew May Sinclair (1863–1946), a feminist writer and member of the Women Writers Suffrage League, whose book *Feminism* was in fact published by that organization in 1912. It would not be surprising if Broughton knew a writer active in an organization in which her friend Marie Belloc Lowndes was a prominent member, and Lowndes in fact mentions May Sinclair in her memoir *Passing World* (1948: 196–97).

9. Similarly, in a letter to Florence Henniker (8 November 1916, Jack Mooney Collection of Rhoda Broughton, Box 5), Broughton confessed that her age influenced her reaction to a contemporary novel: "the high minded chaste heroine's response to her roué lover [...] that she would like to <u>make him the father of her son</u>, made my mid-Victorian head go round!"

Chapter 1

10. For more on the publication history of *Not Wisely*, see Heller, "Introduction" (2013: 5–6, 15–25).
11. See Fahnestock, 1981: 342 for a reference to Kate Chester.
12. See Ofek, 2006: 109–13.
13. Poem by Tennyson (1842).
14. See Michie, 1987: 17–22 for more on "ladylike anorexia."
15. Broughton's dismissal of corsets as unhealthily restrictive employs a rhetoric similar to that which characterised the nineteenth-century dress reform movement; for a history of this movement that underscores its feminist elements, while also providing some background on medical objections to the corset, see Cunningham (2003).
16. Jewsbury's moral disapproval of *Not Wisely* is ironic, given the controversy occasioned several decades earlier by her own novel, *Zoë* (1845), which depicted the love between a married woman and a Catholic priest. A feminist and fan of George Sand, Jewsbury was a fascinatingly complex figure; her role as moral gatekeeper in the 1860s—a role she filled both as reader for Bentley's and reviewer for the conservative journal *The Athenæum*—conflicted with her heterodox persona. Abigail Burnham Bloom theorises that the influence of Thomas Carlyle—who believed that women should focus on duty rather than on love—was in some measure responsible for Jewsbury's dislike of romantic fiction such as Broughton's (2020: 38, 125–26). See also Fahnestock, 1973 for more on Jewsbury's work as reader for Bentley's, including her response to *Not*

Wisely. For Jewsbury's role as reviewer for *The Athenæum*, see Fryckstedt 1986.
17. For more on ambivalence about the female body in *Not Wisely*, see Heller 2006: 92–96.
18. See Hager, 2007 for a related discussion of the gender and class politics of "slumming" in a later work of Broughton's, *Dear Faustina* (1897).
19. Crinolines—a fashion popular among women across the class spectrum—were controversial for a number of reasons, including safety issues (tales abounded of women burned to death when their crinolines caught fire). Perkin notes that the crinoline was considered immodest when women bent over (1993: 96), a point made by Florence Nightingale in 1860 in *Notes on Nursing*, where she inveighs against the "indecency" of the fashion (1860: chapter 4, n. 1).
20. Thornton (1994: 163–68) discusses the actual history of Circassian women in nineteenth-century harems, as well as reproducing paintings which depict them, naked, in harems or on display for male purchasers in slave markets. See also Pal-Lapinski for more on how white women were "exoticized" in orientalist discourses of the period (2005: xv-xvi).
21. See Leith 2005, for iconic photographs of the Palace taken by Philip Delamotte at the end of the 1850s that include the places to which Broughton refers, including Monti's Fountain of the Syrens (2005: 80) and the Greek Court (2005: 71–72).
22. See Arnold, 1920: 273.
23. This critique of women's reading animates such fictions as Charlotte Lennox's *The Female Quixote* (1752), Gustave Flaubert's *Madame Bovary* (1856), and Mary Elizabeth Braddon's *The Doctor's Wife* (1864).
24. See Debenham, 1996: 10–11 for more on the Ritchie novel as an inspiration.
25. See *NW* 1867 [2013]: 182 for the second reference to *Corinne*.
26. The severe penances performed by the nuns of the Bernardine Convent of the Perpetual Adoration are enumerated in Book Six of *Les Misérables*, "Le Petit-Picpus" (1862 [1976]: 425–34).
27. In addition to Mumm's history of Anglican women's orders, see Vicinus's chapter on the sisterhoods as "one of the most important women's communities in the nineteenth century" (1985: 83).

Chapter 2

28. See Appendix A of *Not Wisely* for the letter to Richard Bentley in which Le Fanu, claiming that *Cometh Up* is "perfectly free" of objectionable elements, approves of Broughton's decision to substitute it for *Not Wisely* (2013: 380).
29. I discuss "disembodied embodiment" on p. xlii of my introduction to *Cometh Up*. See also Garrison (2011: 88–105) for a reading of how Nell's meditations on the afterlife at different points in her life reveal a tension between traditional Christian theology, and its dualistic separation of soul and body, and more holistic spiritualist beliefs.
30. For more on Victorian medical theories of consumption and how they apply to

both *Cometh Up* and Broughton's 1872 novel *Good-bye, Sweetheart!*, see Meyer 2003: 289 (his reading of *Cometh Up* may be found on pp. 291–96).
31. See my discussion of matrophobia in *Dead Secrets* (1992: 19–20).
32. Like *Not Wisely*, *Cometh Up* differs in *DUM* serial form from its triple-decker incarnation. In *Cometh Up*, these changes are primarily intended to lengthen the manuscript for volume publication rather than, as in the case of *Not Wisely*, to tone down offensive material. (Broughton did, however, pare down the serial's use of slang.) One of Broughton's changes was to end the story in Nell's words, rather than, as in the serial, with an awkward third-person account of her death. For more on the changes between the serial and the volume form of *Cometh Up*, see the Pickering and Chatto edition's textual notes (2004: 516–32), which include the text of the original ending.
33. Novel by Frederick Marryat (1836).
34. See my introduction to *Cometh Up* (2004: xl-lxii).
35. For Cohen's reading of Richardson's Clarissa as "literature's original anorectic daughter" (1991: 57), see pp. 52–58.
36. She calls him "King Olaf" on several occasions (for example, 1867 [2004]: 232, 235).
37. Similarly, R. C. Terry's chapter on Broughton's novels—one of the first appreciations of their feminist elements—characterises her male leads as "cads and he-men" (1983: 129). See chapter 4 for more on Victorian critics' reactions to Broughton's male characters.
38. Graziella Stringos is planning to edit an essay collection, *Masculinity under Scrutiny: Women Writing Men in Victorian Popular Fiction*, to which both she and I will contribute essays that challenge the dismissive readings of previous critics of Broughton's male characters.
39. See Wollstonecraft for more on the seraglio 1792 [2007]: 47.
40. See, for example, Brantlinger's discussion of "sexual atrocity" narratives written in the wake of the Mutiny (1988: 209).
41. The lines that Nell adapts are from "Lancelot and Elaine" (*Tennyson's Poetry* 1859 [1999]: 419, ll. 258–59).
42. Tabitha Sparks's chapter on *Cometh Up* in *Victorian Metafiction* also considers the ways in which Nell constructs her "autobiography" as a narrative (2022: 70–90).

Chapter 3
43. Jones 2004: 219 notes similarities between Paul Le Mesurier and Paul Emanuel of *Villette*.
44. Fryckstedt 1995: 27. Fryckstedt provides a useful discussion of the circulating library system; see also Griest.
45. In *How They Strike Me, These Authors* (1877), J. C. Heywood in fact entitles the section on Broughton's fiction "A Crude Novelist", and rather fancifully likens her to "a neglected garden with a rich soil, where flowers and weeds grow

rankly together" (99). An example of Broughton's fiction being described as "coarse" is, unsurprisingly, Geraldine Jewsbury's *Athenæum* review of *Cometh Up*, which refers to the love scenes as "coarse and flippant" (1867 [2003]: 140). The *Athenæum* review of *Good-bye, Sweetheart!* mentions Broughton's "vulgarity" (1872: 586).

46. Pykett's study of sensation writing and New Woman novels derives its title from Austin's phrase "the improper feminine" and she discusses his attack on sensationalism (1992: 24–25). For more on Austin and sensationalism, see Helsinger, Sheets, and Veeder 1983 (3.156–60).
47. Reference to Edmund Spenser's *The Faerie Queene* (1590). In book 1 of this allegorical poem, the virtuous Una, a royal maiden who symbolises the Protestant faith, travels under the protection of the Christ-like Red Cross Knight.
48. For more on the Victorian panic over French fiction in the 1860s, see Flint 1993: 138 and 287–88 (on p. 288 she actually discusses St. John's horror at Esther's reading in *Red as a Rose Is She*). Atkinson 2017: 139–238 discusses the perceived "dangers of French novels."
49. For more on Broughton's portrayal of female sexuality in *Red as a Rose Is She*, see Heller, 2020: 126–30.
50. Gesturing toward a tragic plot trajectory she does not follow, Broughton has St. John's current fiancée, Constance Blessington, arrive on the scene shortly after he kisses Esther. Refusing to believe St. John's explanation of what happened, the jealous Constance threatens to spread the rumour that Esther invited him to her bedroom. While this does not happen—and, indeed, St. John breaks off his engagement to Constance in disgust at her spite—one can imagine a scenario in which Esther loses her job, and is unable to find another due to doubts about her moral character. Of course, another tragic outcome of the scene would be for St. John to assault Esther while she is unconscious, the fate of Samuel Richardson's Clarissa, raped by the decadent aristocrat Lovelace, after he drugs her. That Broughton had Richardsonian narrative in mind is indicated by her allusion to *Pamela*—another Richardson novel in which a rapacious upper-class man tries (in this case, unsuccessfully) to violate a virtuous woman—and which Broughton dryly describes as a series of "hairbreadth escapes from RUIN (in big letters)" (1870 [1899]: 372). As if to suggest that this tale's happy ending is both ludicrous and antiquated, Broughton shows Esther reading, but failing to finish, the book.
51. The advertisement for *Good-bye, Sweetheart!* to which I refer appears at the end of the American edition of the novel from which I cite in this chapter (1872: [440]).
52. For more on Broughton's revision of *Corinne* in *Good-bye, Sweetheart!*, see Heller 2011.
53. See *Not Wisely* 36, 163; for Broughton's references to Corinne's description of the after-dinner conversation of ladies at Mme. Edgermond's house; for the description itself, see de Staël 1807 [1987]: 255–58.

54. For the case of "Anna O.", see Breuer and Freud 1893–95 [1957]: 21–47.
55. For Meyer's reading of *Good-bye, Sweetheart!*, see 2003: 296–300.
56. For more on anorexia and hysteria in *Good-bye, Sweetheart!*, see Heller 2011: 68–71.
57. The translation is by Ariel Goldberger.

Chapter 4

58. Fortunately, Broughton's ghost stories have recently received more critical attention: for more on "The Man with the Nose", see not only Purdue (2020), but Masters (2015). Despotopoulou (2011) addresses a story by Broughton, "Under the Cloak" (1873), published in *Temple Bar* and also included in Broughton's collection of supernatural tales, *Tales for Christmas Eve* (later retitled *Twilight Tales*). Though a thriller rather than a ghost story, "Under the Cloak" is highly Gothic.
59. See Jalland 1986: 79–84.
60. See *Cometh Up* 1867 [2004]: 340, and my note on this passage on p. 491, for more on Broughton's appropriation of a passage from *The Mill on the Floss* (1860).
61. See, for example, Mona Caird's attack on marriage as "woman-purchase" in "Marriage" (1888 [2001]: 193).
62. See Ch. 2, n. 7.
63. See Letter to George Bentley, 13 February 1870: "I have been reveling in Miss Austen's Sense & Sensibility. I wish some portion of her spirit would awake in me" (BA, Pt.2, Reel 22).
64. Linton's comments notwithstanding, Broughton still managed to offend "Mrs. Grundy", or the critics who disapproved of references to illicit love. According to a critic in *The New York Daily Tribune,* Broughton is too much influenced by French fiction, and "now and then seems to be contesting with Ouida the palm of naughtiness" (30 January 1887: 6A). In *The Academy,* George Saintsbury singled out Lady Betty in complaining that the plot of *Doctor Cupid* is largely structured by "the selfish and immoral passion of a married woman for a man who is tired of her" (1886: 391).

Chapter 5

65. See William Sharp's review of the novel in *The Academy* (1892: 605).
66. For more on *Lavinia,* see de Groot 2013: 37–47, 53–54, 65–66. Rupert Campion, the Wildean aesthete, is not only effeminate, but may even be an early literary example of gender dysphoria (we are told he has "always sighed to be" a woman [1902: 272]).
67. See n. 8 in the introduction for more on feminists in Broughton's circle.
68. For Ardis's discussion of the "boomerang" plot, see 1990: 97.
69. Meem's introduction to her edition of Linton's politically radical early novel *Realities* (1851) provides an excellent survey of the ideological shifts and

inconsistencies that marked her career (Meem 2010: 7–21).
70. Eliza Lynn Linton's article "The Shrieking Sisterhood" appeared in *The Saturday Review* 12 March, 1870: 341–42.
71. See Pykett 1989: 74 for more on the convention, in romantic fiction, of a choice between two men.

Afterword

72. For more on the "reverse *künstlerroman*", see my reading of *A Fool in Her Folly* (2009). See also Stringos 2020 for a reading of "aspiring women writers" in both *A Beginner* and *A Fool in Her Folly*.
73. See Woods (2016) for an innovative article on teaching canon formation that includes Broughton's *Cometh Up as a Flower*.
74. In *A Beginner*, the most vitriolic reviewer of Emma Jocelyn's novel assails her for daring to address "'the tremendous subject of heredity'" (126). As, however, Broughton tells us little of the actual plot of the scorned novel, it is not clear how the topic is supposed to be raised.
75. See Peterson 2006: 107–10 for a discussion of Cholmondeley and Broughton's friendship and intellectual bond, which Peterson describes as a relationship between "literary mother and daughter" (2006: 108).
76. See, for example, Stringos 2020: 35 and Bloom 2020: 9.
77. As Shelley put it in "Adonais," "Our Adonais has drunk poison—oh!" (l. 316). For that poem's description of the review and its effect on Keats, see ll. 316–42.
78. Hatcheson's review begins by mentioning reviews of *Endymion*, or, as he puts it, "'the world-famous sentence of Gibson upon Endymion'" (1894 [2005]: 124). Actually, the sentence attributed by Hatcheson to "Gibson"—"'This will never do'"—opened Francis Jeffrey's review of Wordsworth's *The Excursion*. Despite Broughton's confusion of negative reviews received by Wordsworth and Keats, however, she clearly wishes to focus on the response to Keats.
79. Joseph Severn noted that, on his deathbed, Keats requested that this line appear, in place of his name, as the "sole inscription" on his tombstone (quoted in Cacciatore 42).
80. For Peterson's discussion of the growing divide between popular and high-culture literature, see her analysis of Mary Cholmondeley's difficulties in defining herself as a woman of letters (2009: 207–23).

Bibliography

Ardis, Ann, 1990. *New Women, New Novels: Feminism and Early Modernism*. Rutgers, New Jersey: Rutgers University Press.

Arnold, Ethel, 1920. "Rhoda Broughton as I Knew Her", *Fortnightly Review* 114, pp. 262–78.

Atkinson, Juliette, 2017. *French Novels and the Victorians*. Oxford: Oxford University Press.

Auerbach, Jeffrey A., 1999. *The Great Exhibition of 1851: A Nation on Display*. New Haven: Yale University Press.

Auerbach, Nina, 2004. "Ghosts of Ghosts", *Victorian Literature and Culture* 32, 1 (March), pp. 277–84.

Austin, Alfred, 1870. "Our Novels: The Sensational School", *Temple Bar* 29 (June), pp. 410–24.

—, 1874. "The Novels of Miss Broughton", *Temple Bar* 41 (May), pp. 197–209.

Bennett, E. A. [Arnold], 1901. *Fame and Fiction: An Enquiry into Certain Popularities*. London: Grant Richard.

[Bentley Archives, BA], 1976. *Archives of Richard Bentley and Son 1829–1898*, Pt. 2, Reel 22. Cambridge: Chadwyck-Healey; Teaneck, New Jersey: Somerset House.

Bernstein, Susan, 1994. "Dirty Reading: Sensation Fiction, Women, and Primitivism", *Criticism* 36, pp. 213–30.

Black, Helen C., 1893 [1972]. *Notable Women Authors of the Day*. Freeport, New York: Books for Libraries Press.

Bleiler, Everett F., 1981. Headnote to Rhoda Broughton, "The Man with the Nose", in Everett F. Bleiler (ed.), *A Treasury of Victorian Ghost Stories*. New York: Charles Scribner's Sons, p. 127.

Blewett, Kelly, 2013. "'The Mightiest and Sweetest of Singers': Rhoda Broughton's Ambivalent Use of Tennyson in *Not Wisely, But Too Well*" (unpublished manuscript).

Bloom, Abigail Burnham, 2020. *Geraldine Jewsbury*. Brighton: Edward Everett Root.

Bordo, Susan, 1993. *Unbearable Weight: Feminism, Western Culture, and the Body*. Berkeley: University of California Press.

Brantlinger, Patrick, 1988. *Rule of Darkness: British Literature and Imperialism, 1830–1914*. Ithaca, New York: Cornell University Press.

Breuer, Josef and Sigmund Freud, 1893–95 [1957]. *Studies on Hysteria*. James Strachey (translator and ed.). Hogarth Press/Basic Books.

Brontë, Charlotte, 1847 [1996]. *Jane Eyre*. Beth Newman (ed.). 3rd edn. Boston: Bedford/St. Martin's.

Broughton, Rhoda, 1865–66. *Not Wisely, but Too Well*, Dublin University Magazine, 66, 392 (August 1865), pp.123–45 – 68, 403 (July 1866), pp. 58–75.

—, 1866–67. *Cometh Up as a Flower*, Dublin University Magazine, 68, 403 (July 1866), pp. 24–41 – 69, 409 (January 1867), pp. 38–50.

—, 1867 [2004]. *Cometh Up as a Flower*, Tamar Heller (ed.), in Andrew Maunder (gen.ed.), *Varieties of Women's Sensation Fiction, 1855–1890*, Vol. 4B, London: Pickering & Chatto.

—, 1867 [2010]. *Cometh Up as a Flower*. Pamela K. Gilbert (ed.). Peterborough, Ontario: Broadview.

—, 1867 [2013]. Letters to Richard and George Bentley relating to *Not Wisely, but Too Well* in *Not Wisely, but Too Well*, Tamar Heller (ed.). Brighton: Victorian Secrets Press, pp. 376–84.

—, 1867 [2013]. *Not Wisely, but Too Well*. Tamar Heller (ed.). Brighton: Victorian Secrets.

—, 1870. Letter to George Bentley, 13 February, in *Archives of Richard Bentley and Son 1829–1898*, 1976, Pt. 2, Reel 22. Cambridge: Chadwyck-Healey; Teaneck, New Jersey: Somerset House.

—, 1870 [1899]. *Red as a Rose Is She*. London: Macmillan.

—, 1872. *Good-bye, Sweetheart!* New York: D. Appleton and Company.

—, 1872 [1981]. "The Man with the Nose," in Everett F. Bleiler (ed.), *A Treasury of Victorian Ghost Stories*. New York: Charles Scribner's and Sons, pp. 128–43.

—, 1873 [2005]. *Nancy*. 2 volumes. Boston: Adamant Media/Elibron Classics.

—, 1876 [1877]. *Joan*. London: Richard Bentley and Sons.

—, 1883 [1984]. *Belinda*. London: Virago.

—, 1886. *Doctor Cupid*. New York: F. M. Lupton.

—, 1890 [n.d.]. *Alas!* New York: Geo. Munro.

—, 1892. *Mrs. Bligh*. 2nd edn. London: Richard Bentley and Son.

—, 1894 [2005]. *A Beginner*. Elibron Classics.

—, 1897. *Dear Faustina*. London: Bentley's. https://archive.org/details/dearfaustinabyr00brougoog/page/n408/mode/2up?view=theater Accessed: 27 July 2022.

—, 1899. *The Game and the Candle*. New York: Appleton.

—, 1902. *Lavinia*. London and New York: Macmillan. https://archive.org/details/lavinia00brourich. Accessed: 9 July 2022.

—, 1912. *Between Two Stools*. Leipzig: Bernhard Tauchsnitz. https://babel.hathitrust.org/cgi/pt?id=coo.31924013441252&view=1up&seq=11&skin=2021. Accessed: 9 July 2022.

—, 1914. *Concerning a Vow.* London: Stanley Paul.
—, 1916. Letter to Florence Henniker, 8 November, The Jack Mooney Collection of Rhoda Broughton, University of South Carolina. Box 5.
—, 1920a. *A Fool in Her Folly.* London: Odhams.
—, 1920b. "Girls Past and Present", *Ladies Home Journal* (Sept.): 38, 141.
Browning, Robert, 1845 [2000]. "My Last Duchess", in Thomas J. Collins and Vivienne J. Rundle (eds), *The Broadview Anthology of Victorian Poetry and Poetic Theory, Concise Edition.* Peterborough: Broadview Press, pp. 224–25.
Cacciatore, Vera, 1970 [1973]. *A Room in Rome.* Rome: The Keats-Shelley Memorial Association.
Caird, Mona, 1888 [2001]. "Marriage", in Carolyn Christensen Nelson (ed.), *A New Woman Reader.* Peterborough, Ontario: Broadview Press, pp. 185–99.
Cholmondeley, Mary, 1920. "Personalities and Powers: The Late Miss Rhoda Broughton", *Time and Tide* 27 (August), pp. 324–25.
—, 1899 [1985]. *Red Pottage.* London: Virago Press; New York: Penguin Books.
Cohen, Paula Marantz, 1991. *The Daughter's Dilemma: Family Process and the Nineteenth-Century Domestic Novel.* Ann Arbor: University of Michigan Press.
Coleridge, Samuel Taylor, 1817 [2006]. "The Rime of the Ancient Mariner", in Susan Wolfson and Peter Manning (eds), *The Longman Anthology of British Literature,* Volume 2A, *The Romantics and Their Contemporaries.* 3rd edn. New York: Longman, pp. 580–95.
Collins, Wilkie, 1860 [1996]. *The Woman in White.* John Sutherland (ed.). Oxford: Oxford University Press.
Cunningham, Patricia, 2003. *Reforming Women's Fashion, 1850–1920: Politics, Health, and Art.* Kent, Ohio: Kent State University Press.
Davidoff, Leonore, 1983. "Class and Gender in Victorian England", in Judith L. Newton, Mary E. Ryan, Judith R. Walkowitz (eds), *Sex and Class in Women's History.* London: Routledge and Kegan Paul, pp. 17–71.
Debenham, Helen, 1996. "*Not Wisely but Too Well* and the Art of Sensation", in Ruth Robbins and Julian Wolfreys (eds), *Victorian Identities: Social and Cultural Formations in Nineteenth-Century Literature.* Hampshire: Macmillan/New York: St. Martins, pp. 9–24.
Despotopoulou, Anna, 2011. "Trains of Thought: The Challenges of Mobility in the Work of Rhoda Broughton", *Critical Survey* 23,1, pp. 90–106.
Faber, Lindsey, 2006. "One Sister's Surrender: Rivalry and Resistance in Rhoda Broughton's *Cometh Up as a Flower*", in Kimberly Harrison and Richard Fantina (eds.), *Victorian Sensations: Essays on a Scandalous Genre.* Columbus: Ohio State University Press, pp. 149–59.
Fahnestock, Jeanne, 1973. "Geraldine Jewsbury: The Power of the Publisher's Reader", *Nineteenth-Century Fiction* 28, pp. 253–72.
—, 1981. "The Heroine of Irregular Features: Physiognomy and Conventions of Heroine Description", *Victorian Studies* 24, pp. 325–50.
Flint, Kate, 1993. *The Woman Reader, 1837–1914.* Oxford: Oxford University Press.

"The Form of Solemnization of Matrimony", 1662. *The Book of Common Prayer*, http://www.eskimo.com/~lhowell/bcp1662/occasion/marriage.html. Accessed 30 November 2021.

Fryckstedt, Monica, 1986. *Geraldine Jewsbury's Athenæum Reviews: A Mirror of Mid-Victorian Attitudes to Fiction.* University Press, Uppsala: Almqvist & Wiksell.

—, 1995. "Food for Thought: Mudie's Select Library and the Fiction of the 1860s", *Australasian Victorian Studies Annual* 1,1, pp. 23–30.

Gallagher, Catherine, 1986. "George Eliot and *Daniel Deronda*: The Prostitute and the Jewish Question", in Ruth Bernard Yeazell (ed.), *Sex, Politics, and Science in the Nineteenth-Century English Novel.* Baltimore: Johns Hopkins University Press, pp. 39–62.

Garrison, Laurie, 2011. *Science, Sexuality and Sensation Novels: Pleasures of the Senses.* London: Palgrave Macmillan.

Gilbert, Pamela K., 1997. *Disease, Desire and the Body in Victorian Women's Popular Novels.* Cambridge: Cambridge University Press.

Godfrey, Esther, 2009. *The January-May Marriage in Nineteenth-Century British Literature.* New York: Palgrave Macmillan.

Griest, Guinevere L., 1970. *Mudie's Circulating Library and the Victorian Novel.* Bloomington, Indiana: Indiana University Press.

Groot, Cindy de, 2013. "Sensational or Conventional: Effeminacy and the Representation of Gender in Rhoda Broughton's Fiction". Masters Thesis, Ghent University.

Hager, Lisa, 2007. "Slumming with the New Woman: *Fin-de-Siècle* Sexual Inversion, Reform Work and Sisterhood in Rhoda Broughton's *Dear Faustina*", *Women's Writing* 14, pp. 460–75.

Hallum, Kirby-Jane, 2015. *Aestheticism and the Marriage Market in Victorian Popular Fiction: The Art of Female Beauty.* London: Pickering & Chatto.

Hatten, Charles, 2010. *The End of Domesticity: Alienation from the Family in Dickens, Eliot, and James.* Newark, Delaware: University of Delaware Press.

Heller, Tamar, 1992. *Dead Secrets: Wilkie Collins and the Female Gothic.* New Haven, Connecticut: Yale University Press.

—, 2004. Introduction, *Cometh Up as a Flower.* Tamar Heller (ed.), in *Varieties of Women's Sensation Fiction, 1855–1890,* Andrew Maunder (gen. ed.), Vol. 4B, London: Pickering & Chatto, pp. xxxiii-l.

—, 2006. "'That Muddy, Polluted Flood of Earthly Love': Ambivalence about the Body in Rhoda Broughton's *Not Wisely but Too Well*", in Kimberly Harrison and Richard Fantina (eds.), *Victorian Sensations: Essays on a Scandalous Genre.* Columbus: Ohio State University Press, pp. 87–101.

—, 2009. "Disposing of the Body: Literary Authority, Female Desire and the Reverse Künstlerroman of Rhoda Broughton's *A Fool in Her Folly*", in Melissa Purdue and Stacey Floyd (eds.), *New Women Writers, Authority and the Body.* Cambridge: Cambridge Scholars Publishing, pp. 139–57.

—, 2011. "Rewriting *Corinne:* Sensation and the Tragedy of the Exceptional Woman in Rhoda Broughton's *Good-bye, Sweetheart!*", *Critical Survey* 23, 1, pp. 58–74.

—, 2013. "Introduction", in Rhoda Broughton, *Not Wisely, but Too Well.* Brighton: Victorian Secrets Press, pp. 5–30.

—, 2020. "[F]leshly Inclinations: The Nature of Female Desire in Rhoda Broughton's Early Fiction", in Adrienne E. Gavin and Carolyn W. de la L. Oulton (eds.), *British Women's Writing from Brontë to Bloomsbury,* Volume 2: 1860s and 1870s. London: Springer/Palgrave Macmillan, pp. 119–34.

Helsinger, Elizabeth K., Robin Lauterbach Sheets, and William Veeder, 1983. *The Woman Question: Society and Literature in Britain and America 1837–1883.* 3 volumes. Chicago: University of Chicago Press.

Heywood, J. C., 1877. *How They Strike Me, These Authors.* Philadelphia: J. B. Lippincott.

Hugo, Victor, 1862 [1976]. *Les Misérables.* Translator: Norman Denny. Harmondsworth: Penguin.

Humpherys, Anne, 2007. "The Three of Them: The Scene of 'Divorce' in Nineteenth-Century English Fiction", in Kay Leydecker and Nicholas White (eds.), *After Intimacy: The Culture of Divorce in the West Since 1789.* Oxford: Peter Lang, pp. 113–34.

Jalland, Pat, 1986. *Women, Marriage, and Politics, 1860–1914.* Oxford: Oxford University Press.

Jewsbury, Geraldine, 1866. Correspondence with Richard Bentley relating to *Not Wisely, but Too Well,* in Rhoda Broughton, *Not Wisely, but Too Well,* Tamar Heller (ed.). Brighton: Victorian Secrets Press, pp. 378–79.

—, 1867 [2003]. Review of *Cometh Up as a Flower,* by Rhoda Broughton. *Athenæum* 2060. Rpt. in Solveig C. Robinson (ed.), *A Serious Occupation: Literary Criticism by Victorian Women Writers.* Peterborough: Broadview Press, pp. 138–43.

Jones, Shirley, 2004. "'LOVE': Rhoda Broughton, Writing and Re-writing Romance", in Kay Boardman and Shirley Jones (eds.), *Popular Victorian Women Writers.* Manchester: Manchester University Press, pp. 208–36.

Kaye, Richard, 2002. *The Flirt's Tragedy: Desire Without End in Victorian and Edwardian England.* Charlottesville: University of Virginia Press.

Kortsch, Christine Bayles, 2009. *Dress Culture in Late Victorian Women's Fiction: Literacy, Textiles, and Activism.* London: Routledge.

Koven, Seth, 2004. *Slumming: Sexual and Social Politics in Victorian London.* Princeton: Princeton University Press.

Le Fanu, J. S., 1851 [1964]. "Schalken the Painter", in E. F. Bleiler (ed.), *Best Ghost Stories of J. S. Le Fanu.* New York: Dover, pp. 29–46.

Leith, Ian, 2005. *Delamotte's Crystal Palace: A Victorian Pleasure Dome Revealed.* Swindon: English Heritage.

Linton, Eliza Lynn, 1868 [1995]. "The Girl of the Period", in Susan Hamilton (ed.),

Criminals, Idiots, Women, & Minors: Victorian Writing by Women on Women. Peterborough: Broadview Press, pp. 172–76.

—, 1880 [2002]. *The Rebel of the Family.* Deborah T. Meem (ed.). Petersborough, Ontario: Broadview Press.

—, 1887. "The Novels of Miss Broughton", *Temple Bar* 80 (June), pp. 196–209.

[Lockhart, John Gibson], 1817. "On the Cockney School of Poetry", No. II, *Blackwood's Edinburgh Magazine* 2, 8, pp. 194–201. https://lordbyron.org/doc.php?choose=JoLockh.1817.Cockney2.xml. Accessed: 18 July 2022.

—, 1819. "On the Cockney School of Poetry", No. IV, *Blackwood's Edinburgh Magazine* 3, 17, pp. 519–24. https://lordbyron.org/doc.php?choose=JoLockh.1818.Cockney4.xml. Accessed: 18 July 2022.

Lowdnes, Marie Belloc, 1920. Foreword to *A Fool in Her Folly*, by Rhoda Broughton. London: Odhams, pp. 5–6.

—, 1948. *Passing World.* London: Macmillan.

Lubbock, Percy, 1928. *Mary Cholmondeley: A Sketch from Memory.* London: Jonathan Cape.

Mansfield, Katherine, 1920. "Victorian Elegance", review of *A Fool in Her Folly*, by Rhoda Broughton, *Athenæum* (20 August 1920), pp. 241–42. https://archive.org/details/sim_Athenæum-uk_1920-08-20_4712/page/240/mode/2up. Accessed: 10 July 2022.

Masters, Joellen, 2015. "Haunted Gender in Rhoda Broughton's Supernatural and Mystery Tales", *Journal of Narrative Theory* 45, 2, pp. 220–50.

Maunder, Andrew, 2004. "Introduction", in Andrew Maunder (gen. ed), *Sensationalism and the Sensation Debate.* Vol. 1. *Varieties of Women's Sensation Fiction 1855–90.* London: Pickering and Chatto, pp. xxxiii-xlvii.

Meem, Deborah T., 2002. "Introduction", in Eliza Lynn Linton, *The Rebel of the Family.* Petersborough, Ontario: Broadview Press, pp. 9–16.

—, 2010. "Introduction", in Eliza Lynn Linton, *Realities.* Richmond, Virginia: Valancourt Books, 2010, pp. 7–21.

Menke, Richard, 2013. "The End of the Three-Volume Novel System, 27 June 1894", *BRANCH: Britain, Representation, and Nineteenth-Century History.* https://branchcollective.org/?ps_articles=richard-menke-the-end-of-the-three-volume-novel-system-27-june-1894. Accessed 4 May 2022.

Meredith, Owen, 1861 [1883]. *Tannhäuser; or, the Battle of the Bards,* in *The Poetical Works of Owen Meredith (Robert, Lord Lytton).* New York: John B. Alden, pp. 312–48.

Meyer, Basil, 2003. "Till Death Do Us Part: The Consumptive Victorian Heroine in Popular Romantic Fiction", *Journal of Popular Culture* 37, 2, pp. 287–308.

Michie, Helena, 1987. *The Flesh Made Word: Female Figures and Women's Bodies.* New York: Oxford University Press.

—, 1992. *Sororophobia: Differences Among Women in Literature and Culture.* Oxford: Oxford University Press.

Mitchell, Sally, 1981. *The Fallen Angel: Chastity, Class and Women's Reading.* Bowling

Green, Ohio: Bowling Green State University Popular Press.

Mumm, Susan, 1999. *Stolen Daughters, Virgin Mothers: Anglican Sisterhoods in Victorian Britain*. London: University of Leicester Press.

Murphy, Patricia, 2000. "Disdained and Disempowered: The 'Inverted' New Woman in Rhoda Broughton's *Dear Faustina*", *Tulsa Studies in Women's Literature* 19, 1, pp. 57–79.

Nightingale, Florence, 1860. *Notes on Nursing: What It Is, and What It Is Not*, https://en.wikisource.org/wiki/Notes_on_Nursing:_What_It_Is,_and_What_It_Is_Not/Chapter_IV. Accessed: 9 July 2022.

"Novels of the Week", 1873. *The Athenæum* 2402 (8 November), p. 592.

Ofek, Galia. 2006. "Sensational Hair: Gender, Genre, and Fetishism in the Sensational Decade", in Kimberly Harrison and Richard Fantina (eds.), *Victorian Sensations: Essays on a Scandalous Genre*, Columbus: Ohio State University Press, pp. 102–14.

Oliphant, Margaret, 1867. "Novels", *Blackwood's Edinburgh Magazine* 102 (Sept.), pp. 257–80.

Orwell, George, 1939. "Charles Dickens", https://www.orwellfoundation.com/the-orwell-foundation/orwell/essays-and-other-works/charles-dickens/. Accessed: 4 May 2022.

Pal-Lapinski, Piya, 2005. *The Exotic Woman in Nineteenth-Century British Fiction and Culture: A Reconsideration*. Durham, New Hampshire: University of New Hampshire Press.

Pater, William, 1873 [2000]. *The Renaissance*, excerpted in Carol T. Christ, M. H. Abrams, Stephen Greenblatt (eds.), *The Norton Anthology of English Literature*, Vol. 2B: *The Victorian Age*, 7th ed. New York: Norton, pp. 1538–44.

Perkin, Joan, 1993. *Victorian Women*. Washington Square, New York: New York University Press.

Peterson, Linda, 2006. "Mary Cholmondeley (1859–1925) and Rhoda Broughton (1840–1920)", in Jennifer Cognard-Black and Elizabeth MacLeod Walls (eds.), *Kindred Hands: Letters on Writing by British and American Women Authors, 1865–1935*. Iowa City: University of Iowa Press, pp. 107–19.

—, 2009. *Becoming a Woman of Letters: Myths of Authorship and Facts of the Victorian Marketplace*. Princeton: Princeton University Press.

Piggott, J. R., 2004. *Palace of the People: The Crystal Palace at Sydenham 1854–1936*. Madison: University of Wisconsin Press.

Purdue, Melissa, 2020. "'His eyes *commanded* me to come to him': Desire and Mesmerism in Rhoda Broughton's 'The Man with the Nose'", in Adrienne E. Gavin and Carolyn W. de la L. Oulton (eds.), *British Women's Writing from Brontë to Bloomsbury*, Volume 2: 1860s and 1870s. London: Springer/Palgrave Macmillan, pp. 183–93.

Pykett, Lyn, 1989. *Emily Brontë*. Savage, Massachusetts: Barnes & Noble.

—, 1992. *The 'Improper' Feminine: The Women's Sensation Novel and the New Woman Writing*. London: Routledge.

"Recent Novels", 1884. *The Times* (1 January), p. 2.

Review of *Between Two Stools*, by Rhoda Broughton, 1912. *Times Literary Supplement* (21 March), p. 118B.

Review of *Doctor Cupid*, by Rhoda Broughton, 1887. *New York Daily Tribune* (30 January), p. 6A.

Review of *Good-bye, Sweetheart!* by Rhoda Broughton, 1872. *The Athenæum* 2324 (11 May), pp. 585–87.

Review of *Nancy*, by Rhoda Broughton. 1873, *The Pall Mall Gazette* (25 November), p. 1824–26.

Review of *Nancy*, by Rhoda Broughton, 1873, *The Times* (5 December): 5D.

Review of *Not Wisely, but Too Well*, 1867 [2013]. *The Spectator* 19 October: 1172–74, excerpted in Rhoda Broughton, *Not Wisely, but Too Well*. Brighton: Victorian Secrets Press, pp. 436–39.

Review of *Red as a Rose Is She*, by Rhoda Broughton, 1870, *The Times* (7 March), p. 4.

Sadleir, Michael, 1944. "Rhoda Broughton", in *Things Past*. London: Constable, pp. 84–116.

Saintsbury, George, 1886. "New Novels", *The Academy* 762 (11 December), pp. 391–92.

Shakespeare, William, 1603–04 [1998]. *The Tragedy of Othello: The Moor of Venice*. Alvin Kernan (ed.). New York: Signet.

Sharp, William, 1892. Review of *Mrs. Bligh*, by Rhoda Broughton, *The Academy* 1078 (31 December), p. 605.

Shelley, Percy Bysshe, 1821 [1994]. "Adonais: An Elegy on the Death of John Keats", in *The Complete Poems of Percy Bysshe Shelley*, New York: The Modern Library, pp. 485–99.

Sheridan, Richard Brinsley, 1779 [1905]. *The Critic*. New York: E. P. Dutton; London: William Heinemann. https://www.google.com/books/edition/The_Critic/YCFTxqUXuXAC?hl=en&gbpv=1&printsec=frontcover. Accessed: 27 July 2022.

Silver, Anna Krugovoy, 2002. *Victorian Literature and the Anorexic Body*. Cambridge Cambridge University Press.

Sparks, Tabitha, 2022. *Victorian Metafiction*. Charlottesville: University of Virginia Press.

—, 2021. "When Rhoda Broughton was Postmodern: Metafictionality in *Cometh Up as a Flower* (1867) and *A Fool in Her Folly* (1920)" (unpublished conference paper), Victorian Popular Fiction Association, Rhoda Broughton Study Day: *Rhoda Broughton: A Centenary Conference*, online conference, 11 September 2021.

Staël, Germaine de, 1807 [1987]. *Corinne, or Italy*. Translator: Avriel H. Goldberger. Rutgers, New Jersey: Rutgers University Press.

Stringos, Graziella, 2020. "Young Aspiring Women Writers, Romantic Love and Disillusionment in Rhoda Broughton's *A Beginner* (1894) and *A Fool in Her*

Folly (1920)", *Victorian Popular Fictions* 2, 1, pp. 24–42.

Stutfield, Hugh, 1895 [2000]. "Tommyrotics", excerpted in Sally Ledger and Roger Luckhurst (eds.), *The Fin de Siècle: A Reader in Cultural History c. 1880–1900*, Oxford: Oxford University Press, pp. 120–26.

Talairach-Vielmas, Laurence, 2007. *Moulding the Female Body in Victorian Fairy Tales and Sensation Fiction*. Aldershot: Ashgate.

Tennyson, Alfred Lord, 1859 [1999]. "Lancelot and Elaine" and "Guinevere", in Robert W. Hill, Jr. (ed.), *Idylls of the King*, in *Tennyson's Poetry*. New York, Norton, pp. 413–44, 495–510.

Terry, R. C., 1983. *Victorian Popular Fiction, 1860–80*. London: Macmillan.

Thackeray, Anne Isabella [Lady Anne Thackeray Ritchie], 1863 [1995]. *The Story of Elizabeth*, in *The Story of Elizabeth & Old Kensington*. London: Thoemmes Press, pp. 1–195.

The Jack Mooney Collection of Rhoda Broughton, University of South Carolina Library, Columbia, South Carolina.

Thornton, Lynne, 1994. *Women as Portrayed in Orientalist Painting*. Paris: ACR/ PocheCouleur.

Vicinus, Martha, 1985. *Independent Women: Work & Community for Single Women 1850–1920*. Chicago: University of Chicago Press.

Wagner, Tamara S., 2013. "The False Clues of Innocent Sensations: Aborting Adultery Plots in Rhoda Broughton's *Nancy* (1873)", *Women's Writing* 20, 2, pp. 202–18.

Warkentin, Elyssa, 2015. "Introduction", *The Lodger*, by Marie Belloc Lowndes. Newcastle-on-Tyne: Cambridge Scholars Press, pp. xi-xxx.

Winter, Alison, 1998. *Mesmerized: Powers of Mind in Victorian Britain*. Chicago: University of Chicago Press.

Wollstonecraft, Mary, 1792 [2007]. *A Vindication of the Rights of Woman and The Wrongs of Woman, or Maria*. Anne K. Mellor and Noelle Chao (eds.). New York: Pearson/Longman.

Woolf, Virginia, 1929 [1957]. *A Room of One's Own*. New York: Harcourt Brace Jovanovich.

—, 1931 [1979]. "Professions for Women", in Michèle Barrett (ed.), *Women and Writing*. New York: Harcourt Brace Jovanovich, pp. 57–63.

Wood, Marilyn, 1993. *Rhoda Broughton: Profile of a Novelist*. Stamford: Paul Watkins.

Woods, Livia Arndal, 2016. "Practicing Canon-Formation in the Digital Classroom", *Nineteenth-Century Gender Studies* 12, 2 (Summer). https://www.ncgsjournal. com/issue122/woods.html. Accessed: 30 June 2022.

Yeazell, Ruth Bernard, 1991. *Fictions of Modesty: Women and Courtship in the English Novel*. Chicago: University of Chicago Press.

Index

American Civil War, 72
Angel in the House, 1–3, 67, 129, 130, 160, 164, 166, 169, 170–71, 182
Anorexia, 29, 63, 73–74, 108–09, 190 n.14, 194 n.56
Ardis, Ann, 152, 153
Arnold, Ethel, 11
Arnold, Matthew, 10
Athenæum, The, 18, 34, 54, 61, 89, 90–91, 102, 106, 122, 127–28, 129–130, 173, 190–91 n.16, 193 n.45
Auerbach, Jeffrey, 41
Auerbach, Nina, 113
Austen, Jane, 6, 80, 144, 173; *Sense and Sensibility*, 137–38
Austin, Alfred, 91–93

Bakhtin, Mikhail, 6
Bentley, George, 23–25, 27, 35, 102, 112, 121, 194 n.63
Bentley, Richard, 2, 24, 30, 32, 51, 61, 89–90, 191 n.28
Bernstein, Susan, 14, 36, 64
Black, Helen C., 15
Bleiler, Everett F., 3
Bloom, Abigail Burnham, 190 n.16
Bordo, Susan, 109
Braddon, Mary Elizabeth, 191 n.23; *Lady Audley's Secret*, 68, 83
Brantlinger, Patrick, 40, 115, 192 n.40

Breuer, Josef, 108, 194 n.54
Brontë, Charlotte, 6, 16, 17, 50, 78, 86; *Jane Eyre*, 7, 16–18, 49–51, 78, 86, 112; *Villette*, 6, 15, 16, 86, 192 n.43
Brontë, Emily, 6
Broughton, Rhoda,
— adultery, representation of, 21, 76, 83, 87, 97, 110, 111–14, 118, 128, 130, 135–36, 159, 160, 165–66, 175, 178
— anonymous publication of early novels, 14
— anti-Semitism, 11, 65
— critical reception of works: 20, 91–93, 192–93 n.45; 132, 136 (*Belinda*); 159 (*Between Two Stools*); 13, 15, 16, 29–30, 60, 86, 89, 193 n.45 (*Cometh Up as a Flower*); 194 n.64 (*Doctor Cupid*); 173–74 (*Fool in Her Folly, A*); 18, 90–91, 102, 106, 193 n.45 (*Good-bye, Sweetheart!*); 194 n.65 (*Mrs. Bligh*); 90, 121–22, 127 (*Nancy*); 15, 25, 29–30, 34, 86, 89 (*Not Wisely, but Too Well*); 93 (*Red as a Rose Is She*)
— "disembodied embodiment", 20, 62–63, 191 n.29
— female desire, representation of, 3, 4, 17, 19, 23, 25, 28, 30, 42, 57, 61, 63, 73, 94, 113, 119, 140

— feminism, ambivalence about, 11, 146–48
— intertextuality, 5–6, 9, 18, 27, 43, 44, 63, 82, 95
— male characters, portrayal of, 77, 136, 192 n.37, 192 n.38
— marriage, critique of, 5, 8–9, 20, 21, 57, 146, 154–55
— metafictional elements of work, 5, 22, 63, 82, 174–77, 179, 183, 189 n., 3, 189 n.4, 192 n.42
— romance and marriage plots, revision of, 9, 13, 18–19, 21, 113, 144–46, 152, 183
— romance fiction, as writer of, 8, 18, 20, 87, 104, 113, 145
— sale of copyrights, 15, 27
— self-presentation as author, 14–15
— slang, use of, 2, 24, 31–32, 90–91, 92, 122, 192 n.32
— Tory politics, 11
— works (*see also* critical reception of works):
  Alas!, 143–44
  Beginner, A, 5, 22, 174–78, 179–81, 183, 185–87, 195 n.72, 195 n.74
  Belinda, 7, 21, 54, 111–13, 114, 130–37, 138, 159
  Between Two Stools, 146, 158–64, 168, 172, 189 n.6
  Cometh Up as a Flower, 2–6, 11, 13, 15, 16, 17, 19–20, 24, 30, 54, 57, 59–84, 89–91, 101, 108, 123, 124, 132, 133, 135, 159, 189 n.4, 191 n.28, 191 n.29, 191–92 n.30, 192 n.32, 192 n.34, 192 n.42, 193 n.45, 194 n.60, 195 n.73
  Concerning a Vow, 21, 146, 158, 164–71
  Doctor Cupid, 21, 111, 112, 113, 137–41, 159

Fool in Her Folly, A, 5, 12, 14, 22, 50, 80, 155, 173–83, 187, 189 n.6, 195 n.72
Game and the Candle, The, 143, 147, 165
"Girls Past and Present", 8, 10, 11, 12, 56, 147, 155, 174
Good-bye, Sweetheart!, 7, 18, 20–21, 84, 85–88, 101–10, 111, 114, 122, 130, 186, 192 n.30, 194 n.55, 194 n.56
Joan, 10, 21, 111, 135–37
Lavinia, 145–46, 194 n.66
Mamma, 145–46
"Man with the Nose, The", 112–21, 126, 123, 194 n.58
Mrs. Bligh, 144–45, 148, 152, 156, 159, 189 n.6
Nancy, 21, 90, 111, 112, 114, 120–30, 131, 132, 134, 135, 137, 138, 140
Not Wisely, but Too Well, 2–7, 11, 13, 15, 16, 19, 20, 23–57, 60, 61, 63, 76–79, 80, 82, 83, 89, 90, 102, 119, 144, 145, 154, 155, 189 n.2, 189 n.7, 190 n.10, 190 n.16, 191 n.17, 191 n.28, 192 n.32, 193 n.53
Red as a Rose Is She, 8, 20, 84, 85–88, 93–101, 104, 111, 114, 115, 126, 130, 193 n.48, 193 n.49, 193 n.50
Second Thoughts, 112, 131, 134, 135
"Under the Cloak", 194 n.58
Widower Indeed, A, 143
Browning, Elizabeth Barrett, 49, 107
Browning, Robert, 45
Byron, George Gordon, Lord, 38, 46, 48

Caird, Mona, 134, 146, 194 n.61
Carlyle, Thomas, 135, 190 n.16

INDEX

Cholmondeley, Mary, 11, 179–81, 190 n.8, 195 n.75, 195 n.80; *Red Pottage*, 22, 147, 179–81
Circassian women, 40, 78, 191 n.20
Cohen, Paula Marantz, 73, 126
Comedy, traditional definition of genre, 9, 28, 48, 51, 56, 63, 79–80, 84
Corday, Charlotte, 107
Corinne (*see* Staël, Madame de)
Corsets, 29, 190 n.15
Crinoline skirts, 37–38, 191 n.19
Crystal Palace, 32, 35–37, 41–42

Davidoff, Leonore, 37
Debenham, Helen, 3, 6, 26–27, 33, 50, 189 n.1, 189 n.5, 191 n.24
Delamotte, Philip, 191 n.21
Dickens, Charles, 170–71
Divorce, 112, 128
Domestic ideology (*see also* Angel in the House), 1, 2, 48, 64, 170, 182
Dublin University Magazine, The, xiii, 23–24, 52

East Lynne (Ellen Wood), 83, 112
Egerton, George, 149
Eliot, George, 7, 16–17, 25, 49, 103, 107, 187; *Daniel Deronda*, 74–75; *Middlemarch*, 7, 113, 123, 132, 136; *Mill on the Floss, The*, 7, 15, 16, 132, 194 n.60
Ellis, Havelock, 150

Faber, Lindsey, 5, 70, 189 n.4
Fahnestock, Jeanne, 28, 190 n.11, 190 n.16
Female genius (*see also* woman of letters), 15–18, 103, 186
Female Gothic (*see also* Gothic), 68–69
Feminism, Victorian and early twentieth-century (*see also* suffragette movement), 9, 10, 11, 17–18, 49, 92, 146–47, 166, 189–90 n.8
Flaubert, Gustave, 191 n.23
Flint, Kate, 6, 193 n.48
Freud, Sigmund, 108, 115, 194 n.54
Fryckstedt, Monica, 13, 89, 191 n.16, 192 n.44

Garrison, Laurie, 191 n.29
Gilbert, Pamela, 3, 8, 11, 26, 38, 72, 183, 189 n.1, 189 n.3, 189 n.7
Godfrey, Esther, 126, 131–32
Gothic (*see also* female Gothic), 8, 40, 56, 75, 113, 119, 130, 131–33, 136, 194 n.58
de Groot, Cindy, 194 n.66

Hager, Lisa, 150, 152, 154, 191 n.18
Hallum, Kirby-Jane, 65
Hardy, Thomas, 10, 139; *Jude the Obscure*, 112–13, 131–32
Hatten, Charles, 172
Heller, Tamar, 108, 189 n.1, 189 n.3, 190 n.10, 191 n.17, 193 n.49, 193 n.52, 194 n.56
Humpherys, Anne, 112
Hysteria, 108–09, 160–61, 168, 171, 194 n.56

"Indian Mutiny", 79, 115

Jalland, Pat, 126, 194 n.59
James, Henry, 10, 39; *Bostonians, The*, 147, 151
Jewsbury, Geraldine, 19, 24, 26, 30–31, 34, 60–61, 89, 184, 190–91 n.16, 193 n.45
Jones, Shirley, 104, 130, 192 n.43

Kaye, Richard, 39
Keats, John, 185–86 195 n.77, 195 n.78, 195 n.79
Koven, Seth, 36

Lee, Vernon, 154
Le Fanu, J. S., 61, 191 n, 28; "Schalken the Painter", 114–15
Leighton, Sir Frederick, 157
Lennox, Charlotte, 191 n.23
Les Misérables (Victor Hugo), 55, 191 n.26
"Liminal woman", 21, 147–48, 158
Linton, Eliza Lynn, 9, 139, 140, 147, 154, 155, 194 n.64, 194–95 n.69, 195 n.70; "Girl of the Period, The", 9, 20, 32, 39, 67, 87, 91–95; *Rebel of the Family, The*, 147, 151–52, 154
Lowndes, Marie Belloc, 11, 14, 18, 80, 147, 173, 177, 189–90 n.8
Lubbock, Percy, 9–10

Mansfield, Katherine, 173–74, 176–77
Masters, JoEllen, 194 n.58
Matrimonial Causes Act, 113, 128
Meade, L. T., 154
Meem, Deborah, 151, 152, 194–95 n.69
Menke, Richard, 144
Meredith, Owen, 45
Meyer, Basil, 108, 191–92 n.30, 194 n.55
Michie, Helena, 68, 190 n.14
Millais, John Everett, 81
Mitchell, Sally, 31, 33
Modernism, 9, 19, 174–77
Moonstone, The (Wilkie Collins), 115
Mudie's Circulating Library, 89
Mumm, Susan, 56
Murphy, Patricia, 150

New Woman, The, 9, 11, 21, 22, 25, 56, 102, 107, 134, 143, 147, 148–50, 152, 166, 175, 179, 193 n.46
Nightingale, Florence, 191 n.19

Oliphant, Margaret, 2, 13, 17–18, 20, 50, 59, 60–62, 64, 75–76, 123, 178
Ophelia (*Hamlet*, William Shakespeare), 81
Orwell, George, 171
Ouida (Marie Louise de la Ramée), 74, 194 n.64

Pall Mall Gazette, The, 90, 121–22, 128
Pattison, Mark, 131
Peterson, Linda, 16, 17, 175, 180, 186, 190 n.8, 195 n.75, 195 n.80
Postmodernism, 177
Pre-Raphaelite art, 28, 81
Purdue, Melissa, 118

Radcliffe, Ann, 68
Rhoda Broughton Centenary Conference, 3, 189 n.1, 189 n.4
Richardson, Samuel, 73, 192 n.35, 193 n.50
Ritchie, Anne Thackeray, 7, 49, 189 n.5; *Story of Elizabeth, The*, 7, 189 n.5, 191 n.24
Roland, Madame, 107
Romer, Robert, 34–35, 89

Sadleir, Michael, 77
Sensation fiction, 2–4, 7–8, 17–18, 20, 21, 28, 34–35, 43, 46, 48, 50, 60, 68, 77, 79, 82–84, 88–89, 90, 91, 93, 94, 98, 127, 129, 144, 178, 193 n.46; controversy over, 13–15, 36, 64, 94, 97, 175–76
Severn, Joseph, 195 n.79
Shakespeare, William, 45, 46, 47; *Othello*, 51
She (Rider Haggard), 115
Shelley, Percy Bysshe, 78; *Adonais*, 185, 195 n.77
Sheridan, Richard Brinsley, 81–82

Sichel, Walter, 9, 10, 107, 147
Sinclair, May, 190 n.8
Sparks, Tabitha, 5, 189 n.4, 192 n.42
Spectator, The, 15–17, 25, 29, 30, 86, 88, 89, 187
Spenser, Edmund, 193 n.47
Staël, Madame de, *Corinne*, 7, 17, 18, 21, 49, 102–03, 105–06, 107, 109, 186, 193 n.53
Stringos, Graziella, 189 n.1, 189 n.3, 192 n.38, 195 n.72, 195 n.76
Stutfield, Hugh, 149
Suffragette movement (*see also* feminism, Victorian and early twentieth-century), 92, 146, 153, 166, 190 n.8

Tailarach-Vielmas, Laurence, 11, 36, 189 n.7
Temple Bar, 13, 91, 93, 120, 139, 194 n.58
Tennyson, Alfred Lord, 45, 47, 57, 82, 190 n.13, 192 n.41
Terry, R. C., 192 n.37
Train travel, 14
Trollope, Anthony, 3

Vicinus, Martha, 191 n.27
Victorian woman writer, the; cultural anxieties about, 12–13, 177–78; paradoxical position of, 13–14; uneasy relationship to domestic fiction, 7

Wagner, Tamara, 127
Whyte-Melville, George, 47
Wollstonecraft, Mary, 62, 78, 154; *Vindication of the Rights of Woman, A*, 69, 71, 192 n.39
Woman in White, The (Wilkie Collins), 29, 74
Woman of letters (*see also* female genius), 16–17, 103, 186, 195 n.80
Woman Question, the, 64, 87, 102
Wood, Marilyn, 3, 101, 122, 130, 164
Woods, Livia, 195 n.73
Woolf, Virginia, 1–5, 9, 12, 22, 168, 174, 176; "Professions for Women", 1–2, 3, 4, 12, 22, 176, 182; *Room of One's Own, A*, 1, 5, 9, 22, 168, 174, 176, 181

Yeazell, Ruth, 94

Also in the series......

Key Popular Women Writers Series
Carolyn Lambert
FRANCES TROLLOPE

Key Popular Women Writers Series
Catherine Pope
FLORENCE MARRYAT

Key Popular Women Writers Series
Valerie Sanders
MARGARET OLIPHANT

Key Popular Women Writers Series
Fiona Snailham
ELIZA LYNN LINTON

www.ingramcontent.com/pod-product-compliance
Lightning Source LLC
Chambersburg PA
CBHW052039300426
44117CB00012B/1893